THE WISE OLD WOMAN SPIRIT

Help as a Partnership

Susan K. Faron

 CHIRON PUBLICATIONS • ASHEVILLE, NORTH CAROLINA

© 2023 by Chiron Publications. All rights reserved. No part of this publication may be reproduced, stored in a retrieval system, or transmitted, in any form by any means, electronic, mechanical, photocopying, recording, or otherwise, without the prior written permission of the publisher, Chiron Publications, P.O. Box 19690, Asheville, N.C. 28815-1690.

www.ChironPublications.com

Interior and cover design by Danijela Mijailovic
Front cover sculpture created by Susan Faron
Printed primarily in the United States of America.

ISBN 978-1-68503-187-9 paperback
ISBN 978-1-68503-188-6 hardcover
ISBN 978-1-68503-189-3 electronic
ISBN 978-1-68503-190-9 limited edition paperback

Library of Congress Cataloging-in-Publication Data Pending

In Remembrance and Celebration

Five whose feminine wisdom shined upon me!

Daniel Milton Faron, 1940–1954
Companion, guide, protector

Florence Grossenbacher, 1921–2009
Present, thoughtful, wise

Margaret Ryan, 1949–2019
Funny, open-hearted, brilliant

Betty Smith, 1924–2021
Gifted, warm, soulful

James Brandenburg, 1943–2023
Friend, colleague, the real McCoy

A tribute to my mom and dad ...
they always loved and believed in me

This book is dedicated to Gary Toub—analyst, consultant, author, and spiritual guide.

"Words as Eggs," as Lockhart writes, might be letters or names to describe rebirthing experiences, not unlike my weekly session with Gary Toub; every week, something is born, something is new, something is gifted. Of course, no words capture a true understanding of the mystery of a friend and mentor who invariably rebalanced, comforted, empathized, challenged, reflected, grieved, encouraged, invited, celebrated, explored, accepted, supported, and modeled just exactly what I needed. Through search and discovery, through work and training, through a relationship that brought out the best in me, I am surely humbled to have studied and worked with what often emerged as the wisdom of the archetype of the Wise Old Man, Gary Toub!

This book is also dedicated to the Wise Old Woman spirit.

The wellspring of this book is the Wise Old Woman spirit. You'll read how she gentled her way into my psyche over a lifetime, relating to me even while she was still unknown to me. She is the roots and branches of this opus, the writing of which came from her as we met every morning, and sometimes in between. She is not only the focus of this book, but also the reality and *experience* in our lives of the *eros* and *emptiness* that she is. In sum, the Wise Old Woman spirit holds all credit for the magic that reading about her invites.

She is hardly known but she is everywhere and influential! There is no defining her any more than we can define ourselves. However, we might consider this book a worthy start.

It is a reaching out, filled by some urge to convey what a partnership with the Wise Old Woman spirit can reveal—a way of living without violence, a way of balance, beauty, unity and peace.

Who am I to offer this? Why did she come to me? Not by my choice; no, it was not a choice. But a joyful and hopeful feeling companioned by my wanting to tell about her. I can't exactly do that; I'm not a preacher. So I wrote this book.

Contents

Acknowledgments

As you will read in the preface, the "Original Seven" were those women and men whose lives expressed the wisdom of the feminine and whose visits flooded my dreams at the beginning of this book. They were Betty Mallet Smith, Greek mythologist, leader, and author; Brigitte Frolich-Jacobs, faculty and researcher at the Jung and von Franz Centre and dream woman first to be consciously recognized as the Wise Old Woman spirit; Florence Grossenbacher, analyst, friend, and consultant for more than twenty years; Nana, my beloved and psychic grandmother; and three men, Gary Toub and Hansueli Etter, both analysts, teachers, leaders and authors; and Daniel Milton Faron, beloved brother who died at age fourteen. These seven, with their Wise Old Woman ways, entered my dreams as the Wise Old Woman spirit was emerging in my conscious life.

During this time, I was honored to meet with Andreas and Vreni Jung. Andreas and Vreni warmheartedly invited me into their home, and Andreas shared memories about his grandmother, Emma Jung. The interview took place in the home where Jung and Emma had lived, and the quality of the entire afternoon was surely numinous. Andreas and Vreni Jung are friends who have given me and the world the lasting treasure of a view of Emma's life seen clearly expressing the spirit of the Wise Old Woman.

My good fortune continued when I began working with Margaret Ryan in 2018, an extraordinary and beloved editor at *Psychological Perspectives*. Sadly, eighteen months later, Margaret Ryan died in late 2019. Our time together began with a felt connection between us that was immediate and joyful yet somehow anticipatory of her all-too-soon departure from this life. It was Margaret who led me in the right way with warmth and kind directedness from the beginning. I loved Margaret, and thank my lucky stars that I knew her for a brief but wonderful time.

Nothing short of a miracle, I found another fantastic editor, LeeAnn Pickrell, managing editor of *Jung Journal: Culture & Psyche*. She gracefully entered the space opened by Margaret's loss. LeeAnn's remarkable expertise and patience reside in the context of her vast experience, not only in the fields of writing and psychology, but also by her own vital relationship with a feminine wisdom figure. It's no surprise that LeeAnn is a soulful poet as well. It is a delight to read her creative work—that same imaginative energy also lends itself to her editing.

LeeAnn encouraged me from the beginning and all along the way, reinforcing what I did right, reassuring and praising new inspirations that invariably arose from the Wise Old Woman spirit. She matter-of-factly corrected my missteps, gently guiding me back on course. Our shared history of relationship with the spirit of the Old Woman enlivened and potentiated the enterprise. The two of us were like a beating heart tending to the work. Moreover, LeeAnn saw right away the shining star of Chapter 6.

Thus, Chapter 6 is the cherry on the pie. Thirteen contributors from all around the world sent dreams and active imaginations depicting the Wise Old Woman spirit in action and in non-action. Their stories comprise a kaleidoscope of the Wise Old Woman spirit—colorful, astonishing true-to-life experiences of how she appears in our lives. I am deeply indebted to each of them and feel forever grateful. That's all I'll say for now; Chapter 6 will speak for itself.

I also want to bow to my husband and all my children and grandchildren who have been, and continue to be, a constant source of spiritual strength and unlimited fountain of loving *eros*. An email about the latest, a text of cheer, a heart emoji, a visit on Zoom, faithful coming togethers (of course, with self-tests, vaccines and boosters, masks, distancing, and carefulness), exams, graduations, job interviews and hires, near-misses, and travels have comprised the outside of my inside life, particularly in the last three years through the course of the pandemic. I am most grateful for all the children, grand and otherwise, near and far, for continuing to live with gusto and sometimes discouragement, without always knowing what to do in these most difficult of times. I want to thank them for their amazing courage and soul, spirit, heart and brilliance!

I also want to thank the eldest grandchild who couldn't be present concretely, but is always with me in my heart.

Double this grace for the six children that bore such loving offspring! The "children's" work buoys me just to watch them, from Environmental Biologist; Senior Director for digital payments to ease our way; Graduate Faculty, Leadership and Consultation; Computer Expert, Software Engineer and Inventor; Middle School Educator, Drama and Leadership; Community College Vice President and Leadership; Tenured Faculty, Counseling and Leadership at a City College; Tax Specialist and Consultant; Social Worker to mend and create families; Philanthropy Manager for promoting others' well-being; to Judge and law of the highest order, each of them serving others. I particularly want to thank them for how they have modeled for me. As I move into older age, they are soon the backbone of the family, and I am exceedingly grateful to be leaving it for them as they continue to care for each other and the world.

As my husband Herb says, he "keeps it all going," as the chief chef and bottle washer, along with unending "honey-dos." Herb went to the post office or the bank, with mask and caution, and cared for meals as well as home supplies, all while running a business. Moreover, he read and re-read parts of the manuscript, also hearing many versions of many drafts, sometimes listening in his sleep. Toward the text's completion, he gave me the best compliment ever with his enthusiastic reading of the preface! With patience and grace, he bore the agony of having a mate who has been writing a book—eleven plus years.

Finally, the completing lysis of this story about the Wise Old Woman spirit is captured by my analysands with all their ways of relating, revealing the *eros* in their lives and a most deeply moving intimacy held by our valuing of emptiness. Their own development translates into further widening of my understanding of the WOW (Wise Old Woman) and how she enters the psyches of their lives. In recognition of their very real selves, their soulful selves as imaged through their dreams, I wish to bow to these most vital stories of all.

All this depth and richness was and is the context of my life: their loving *eros* surrounds and holds me every day. I can feel the Wise Old Woman spirit hovering among them all and feel glad for the bond of lively friends and family as well for the inner community. Likewise, *emptiness* is a constant companion, a part of every day, reminding me that she is there when no one else is. *Emptiness* offers its own personal experience

3

of the Wise Old Woman spirit, unique to each of us and meant to invite rest, protection, reflection, renewal and rebirth.

List of Illustrations

Preface
1. Original WOW spirit sea sculpture made of driftwood and shells

Chapter 1
1. Same original WOW posed in front of mirror
2. Early sculpture of brown, bejeweled, green-haired troll WOW
3. WOW crescent sea sculpture
4. *"Something to Say"*

Chapter 2
1. Venus of Willendorf
2. Winged Isis
3. Ancient Roman statue of Isis

Chapter 3
1. The Three Spinners

Chapter 5
1. Jung family home from the water
2. Walkway to Jung family home
3. Emma and her little sister, circa 1887
4. Emma as a bride
5. Emma and Carl engagement picture
6. Emma as a young mother
7. Family picture Château d'Oex
8. Veranda of Jung family home
9. Emma and Carl at Eranos
10. Emma and Toni with group of professionals

Original Wise Old Woman spirit emerging from active imagination
as a sea sculpture and standing on a 500-piece puzzle.
Her crown of coral appears as sulci and gyri.

Preface

The story for this book began long before I was born. After all, it's all about the Wise Old Woman spirit and she is eternal! Moreover, I am grateful every day for her guidance and confidence that I could do the job.

She came to me, you see, in the same way she comes to everyone ... personally, engaging, and, for me, a beckoning that could not be ignored. She first sneaked into the door of my soul, drumming and dancing and chanting her ways.

In my earliest memory I was two years old, sitting on the bleachers inside a huge tent, and focused on a large old Navajo man. He sat alone in the middle of the circular arena singing monotone sounds; as a toddler I was unimpressed. I do, though, remember wondering, "What does this mean? What is this about?"

How could I have known that the ritual I was watching was only the beginning of a series of emersions into the mystique of Native American myth and ritual. As we visited reservations, ceremonies, and pueblo towns, these early life experiences seeded my love for Mother Earth and for life itself.

Similarly, dreams throughout my life, particularly in later life, have served as stepping-stones leading me further along the path toward this opus. Although there were many, a few key dreams have illuminated the way.

A dream from 1996 remains a guiding inspiration for me. It began as a dream about the spirit of the Wise Old Man, and he was wonderful! *Visualize an old professor-type who showed me a graph on his monitor—* we didn't have laptops in those days—*revealing how the world would increase sevenfold over the next seven years. Then he took me outside—I* remember this vividly—*and the horizons of the world appeared as he gestured with his hand in seven arc-like movements. Motioning from left to right, up and over, the Wise Old Man showed the Earth growing seven times larger.*

A short time after that, I dreamed about the Wise Old *Woman* spirit. I didn't know her name at the time. *A kindly old woman, whom I met on a country road, came pushing a gate like it was a walker. It was a gate, though, and the marvelous thing about it was that it could open to unknown worlds ... to all new worlds. So here in this wide expanse, amid the rolling hills of nothingness, with only a dirt road to mark the path, a little old lady appeared with what was basically an invitation to everything I had yet to discover.*

Seven years after the 1996 dream I went to my first study group at the C.G. Institute of Colorado. There, I initially learned from another member about the Jung and von Franz Centre in Switzerland (The Research and Training Centre for Depth Psychology According to C.G. Jung and Marie-Louise von Franz). It was also in this group that I was favored by destiny to meet and study with Gary Toub, outstanding analyst, teacher, and author. Surely it was a synchronicity that we connected when he was the one who answered the phone when I called to register for the study group. For fifteen years before we met, I gave out a wonderful paper

8

he wrote to many patients and colleagues. I feel most fortunate to have continued consulting with him for more than nineteen years!

A significant dream in 2005 served as a further bridge on my path forward. It occurred in Delphi, Greece, the very same morning I had planned to visit the oracle at Apollo's temple.

I'm sitting in the driver's seat of my car, fearful and immobile. I had pulled into the driveway and seen a burglar in my house through the picture window. Unable to move as he approached me, I was "scared stiff," so to speak. Later, I am at a jail station identifying the intruder, only to ask if he were good with tools? He apparently said "yes," because I wound up hiring him as my gardener!

The unconscious seemed to have another idea. Indeed, the message of the oracle was way ahead of me, entering my dreams and answering my question by the next morning. I awoke with a nod to my inquiry of applying for analytic training at the Centre.

I began my training at the Centre in 2007, and by 2010, I had done a bit of digging and planting. Near the end of July, I had the following vision:

It was about 2 a.m. and I had been studying for the Propaedeuticum exams, looking out the open window into the night before I went to bed.

Amazed, I saw in the hills ahead, a few miles away, a bright neon-like star ... no, stars ... as big as buildings or bigger ... four ahead, two or three to the right ... and left also ... but big and not in the sky ... rather in the hills across from our home.

I was so taken aback that I woke my husband, and he got up and saw them too ... primarily white ... no, gold ... maybe a blue, too, but bright and large, maybe 10 or 20 times larger than the stars in the sky, about half the size of one of the hills.

The numinosity and power of this experience preceded a dream three days later, on August 1, 2010, about a seven-pointed star. It was in that dream that Brigitte Jacobs-Fröhlich (B.J.), an analyst in the outer world and faculty member at the Centre, tested me on the "religion" exam, together called the *Propaedeuticums*, which came at about the halfway point in the training. As it was, we had already planned the religion examination for nine months later. Perhaps part of the dream's message was to draw attention to the "nine-month" incubation ahead. Of course, the unconscious has its own time and is not necessarily in sync with the outer world.

The dream is as follows:

As Ms. Jacobs begins the examination, she says, "Tell me about the seven-pointed star?" I replied, "I don't really know about the seven-pointed star." Ms. Jacobs responded, "Well, maybe later." I didn't want that, and so I persevered. Realizing I didn't have any paper or pen with me, I was blessed to find something that already had typing on it and borrowed a pen. During the examination, I wound up writing on the spaces between the lines! The specific question for the examination in religion was as follows:

"How does the seven-pointed star affect the two houses around the corner?"

First, the dream is all about relationship. Moreover, I wrote about how the tension of this formation "held" the two houses in place, with the tension keeping them in balance. Although a full interpretation of this dream is beyond the scope of this study, here is a glimpse of what the dream may be talking about. It seems to speak directly to Jung's description of bearing the tension of the opposites and its saving grace. In this regard, according to a 2009 lecture by Jacobs-Fröhlich, Jung frankly states that the only way to avoid a third world war depends upon enough people being able to bear the tension of the opposites.

How the seven-pointed star "held" the two houses in tension was not described. Nevertheless, the "two houses" would be held and contained by the star. Surely there are many ways to consider and interpret this dream, but the most *important part* of its understanding is that it is my first *conscious* recognition of the Wise Old Woman spirit! She appeared to me in the form of Ms. Brigitte Jacobs, my chosen examiner for religion.

B.J. is a beautiful older woman in the outer world, an analyst and teacher, symbolizing a positive aspect of the Great Mother, the Wise Old Woman spirit. As we enter the dream, a sacred examination and deep conversation is taking place between the Wise Old Woman and me.

So here it is. The Wise Old Woman spirit is speaking right now. She is ever-present and ready to help and certainly we need it *yesterday*. This book *is* the conversation!

Following the dream, I wrote the answer in my journal, which I leave intact here. That is, the Wise Old Woman is asking me to answer that which has no answer. Maybe it is like *the legends of the holy grail*, the stories in which the hero or heroine of the venture must ask the right question, rather than give *the* answer.

It is interesting that the tension is accredited to the star, not to the two houses. They don't seem to be oppositional. Maybe that's because they have the star. It appears that the star has or takes the tension upon itself, giving the houses a more comfortable relationship, allowing a loving cooperation.

In the dream, there is an evaluation or psychological testing in the life of the feminine, perhaps a kind of deep exploration, that moves onward with perseverance and ends with writing "on the white spaces." Interestingly, the motif of space in the dream, when I wrote in the spaces between the lines, anticipates *emptiness,* one of the two central symbols unique to the Wise Old Woman spirit.

This dream could be viewed as a rite of passage, a solemn ceremony held in a sacred setting, conducted by a Wise Old Woman, and performed by recording, remembering, reflecting, capturing, and giving it visibility, "putting it in writing," so to speak, writing creatively where nothing has been written before.

Moreover, there is a time issue, not an ordinary time limit to the test, but one with a sense of insistence. In the dream's examination, it is important to write the response immediately as one would when drafting an agreement or commitment. At the end of the dream, the examination is still in process.

Could it be that the appearance of the seven-pointed star is an expression of the divine feminine touching the earth of my life? If I, indeed, were touched by the feminine face of God, wouldn't this also connect with the dream, which began with Ms. Jacobs, the feminine who symbolized the Wise Old Woman spirit?

The unconscious seemed to be leading me toward her. That is, the unconscious was pointing toward the archetype of the Wise Old Woman— the one who can experience, contain, and remember those moments of wisdom and grace. I wondered to myself, "Am I to learn about her? Learn about my own aging woman self? Does the seven in the star represent a stage in my own psychological development and the promise of greater wisdom and spiritual evolution?"

As I continued my research into Jung's discovery of the spirit of the Wise Old Man, I found myself asking, "What about the archetype of the Wise Old *Woman*?" The more I read of Jung's discovery of the masculine wisdom figure, the more I felt drawn to learning what he may have said about the feminine. "Earth Mother" was as far as it got for Jung and didn't quite translate into the wisdom that the Wise Old Woman spirit holds.

That's when I began to learn about *eros* and *emptiness* as unique to the feminine principle. As you will read, Jung has observed that the *complexio oppositorum* is missing in today's consciousness. Specifically, the feminine qualities in men and women, which have been denied and disparaged by the collective for thousands of years, are the very characteristics that are urgently needed today.

Joyful images of older women and men began to flood my dreams. These are the elders who most inspired me. "The original seven," I called them, so named in the book's acknowledgments. I didn't realize it fully at the time, but they were repeated expressions of the Wise Old Woman spirit! It seems the unconscious wanted to get my attention.

At the same time, I was confronted by the never-ending and increasing violence of the times. When news came of the Sandy Hook shooting in Newtown, Connecticut, of the little first graders in December 2012, I grieved with all the others across the country from that day forward. Looking back, the inner history of this study about the Wise Old Woman spirit's emergence parallels the explosion in outer violence, especially here in the United States.

Also, in late 2012, while attending the Centre in Switzerland, I awoke to the idea of Emma Jung and dreamed of her family! Hansueli Etter, my Swiss analyst, kindly helped me connect with Andreas Jung, Emma's grandson. With his encouragement I was able to reach Andreas simply by phoning his home at Seestrasse 228 in Küsnacht. Andreas and I had arranged an interview time, which I keenly anticipated. I even practiced taking the correct train and wearing boots to negotiate the snow.

On March 13, 2013, Andreas Jung and I met in that very house, the former home of Emma and C.G. Jung. Andreas Jung is their fifteenth grandchild. He and his wife graciously welcomed me into their home.

Andreas Jung was an easy man to talk with. We initially planned a forty-five-minute interview that, nevertheless, unfolded into four-plus hours as I received a firsthand and personal experience of his grandmother. Within the place that Emma lived, I could feel what it might have been like to be there with her. Moreover, I felt Emma through Andreas and throughout the interview. I dreamed of Emma's broach, a photo you will see later, and think of it as *the message of herself in diamonds.* Andreas and I have continued the deep and sacred conversation about the Wise Old Woman spirit through the connection that we made and the wonder of what he had to tell me about his grandmother.

More formally, this book originates from my thesis and study at the Jung and von Franz Centre in Zürich, Switzerland. It is born out of classical Jungian thought. It is the heart of my studies in Switzerland and has continued beating into this day and beyond. In fact, this heart is her, the Wise Old Woman spirit, as it speaks the language of *eros* and *emptiness!*

This book tells the story of the Wise Old Woman archetype and how her spirit has developed more consciously. Beginning with the evidence of a 4,000-year-old culture of peace, with its complete refusal of violence, it appears these people understood that such brutality is unacceptable. Barbarity opposes human survival. The fountain of divine wisdom, evolving over time, is emerging within, as we honor the middle way. Moving through the history of the ancient goddesses, to the vignettes of Emma's Wise Old Woman ways, and onto the thirteen dreams from around the world, she affirms her ever-presence.

Therefore, this narrative may, indeed, be considered a deep conversation that begins with a question in search of soul and survival. As a response to Jung's imploring "Is he [are we] related to something Infinite or not?" this study is of a spiritual nature (Jung, 1989, p. 325). Your reading today might be understood as a budding partnership; the second part of the title of this book *is* "Help As a Partnership." And so I'm planning for us to be together in this and learn about the Wise Old Woman spirit in unison.

In sum, the Wise Old Woman spirit is upon us. She really does exist, consciously in waking fantasies and unconsciously in dreams from around the world. Even in the face of the 2020 pandemic and amid the looming and ongoing climate crisis, Russia's war on Ukraine in 2022, increasing incidents of civilian violence, worldwide threats to democracy, and the catastrophic loss of women's reproductive freedoms, she is present.

The fate of the human race is in gravest question. The scales seemed tipped to eradicate us all; balance is lost. It is unknown at this time how human life will survive. Perhaps the Wise Old Woman spirit will infiltrate our psyches and pry open the unused, untouched *eros* and *emptiness* that has been left out and left behind for far too long. Long enough to come too close to perishing altogether.

Perhaps one hope can be found in Rapunzel's tale, which I relate in Chapter 3. Rapunzel, as a symbol of the feminine in the culture, not only survives the impossible—kidnapping, loss, isolation, disparagement, seclusion, abandonment, and more—but also discovers her redemption through relationship and her salvation in the *emptiness* of her soul.

It was *eros* or relationship that she felt with her unseen parents, *eros* or relationships with creatures in the garden, *eros* or relationships beginning and becoming in the tower, and *eros* or relationships with even more creatures in the desert. Through *eros* and relationship the Wise Old Woman's spirit enters Rapunzel's psyche. While alone in the desert, Rapunzel births a doubling of new life, twins, both masculine and feminine, emerging out of her suffering the desert extremes, where the complexes leave nowhere to hide.

The emptiness of the tower in particular, the phallic incubator, symbolically shows the feminine in the masculine that is yet to be born. Furthermore, emptiness itself fills much of Rapunzel's life; she is a human, alone almost all the time and confined in one place or another. Imagine the Wise Old Woman spirit *as* the emptiness, *as* the vessel, *as* the nothingness around her, holding her potential until the time is right.

In the end, Rapunzel endures the harshness of shadow and demon-energies that seclude themselves in the psyche's desolate parts, only to emerge as royalty of the highest possible value, made whole and complete through the *coming out* of the *eros* and *emptiness* of the Wise Old Woman spirit.

CHAPTER 1
Introduction to the Wisdom
of the Old Woman Spirit

With the exception of the Hindu and lesser-known religions, the past 5,000 years have witnessed the development of a masculine god-image that has become more and more one-sided; indeed, violent in its extremeness—for example, primitive aggression "in the name of God." Psychological findings suggest it is *complexio oppositorum*— "the opposites" apparently "contained in God"—that is missing in our consciousness (1969a, CW 11, p. 358). The Wise Old Woman spirit is just such a missing part and one with which a healing rebalancing can occur. The Wise Old Woman spirit represents the compensating *imago* of the Feminine Divine so critically needed today.[1]

The incidence and pervasiveness of world violence have been worsening since 3,000 BCE, when the ancient and peace-living goddess-centered culture across Southern Europe (circa 7,000 BCE to 3,000 BCE) began to be overrun by horse-riding conquerors (Gimbutas, 1989, p. xiii). As C.G. Jung said, "The present situation is so sinister that one cannot suppress the suspicion that the Creator is planning another deluge that will finally exterminate the existing race of man" (1960, CW 8, para. 428). Noting that "there is a terrible spiritual famine in our world," Jung concludes, "contemporary history has indeed demonstrated before our own eyes how human lives count for nothing" (1977, pp. 414, 460). In essence, "The world is hanging on a thin thread, and the thread is the psyche of man" (Segaller, S. 1990).

---

[1] The Wise Old Woman spirit may be known as "WOW spirit," "WOW," "Spirit," "archetype," or "Old Woman." She may also be referred to as a wisdom figure or modern expression of the feminine divine.

Same original WOW posed in front of mirror revealing
her base chakra and shell backpack.

The Wise Old Woman spirit is divine but she is not a goddess nor is she worshipped. She does, however, require our participation. She can be thought of as a spirit in what Jung called the collective unconscious and may also be referred to as an archetype. In fact, the wisdom figure of the objective unconscious has been referred to as the archetype of the spirit. Moreover, archetypes can be thought of as the building blocks of the human psyche, inapprehensible by the intellect, in part because they reside in the realm of the irrational. The archetypes serve as a bridge from our unconscious instinctual drives to their spiritual meaning in consciousness. Archetypes are patterns of perceiving inner meaning, and they convey meaning beyond logical reasoning.

At the same time, archetypes are described as typical modes of apprehension and can show themselves to us as symbols. The Wise Old Woman spirit is expressed through such a symbol. She emphasizes the positive side of the feminine principle, and is often depicted in a dream serving in a guiding, helping, or warning role. Amazingly, Jung describes how the wisdom figure is born out of each individual psyche as a psychological and individual reality.

Importantly, a relationship with the Wise Old Woman spirit amplifies all other images of the feminine divine because she is related to all of them. Growing through human development, the Wise Old Woman spirit has evolved into human existence. She is a part of our human psyche and is of human origin. In fact, Jung described our parental images as the origin of the wisdom figures. This is why the Wise Old Woman spirit is likely close to human consciousness.

Like the archetype of the Wise Old Man, the Wise Old Woman spirit is a shapeshifter so recognizing her is based primarily on her behavior and role as well as the context in which she appears. Thus, each of us has a unique individual image of her at any given time. Our image is woven out of our individual experience because she is humanized on an individual basis.

As an emissary of the Self, the Wise Old Woman spirit serves as an experiential psychological reality that Jung described as essentially no different from the traditional concept of the supreme deity. The Wise Old Woman spirit, emerging from the collective unconscious—the objective unconscious psyche of women and men across millennia—can be considered a humanized form or expression of the feminine divine. That is, she is both human and divine. Moreover, every woman and man can have an individual, personal relationship with her.

Through the human imagination and dreams, the Wise Old Woman spirit offers partnership involving a very real intimacy and immediacy. She invites our collaboration with her as she holds that wisdom and offers it personally to us. As such, the Wise Old Woman spirit echoes the ancient message from the collective unconscious of which Jung and von Franz wrote: "Protect me and I will protect you" (Jung 1968d, CW 12, para. 155) and "Help me and I will help thee" (von Franz, 1997b, p. 29).

Although Jung and von Franz suggested that the feminine wisdom figure is more or less a correlate of the Wise Old Man archetype, it is clear the thousands-of-years-old emphasis on the masculine isn't working by itself. Of course, the image of a masculine deity is not to be exiled, any more than the consciousness we have gained, but a rebalancing is clearly needed.

This exploration will differentiate the Wise Old Woman spirit from the masculine wisdom compeer by exploring what *eros* really means as a vital center of the feminine. I also bring to light a lesser-known writing by Jung in which he describes "a great feminine secret," referring to that mystery as "*emptiness*" (1968h, CW 9i, para. 183). These two qualities are uniquely feminine and emphasize the tone and relational aspects of the Old Woman's Wisdom.

In contrast to the contemporary all-good Mother Mary, the Wise Old Woman archetype distinguishes herself not only by reflecting, but also by living the archetype of wholeness through us, reminiscent of the ancient goddesses who embraced all of life, the dark and the light. This is the *complexio oppositorum* that is missing and so needed in the world today. She can be considered as the feminine in both men and women that until the veneration of Mary had "no metaphysical [representation] in the Christian God-image" (von Franz, 1993, p. 1). Appearing in dreams and other manifestations of the unconscious, it is as if she is reaching out. A partnership with Wise Old Woman spirit is a partnership with the wisdom of the ages.

How Are We to Access the Wise Old Woman Spirit?

Of course, a human being can't simply make an archetype constellate, even with the best ego intentions. We can do our best but if the unconscious itself is not activating the feminine spirit, we can only wait and be attentive to our dreams or other signs of her presence. At times we might help to activate it because our energy is required, and surely once the archetype is constellated, it needs our contribution.

The relationship is complex. If the Wise Old Woman spirit is activated, we might not be aware of it or get the response that we want. Perhaps her response is a silent "No." Just because we are in trouble, we may or may not evoke the Wise Old Woman spirit's help. We can only try by asking for guidance and offering a conscious standpoint. Moreover, we don't know if any response will come on ego's terms because we have little or no control over the outcome of our petitions, and there are no guarantees.

At the same time, those who have related to the Wise Old Woman archetype may experience her nearness more often, entering this relationship with greater familiarity and ease, yet always contingent upon her powerful archetypal energy. There appear to be degrees of felt presence and gradations in the experience itself, so that its activation is not necessarily an all-or-none occasion. No matter what strength the archetype of the Wise Old Woman presents, it is always humbling. She is to be taken seriously because the need for her aid is a critical matter. In *Answer to Job*, Jung writes of faith:

Faith is certainly right when it impresses on man's mind and heart how infinitely far away and inaccessible God is; but it also teaches his nearness, his immediate presence, and it is just this nearness which has to be empirically real if it is not to lose all significance. (1969a, CW 11, para. 757)

He further states:

Therefore, the question as to whether the process is initiated by consciousness or by the archetype can never be answered; unless, in contradistinction to experience, one either robs the archetype of its autonomy or degraded consciousness to a mere machine. We find ourselves in best agreement with psychological experience if we concede to the archetype a definite measure of independence, and to consciousness a degree of creative freedom proportionate to its scope. ... Then there arises that reciprocal action between two relatively autonomous factors, which compel us, when describing and explaining the processes, to present sometimes the one and sometimes the other factor as the acting subject, even when God becomes man. (para. 758)

I am also reminded of the ancient rituals meant to activate an archetypal experience. For eons the whole basis of religion has been about creating an archetypal experience through rites focused on music, dance, chanting, and images of beauty. In active imagination, one can call upon the Wise Old Woman spirit; consciousness can initiate the contact, and by continuing the activation over time, a stable relationship can be established.

As a threshold exploration of the Wise Old Woman spirit, whom I consider an emissary of the "self" (Jung, 1969d, CW 7, para. 399), this book offers a framework for the reader's own deeper understanding of and connection with this archetype of wisdom from a feminine perspective. The Wise Old Woman archetype, as complement to that of the Wise Old Man, could round him out, even potentiate him—and also emphasize the necessary feminine qualities for achieving world Tao.

Aspects of what's been written about both archetypes of the feminine divine and the Great Mother apply to the Wise Old Woman spirit discussed here. Although the Wise Old Woman spirit is indefinable, as is the god-image in any form, a multiplicity of descriptors is used in this book to emphasize her infinite and subtle complexities. Needless to say, the possibilities are inexhaustible, just as this exploration is only a partial and beginning effort to understand her better.

Help as a Partnership

Both Jung and von Franz would tell us that help is available and always has been. Their descriptions of the powers of the unconscious include mutual help and protection. This suggests that a partnership be formed—not a partnership of equal powers—but a partnership that is "a cooperative relationship" between those "who agree to share responsibility for achieving some specific goal" (Advanced English Dictionary, 2008–2015). As Birkhäuser-Oeri writes, "Perhaps only gods are truly creative, but they need human help" (1988, p. 149). The unconscious seems to be beckoning a collaborative relationship—in this case, with the Wise Old Woman archetype—one in which both parties need to be intimately involved. Indeed, the unconscious appears to hold a "higher" intelligence and seemingly unlimited power. Von Franz writes about the "active intelligence of the unconscious":

It [the unconscious] sometimes manifests in the most strange arrangements of fate, in synchronicities, and in all those experiences where one has an uncanny feeling that one is being manipulated by a higher intelligence. Sometimes it appears in an evil trickster form to make you fall down, and sometimes in

20

a helpful form, but always it comes most surprisingly. (1997b, p. 28)

On the other side, the unconscious seems less focused and needs the bright light of our limited ego consciousness. This is why Jung wrote in *Answer to Job* that Yahweh doesn't seem to know everything (1969a, CW 11, paras. 560, 638). He lacks *eros* and relationship to values (para. 621), and needs our conscious input to learn right and wrong from a human perspective. Jung writes extensively about this confrontation with the god-image in *Answer to Job*.

In addition, von Franz suggests, that from a human point of view, "the psychic nature in man [humans] … wants to become more human and less cruel, [and] … has a secret longing to get out of that" (1993, p. 194). This perspective suggests that the unconscious is, at least at times, conscious of itself. Jung describes this phenomenon as "an unconscious ego and hence a second consciousness" that may be present (1960, CW 8, para. 385). This may suggest that the Wise Old Woman sometimes knows that she doesn't know—which might be her wisest way of all—knowing the existence of her own unconsciousness.

This second consciousness may also explicate, at least in part, how the Wise Old Woman archetype may appear as an older, wiser presence, even if not to our immediate awareness. Thus, the archetype of Wise Old Woman (or Wise Old Man) may come to help us "get out of that," appearing in a dream or an active imagination, and arriving as a response to ego's coming up short in a difficult situation (von Franz, 1997b, p. 28).

Von Franz also notes "Mother Nature's attitude depends on the human being" (1993, p. 188). Both works and grace are required for help (von Franz, 1997b, p. 27). We are required to be adventuresome, courageous, and generous in our attitude toward the higher powers. Von Franz says that what we're "meant for" comes in the form of the wisdom figures. They are said to know about our myths and hold the information about our individual destinies (Toub, personal communication, April 21, 2015). Von Franz continues by saying that if we don't "pay attention to the unconscious, then it can't do a thing" (1997b, p. 29).

The Origin of the Wisdom Archetypes and Mana Transformed

According to Jung, the wisdom archetypes originally arose from the all-powerful, all-magical, and all-authoritative experiences of the mother and father images in the human psyche. In turn, the *mana* associated with them becomes an autonomous complex, the animus or anima within us, which when conquered, or made conscious, is transformed into a psychological function of relationship between the conscious and the unconscious. Jung describes this process as a psychological function of an intuitive nature (1969d, CW 7, para. 374).

This relationship establishes a power balance between these two realms because the *mana* does not reside in either, neither, but in both, and could be termed a midpoint of the personality. This invisible *mana* can unite the tension of the opposites, or be the result of conflict between them, thus leading to the birth of personality (Jung, 1969d, CW 7, paras. 381–82). Purposiveness can occur when consciousness actively experiences, or at least understands, these transformative processes.

"The word 'mana' is Melanesian and means holy or full of power" (Crisp, 1999–2010). Jung quotes Lehmann in defining the mana-personality as "extraordinarily potent" (Jung, 1969d, CW 7, para. 388) and possessing superior wisdom and superior will. He speaks of the *mana* being as an archetype appearing through untold ages, as a godlike being manifesting historically in the human world as the hero or priest (paras. 388–89), or later, according to von Franz, as the goddess of nature or love (1964, p. 196). Paradoxically, as an expression of the Great Mother, the Wise Old Woman spirit is first the mother of the animus, and then later appears to be born from the relationship of making the animus or anima conscious (Jung, 1967, CW 5, para. 315).

Keeping to the Middle Way

Of course, inflation through identification is a grave danger. Balance is lost by identifying with an archetype and can only be avoided if one fully admits one's weaknesses and changes one's attitude, realizing and recognizing the sovereign powers of the unconscious. On the other hand, concretization doesn't work either and results in perceiving the *mana* being as having the qualities of absoluteness and supremacy (Jung, 1969d, CW 7, para. 394). Both are one-sided and dishonest. As Jung explains, all value would flow over to the chosen side, with its opposite relegated to an equally extreme compensatory role. Keeping to the middle way appears to be the only path along which to become oneself and develop as a human being. Somehow fairness to both the conscious and the unconscious is required (para. 397). As Jung states:

> Thus, the dissolution of the mana-personality through conscious assimilation of its contents leads us, by a natural route, back to ourselves as an actual, living something, poised between two world-pictures and their darkly discerned potencies. This "something" is strange to us and yet so near, wholly ourselves and yet unknowable, a virtual centre of so mysterious a constitution that it can claim anything—kinship with the beasts and gods, with crystals and with stars—without moving us to wonder, without even exciting our disapprobation. This "something" claims all that and more, and having nothing in our hands that could fairly be opposed to these claims, it is surely wiser to listen to this voice. I have called this centre the self. (para. 398)

In other words, Jung recognizes that the wisdom figure represents particular manifestations of the archetype of the Self. He suggests that the old wisdom archetype, functioning as emissary of the Self, needs to be heard. However, Jung reminds us that we can really say nothing of the contents of the Self, because the ego is the only content of the Self that we do know. "The individuated ego senses itself as the object of an unknown and supraordinate subject," and "senses the self as something irrational"; psychological development requires stepping beyond science into the unknown realm of spirit (Jung, 1969d, CW 7, para. 405).

According to von Franz, "Jung defines the spirit/Old Man as the active power of the unconscious which invents or arranges or orders images … a kind of intelligent activity" (1997b, p. 28). Integrating the contents of these images is a key means of facilitating balance in our living according to the middle way. Moreover, Jung emphasizes how the spirit can appear quite spontaneously due to its autonomous nature (Jung, 1968f, CW 9i, para. 395). In fact, the spirit makes the human creative through initiating spontaneous movement and activity, by producing images independent of sense perception and then manipulating these images quite autonomously (para. 393).

Jung's Preconscious Awareness of the Wise Old Woman Spirit

Very little is written about the archetype of the Wise Old Woman, per se. However, Jung clearly acknowledged the image of the divine feminine. For example, when referring to the Assumption of the Virgin Mary, he writes:

> One could have known for a long time that there was a deep longing in the masses for an intercessor and mediatrix who would at last take her place alongside the Holy Trinity and be received as the "Queen of Heaven and Bride at the heavenly court." For more than 1,000 years it has been taken for granted that the Mother of God dwelt there, and we know from the Old Testament that Sophia was with God before the creation. (1969a, CW 11, para. 748)

Jung often writes about these sacred images as an eternal twosome: "Man as the son of the Heavenly Father and Heavenly Mother is an age-old conception which goes back to primitive times" (para. 486). He observes elsewhere, "whereas in fact Father Sun and Mother Earth have allowed it [culture] to grow for their delight in accordance with deep, wise laws" (1969b, CW 7, paras. 427–28). Regarding archetypes in the collective unconscious, Jung offers: "Less frequent is the archetype of the Wise Old Man and the earth mother" (1980a, CW 18, para. 1158).

Throughout "Psychology and Alchemy" (1968d,e,i CW 12), Jung considers the feminine divine in numerous ways: as Sapientia, mother of the wise (para. 465, plate 101); Wisdom (paras. 358, 466); Earth Mother (para. 522); *prima materia* (fig. 135, p. 268; para. 444); Mother Nature (para. 214); old woman (para. 417); Great Mother (para. 329); mother-goddess (para. 148); Prophetess (with magical qualities) (paras. 209, 329); Mercurius as *anima mundi* (para. 470, plate 209). In "Transformation Symbolism in the Mass," he recognizes this archetype as Sophia (1969f, CW 11, paras. 386, 727).

Early sculpture of brown, bejeweled, green-haired troll WOW, complete with a tail. Now living with a Swiss woman.

Although Jung did not explicitly use the words *Wise Old Woman archetype*, he seems to refer to her, psychologically speaking, when he writes about the syzygy between the animus and anima: "the missing fourth element that would make the triad a quaternity is, in a man, the archetype of the Wise Old Man … and in a woman the Chthonic Mother" (1968, CW 9ii, para. 42). Here, Jung offers *Chthonic Mother* as a "counterpart" to the Wise Old Man spirit, presenting her as a mirror reflection of the masculine spirit. Her feminine uniqueness was not described.

In an interview published in *Psychological Perspectives* in 1999, von Franz reported Jung saying that he would not speak further about figures beyond the archetypes of Wise Old Man and Earth Mother, saying,

"People already don't understand" (Wagner, 1999, p. 19). However, it could be said that the spirit of the Wise Old Woman has become more and more activated, as it has become more needed. Not surprisingly, Jung, at the beginning of the next stage of cultural development, would at times conflate characteristics of the Wise Old Woman spirit with those of the Wise Old Man archetype. Jung's use of traditionally feminine characteristics—for example, intuition—likely points to his preconscious or precognitive awareness of the growing necessity worldwide for a positive feminine divine, and for the Wise Old Woman spirit, in particular (1968f, CW 9i, para. 406).

The next section of this chapter reviews Jung's work on the Wise Old Man archetype, not only to get a beginning sense of the Wise Old Woman spirit through their shared characteristics, but also to discover how each wisdom figure might be manifest and uniquely lived out. As Jung has stated, "Without awareness of differences [there is] no consciousness at all" (1968k, CW 13, para. 244).

Jung's "Phenomenology of the Spirit in Fairytales"

Jung begins writing about the spirit in fairy tales by noting a variety of "psychic modes" produced in human consciousness that describe the phenomenon of "spirit," primarily from a masculine point of view and manifest as the archetype of the Wise Old Man (1968f, CW 9i, para. 395, paras. 385ff). He describes the "essentially antithetical nature of the spirit archetype," which often shows a "bewildering play of antinomies all aiming at the greater goal of higher consciousness" (para. 433). Jung describes the Wise Old Man as a shapeshifter, having great plasticity and appearing in dreams or active imaginations. He can manifest, for example, as an old man, a ghost of a dead one, a boy, a dwarf, or an animal (paras. 396, 398).

According to Jung, "It can never be established with one-hundred-percent certainty whether the spirit figures in dreams are morally good. ... we can never know what evil may not be necessary in order to produce a good by enantiodromia, and what good may very possibly lead to evil" (para. 397). Because of their doubling aspect, these archetypes have the power to hinder or help. The wisdom figures, like all archetypes, whether feminine or masculine, have a creative side and a destructive side. For example,

26

instead of helping, von Franz tells us that the old woman or old man figures can also play tricks on us (von Franz, 1997b, p. 28). One description of the negative masculine, according to Jung, is that "occasionally the old man is a very critical old man" (1968f, CW 9i, para. 405).

It depends on whether one pays attention to the unconscious by tending to dreams, talking with dream figures, recognizing synchronicities, or heeding physical symptoms—all ways of relating to the unconscious in some significant way. It is interesting to note that, according to Jung, the lower side of any archetype "points downward," being partly negative and of the nether regions, "but for the rest merely neutral" (para. 413).

The Wise Old Man spirit appeared as a figure Jung observed in analysands' dreams and seemed related to "a certain kind of father complex," namely a positive one (para. 396). Jung explains that the wisdom figure of the Wise Old Man may be said to represent an advanced state of inner development, symbolizing superior insight. As such, the Wise Old Man archetype may train the hero and offer assistance and aid (Jung, 1968f, CW 9i para. 405). He is the helper in dreams and is often represented by a teacher, therapist, physician, or other positive male authority figure (para. 398). Sometimes he may be referred to as a *shaman* and may give gifts to further the hero's journey. Jung also reminds us that, "The tendency of the old man is [to] set one thinking" (para. 405). He describes how the Wise Old Man "asks questions for the purpose of inducing self-reflection and mobilizing the moral forces ... and more often still, the unexpected and improbable power to succeed" (para. 404).

So it is, in times of crisis, that people quickly take stock of everything they've got. A union of physical and spiritual forces can give them resolve to face the issues. "Indeed, the old man is himself this purposeful reflection and concentration of moral and physical forces," and through those forces, people "... develop an unexpected power of endurance, which is often superior to the conscious effort of will" (para. 402). "Always spurring him on, giving him lucky ideas, staying power, 'enthusiasm' and 'inspiration'" are only some of the ways Jung speaks of the gifts brought by the Wise Old Man spirit. As Jung writes, "He himself did not create the spirit, rather the spirit makes *him* creative" (para. 393).

The Wise Old Woman Spirit and Archetype of the Wise Old Man: What Do They Share, How Are They Different, and Why Does It Matter?

In my experience, much of the same could be written of the Wise Old Woman archetype that is written about the Wise Old Man spirit. That is, both of the wisdom figures seem to share certain characteristics. Each offers positive guidance and good advice, for example. Shapeshifting is another common characteristic. For instance, the Wise Old Woman spirit may appear as a wise, prophetic old woman or an ugly evil hag (Gimbutas, 1989, p. 210). The figure of the Wise Old Woman both gives life and takes life, her darkness manifested as the archetype of death.

Jung writes that "spirit and matter might well be one and the same transcendental being" (1968f, CW 9i, para. 392). In fact, he writes of spirit being in matter. He further describes spirit in matter, stating, "Nature is not matter only, She is also spirit" (1968i, CW 12, para. 444). Furthermore, von Franz tells us that the Old Man is a "pure nature phenomenon" (1997b, p. 28) and describes the Wise Old Woman as the "wisdom of nature" (p. 169). From these perspectives, both the Wise Old Woman and Wise Old Man are not only spirit but archetypes of nature. It might also be said that each resides within a spiritual process that is, in itself, a relationship to nature. This spiritual process could be considered a sacred experience—or an experience of holiness that is quite alive and vivifying.

Sometimes this process is one of "being moved by the spirit, swept up by some content of the unconscious, gripped by a religious experience" (von Franz, 1997b, p. 92). Yet, a spiritual process can also be a slow and daily one, a kind of quiet numinosity. Could it be like the process of realizing the presence of an archetypal spirit, for example, the Wise Old Woman or Man, which may accompany and guide us?

Although spirit and matter may be one in the highest sense, their differentiation seems particularly important at this time. Something is missing from both realms in human consciousness, something that could promote the rebalancing that Jung enjoins. He warns again about the necessity of balance and how important it is to differentiate

28

our relationship to spirit simultaneously with how we differentiate our relationship to nature (1968f, CW 9i, para. 393).

Balance was lost, for example, when the Western world one-sidedly grew toward *logos*, the thinking and sensation functions associated with the spirit or masculine principle. Technology, industrialization, and moneymaking have long been the focus. On the other hand, connecting with nature, as in valuing, respecting, and preserving forests and wildlife, emphasizes a beneficial *eros* relationship to Earth.

This involves an experiencing that engages the body, its senses, and the functions of feeling and intuition. Each way of relating to both spirit and nature needs its particular attention from us. Similarly, relating in a distinctive way to our inner spirit and our inner nature is equally important and likewise requires a continual balancing and rebalancing.

Nature and spirit are not the same as feminine and masculine, nor are they the same as female and male. Jung has told us that the feminine and masculine principles are more than important intellectual categories. Indeed, as characterizing the wisdom figures, they offer sacred experiences. Although feminine and masculine ways of being are slowly integrating one another in the outer world, it seems imperative to recognize, psychologically speaking, how the feminine and masculine wisdom figures have distinctive ways of being and helping.

Evidence of the Wise Old Man and Wise Old Woman spirits is everywhere. They come to us in dreams, and are told about in fairytales, myths, and legends. Jung has discerned unique parts of that feminine aspect distinct from the masculine, and in certain ways, even alien to it. *Is it not likely that the missing opposites in today's world are, indeed, these very qualities: the feminine ways of being routinely rejected by the patriarchal and authoritarian dominance of our time?*

Part of our task is to further differentiate the two archetypes because we know that the weight on the masculine principle is not working by itself. Because Jung warned that archetypes are inapprehensible by the intellect, it is promising that emphasizing the feminine irrational spirit in our lives can make a life-saving difference.

It seems likely that how these functions operate could be of significance in telling them apart. It also appears that some distinctions between the two sages are often a matter of preponderance or emphasis in characteristics. Although traditional differences between the feminine and masculine have been manifesting over hundreds of years, the role of the Wise Old Woman archetype has been usurped at times, hardly mentioned on its own and rarely by name.

Similarly lopsided, positive crone figures have seldom appeared in the literature. Thus, the archetypes of the Wise Old Woman and Wise Old Man need to be considered independently for the Wise Old Woman spirit to finally be seen, appreciated, and allowed to consciously breathe. If, indeed, one needs her for survival, then let us find out who she is.

Revealing Complexities of the Wise Old Woman Spirit

Von Franz's writings about the Wise Old Woman spirit likewise describe her as the feminine correlate or parallel of the archetype of the Wise Old Man (1997b, p. 29). However, her descriptions about the archetype often reflect uniquely feminine characteristics for the wisdom woman. Von Franz delineates aspects of the Great Mother: "With the archetype of the Great Mother you have the witch, the devilish mother, the beautiful Wise Old Woman, and the goddess who represents fertility" (1974, p. 31). According to von Franz, "the helpful 'old woman' is a well-known symbol in myths and fairytales for the wisdom of the eternal female nature" (Jacobi, 1964, p. 279). She gives the example of an analysand who spontaneously refers to his dream figure as the "Wise Old Woman" (p. 277). The wisdom figures appear in dreams as a new dominant, she explains, when the analysand is at least partially released from identification with the animus or anima.

Elsewhere, von Franz gives examples of a "superior female figure—a priestess, sorceress, earth mother" that represent the center or the nucleus and personification of the Self in a woman's dreams (1964, p. 196). She describes a specific example of the Wise Old Woman spirit in an Eskimo tale in which a "tiny woman clothed in the 'intestinal membrane of the bearded seal'" tries to warn the heroine (Rasmussen, 1988, p. 212).

Von Franz recognizes the Wise Old Woman spirit both as paradoxical and uniquely feminine. She suggests that the image of the feminine Godhead may be represented by the Russian witch, Baba Yaga, for example, in which the negative and positive are mixed: "Wicked … or

30

wise ... most puzzling of all" she is "sometimes both," describing her makeup of opposites or complexities (von Franz, 1997b, p. 27).

This combination of opposites is also seen in the linguistic origins of Baba Yaga's name. An earlier form of a word or ancestral language, Slavic in this case, cites meanings for *Baba* such as grandmother or mythic cloud woman who makes rain. In contrast, *Yaga* represents the opposite, such as disease or to strangle (Gimbutas, 1989, p. 210). The Russian witch, Baba Yaga, has helped through Russian tales preserve the prehistoric image of the "Killer-Regeneratrix," a motif discovered by archeomythologist, Marija Gimbutas (p. 210).

The *Killer-Regeneratrix* refers to the divine feminine and reveals another image of the opposites, emphasizing again the Wise Old Woman spirit's complexity. However, the *Killer-Regeneratrix* motif was found throughout European folklore not as a formidable goddess but rather as a witch. She had been degraded into "a loathsome caricature" (Gimbutas, 1989, pp. viii, 210). This is exampled by the witch's hooked nose being symbolic and remnant of the ancient bird goddess, conflating the two quite physically (p. 209).

Gimbutas writes that the *Killer-Regeneratrix* is manifest as Old Hag, dry bones, and winter. She states that the Old Hag is a fearsome goddess described in regional folk stories. Her witch part was associated with death in winter and imaged as tall and boney, hence the Old Hag. Gimbutas describes the bare bone as the closest symbol to death and notes there is no life without death, another pair of opposites.

In this sense, the hag and bone are symbolically related, according to Gimbutas, who suggests that the large white bones of ancient Greece were buried for the purpose of providing "a bridge between death and new life" (p. 211). This echoes the ancient cultures' emphasis on rebirth. In fact, traditional images show that there is a great deal more weight on regeneration than death.

The Old Hag of ancient Celtic myths is sometimes referred to as Grania, Annia, Anu, and other goddesses. On one side, "The original meaning of *gráinne* is 'ugliness'. ... The other meanings of *gráinne* are "'grain, seed,' which suggest association with regeneration" (p. 211). So again, the opposites are represented.

Baba Yaga's Baltic name, *Ragana*, derives from *regёti*, "to foresee," and *ragas*, "crescent or horn," and she may be understood as a seer and associated with the moon. Ragana appears to have control over life and death in a cyclic sense, and thus is similarly related to regeneration (pp. 209–210).

WOW sea sculpture made of driftwood and shells: "The Speaker," reminiscent of the moon's crescent. Her photo was emailed to each contributor when updating the book's progress one holiday season.

"Something to say"

32

The Wise Old Woman's complexity is further glimpsed when von Franz points to the spindle, another attribute of both her and her witch-side, again recognizing two opposite aspects of the great goddess at once (1993, pp. 44–45). She amplifies the symbolism of the spindle and describes the sowing of flax, spinning and weaving as the essence of feminine activity, yet within it, is the phallic masculine. Fertility and sexual themes are pointed out, as are other symbolic meanings of the spindle: the mystery of giving birth and mothering, and weaving "a web around her child with her phantasies and feeling expectations" (p. 46). She does not further differentiate the Wise Old Woman archetype from the feminine principle, per se.

The spindle is also related to activities such as knitting and embroidery, which, according to von Franz, allows guilt-free laziness and quiet time for a woman. She suggests this can be a time of relaxation and reflection, and sees this type of activity as enhancing a woman's feminine nature, as self-educative, and as fostering patience. Moreover, she indicates that the woman can create the right atmosphere when her inner-life symbols of spinning and weaving are connected to consciousness in a positive way.

A similar involvement in feminine activity could enhance the man's feminine nature, as well. Roosevelt Grier, for example, retired professional football star, models attention to the development of his feminine energies, the same that reside in all men to observe and feel free to accept, through his hobbies of needlepoint and macramé.

The darker side of spinning is likened to plotting and cunning, as if into an evil web of intrigue. The negative side of the spindle might also be manifest by a pattern of pointed, wounding remarks that misuse this quality in a way that triggers another's complexes. Lastly, von Franz reminds the reader that a woman may be pricked by the spindle of her mother's negative animus when she turns the spindle against herself.

The Killer-Regeneratrix motif appears again when von Franz describes the frightening dark side of "the abysmal shadow of Baba Yaga, an abyss into which one can only look with horror and turn away" (von Franz, 1993, p. 187). In her interpretation of Sleeping Beauty, recognizing the "forgotten godmother" as the one who curses the babe, von Franz notes, "For the time being we can say that she is the dark side of the feminine principle forgotten in our civilization and also the dark, imperfect side of Mother Nature" (p. 44). "She is full of the powers of destruction, of desolation, and of chaos, but at the same time is a helpful figure" (p. 173). Perhaps this is when the Wise Old Woman spirit comes into play. When an individual's ego has done all it can, and the situation is desperate, the archetype of the Wise Old Woman or Man may then appear (pp. 28–29).

For example, a young mother who faced the possibility of great loss, retreated into a sleeping bag for six or so hours a day when the kids were in school. She meditated constantly and prayed that things would be resolved. She told no one of this experience. After two weeks, she felt a shift and a sense of knowing that it would be all right. Nothing in the outer world had changed. She had been aided by the unconscious, helped by an inner wisdom, psychologically speaking, and experienced the needed "separation" from that swallowing depression. She described a deeply felt sense of spiritual help and release from the conflict. Jeffrey Raff calls this kind of experience, the *felt vision* (Raff, 2006, p. 79).

When von Franz wrote about the Wise Old Woman in her analysis of a Grimms's fairytale, "The Straw, the Coal and the Bean," she describes the old woman in a distinctly feminine way:

> In spite of her modest appearance, she represents the archetype of the wise old woman, the wisdom of Nature. She cooks her own meal, so she represents Nature not in her giving form but Nature circling in herself without progress. So, something is bound to happen. (von Franz, 1993, p. 169)
>
> So perhaps we could say that the poor old woman represents an incarnation of Great Mother Nature in her double aspect, representing a feminine humanity that is based on an aspect of nature that promotes consciousness. ... The poor old woman represents Mother Nature's design for humanity ... and promotes our becoming civilized and conscious. (p. 170)

These thoughts echo earlier statements about the wisdom figures' knowledge of our destinies. While this *being-ness* of circling in herself does seem reminiscent of the contemplation and reflection associated with the archetype of the Wise Old Man, it is, nevertheless, somewhat different from the typical active, purposive, and initiating function of the masculine.

Von Franz depicts a repetitive movement, "without progress," which is similar to the kind of stillness or movement in place often associated with the feminine principle. Maybe the old woman is stirring a mandala of patience and waiting. Jung does say that the archetype of the Wise Old Man is sometimes nothing more than a cautious and patient waiting (1968f, CW 9i, para. 397). It seems that the Wise Old Man spirit has feminine characteristics, too.

The quality of intuition is also called up when von Franz points to a foretelling, planning, or knowing function as the Wise Old Woman circles within herself. In writing about the spirit, Jung, however, ascribes intuition to the Wise Old Man (para. 406). Here again, the wise masculine is identified with a principle traditionally associated the feminine function, that of intuition.

CHAPTER 2
Manifestations of the Feminine Divine

So how does one begin to enliven, symbolically speaking, the archetype of the Wise Old Woman? Not finding many descriptions of the Wise Old Woman spirit, the question remains: how is she particularly "woman" or uniquely feminine? If we hypothesize that the feminine principle is a necessary compensation for our troubled world, how do we learn about the parts that remain missing in our current world, especially if these parts are primarily unconscious?

Perhaps we might first acknowledge some feminine deities by citing their names and origins. Through that naming, we might bring forward central aspects of the feminine that are different from the masculine; qualities, which I suggest, are related to the Wise Old Woman. Psychologically speaking, these goddesses are all images of the feminine archetypes that govern a woman's life. As such, a woman's ego is related in the depths of her unconscious to all these divine goddesses. Of course, a man's anima is also connected to these feminine deities.

Behind a human behavior pattern in the outside world are archetypes, which we also experience as pictures in the inner world or images in our dreams. The images are more or less feminine or masculine because the psyche depicts certain qualities with the image of a woman and certain qualities with the image of a man. In other words, the images are female and male, so we call them feminine and masculine. Typically, a woman's genuine nature is most related to the feminine archetype. Hence, I offer a sense of the many feminine deities that have existed over time revealing the archetype, serving as expressions of the "old" in the Wise Old Woman spirit.

It is important to remember, when referring to our human heritage, that women, as well the anima of men, "have descended from a long line of sacred females who have been respected for thousands of years" (Ann

37

& Imel, 1993; Birkhäuser-Oeri, 1988, pp. 18–19). Discovering these goddesses, with their lively images and stories, forms a most remarkable and colorful picture, for they are filled with the very feminine qualities that are needed in our world today. The presence of so many goddesses offers a certain weight, complexity, and tone that comes only from an emphasis on the distinctly feminine. It is noteworthy that the one feature held in common among the Neolithic agrarian economies, in which "the first breakthroughs in material and social technology" occurred, was the worship of the goddess (Baring & Cashford, 1991, p. 105).

Following an introduction of the goddesses, I focus on two of them in particular in greater detail. This close examination is meant to provide a glimpse of how these feminine deities offer, in and of themselves, a feminine way of being. They are the great goddess of the goddess-centered, matricentric culture of Old Europe, seven millennia BCE (Gimbutas, 1989), and Isis, the cosmic feminine goddess who embraces "the aspect of all other feminine goddesses of old Egypt" (von Franz, 1980, p. 510).

Feminine Deities from around the World and throughout History

I was astonished to discover there are so many goddesses all over the world and throughout the whole of recorded human history. Here is a list of some of the multitude of goddesses to provide a continuum and context for our study (Goddess-guide.com, 2007–2022, Esoteric Theological Seminary, n.d.; Circle of Mithras, n.d.):

- Inanna and Nammu, goddesses of Sumer
- Asherah, the goddess from Canaan, as well as the goddess Anath
- Ishtar and Tiamat, the goddesses from Babylon
- Demeter, Cybele, and Aphrodite, goddesses from Greece
- Gaia, Hera, Artemis, and Athena, more goddesses from Greece
- Fortuna and Umbria goddesses from Italy
- Anu and Danu, Irish goddesses
- Nanna and Suni, German goddesses
- Mokosh from Russia and Zyzilia from Poland
- Artio and Bormana from France
- Maat, Hathor, Seshet, and Nut, goddesses of Egyptian mythology
- The goddess-like Shekhinah of the Hebrew tradition
- Mary, Mother of Christ, of the Christian faith

- Sophia, the goddess not only from the Christian Bible, but also from alchemy and the Gnostic, Sufi, Mithras, and pagan religions of antiquity.

One source alone offered thousands of names of goddesses, covering 30,000 years of goddess worship (Ann & Imel, 1993). Another source provided a list of over 132 categories of Goddess origins, including Hawaiian, Native American, Inuit, Celtic, Norse, British, Scandinavian, Japanese, Chinese, Korean, Indo-European, Filipino, Middle Eastern, Indian Hindu, Aztec, Mayan, African, and Central and South American. Other categories include Latvian, Cretan, Himalayan, Nepalese, and Tibetan goddesses. Also listed are goddesses of children and childbirth, fertility and agriculture, islands and oceans. There are moon goddesses and sun goddesses (Chinaroad Lowchen, 2000–2008). In sum, the number of divine goddesses is immense, and they have been part of our existence for many thousands of years.

The Old European Great Goddess

Venus of Willendorf, Natural History Museum of Vienna, Austria, circa 25,000 to 30,000 BCE (Photo: Jakob Halun, CC-BY-SS 4.0).

39

Beginning with the work of Gimbutas, noted emeritus professor of European archeology at the University of California, Los Angeles (UCLA), we learn about this ancient goddess presiding over a "balanced, nonpatriarchal and nonmatriarchal social system" that "reached a true florescence and sophistication of art and architecture in the 5th millennium BCE" (Gimbutas, 1989, p. xx). This culture, as I mentioned previously, thrived for 4000 years in peace and unity. Gimbutas, wanting to write accurately about her findings, reminds us that her research is focused "strictly on European evidence," although she discovered parallels worldwide as she broadened the scope of descriptive archaeology to include interdisciplinary research.

Her work is a study in *archeomythology*, a combination of archaeological findings, comparative mythology, and folklore. "In Europe [the goddess] ruled throughout the Paleolithic and Neolithic eras, and in Mediterranean Europe throughout most of the Bronze Age" (Gimbutas, 1989, p. 321). Jung himself noted findings from Knossos on Crete revealing "the existence of a highly developed prehistoric civilization (around 2,000 BC)" (Jaffé, 1979, p. 48). In 2005, I also witnessed firsthand the beauty and complexity of this goddess-centered culture, still evident in the ancient ruins after hundreds of years.

Gimbutas found evidence of a goddess-centered culture that lived in peace and respected the earth. She writes about a cooperative and egalitarian society manifested in more than 30,000 artifacts from 3,000 sites known at the time of her writing, preserving a "vast body of symbols," 97 percent of which are of the female form (Gimbutas, 1982, p. 11; 1989, pp. xii, xv; Robb, 1992, p. 6). "Their culture was a culture of art" with its "striking absence of images of warfare and male domination, [and] reflects a social order in which women as heads of clans or queen-priestessess played a central part" (Gimbutas, 1989, pp. 321). She also found that "the concept of regeneration and renewal is perhaps the most outstanding and dramatic theme that we perceive in this symbolism" (p. 316). In her view, the goddess served as a symbol of the unity of all life in nature and a celebration of life itself. She describes a "long-lasting period of remarkable creativity and stability, an age free of strife" (p. 321).

Indeed, research shows that "agriculture, building, weaving, potting, writing, poetry, music, the graphic arts, calendars, and mathematics" all appear to have been developed mostly by women (Walker, 1983, p. 684). Elder women among the Hittites (priestesses) "taught the art of writing, kept records, advised kings, and practiced medicine" (p. 685). From early antiquity their "life-loving spirit of affirmation" was evidenced by a culture of nonviolence and cooperation (p. 687).

The culture of the goddess was tragically overrun by "wave upon wave" of invasions of horse-riding, "cattle-herding Indo-European tribes ... from the fourth millennium [BCE]" (Campbell in Gimbutas, 1989, p. xiii). Further, according to Gimbutas, when Christianity introduced "the philosophical rejection of the world," the goddess, "and all she stood for," was rejected too (p. 321).

However, the feminine principle, as manifest in the ancient goddess artifacts discovered by Gimbutas, is concrete testimony to her indelible mark on the psyches of humankind. Gimbutas tells us that some beliefs in the present day are, for example, "archaic aspects of the prehistoric Goddess" and continue to endure in the Western psyche (p. xvii). It is noteworthy that Gimbutas attributes grandmothers and mothers as responsible for passing on these ancient beliefs and keeping them alive.

Isis, the Cosmic Feminine

The second divine goddess described here is the ancient Egyptian goddess, Isis. It is noteworthy that Plutarch translates the name Isis to mean wisdom (Hall, 1928, p. 45). Much of this section on Isis is drawn from a lecture entitled, "The Feminine in Religion," presented by Brigitte Jacobs-Fröhlich (March 2015). She states that Isis represents the search for truth and what is hidden of the godlike wisdom. "Every human has a sense of his [or her] own truth," having wisdom, for example, about the hidden truth behind his or her symptoms. Jacobs likens this inner knowledge to the sun rising.

Isis is connected to Sophia, as they both share images with the feminine archetype in religion (Hall, 1928, pp. 45, 48). In addition, the Shekhinah of the Kabbalah and Gnostic Sophia are directly connected to her. In Proverbs 8, wisdom is described as a woman and could be seen as a feminine personification of the collective unconscious. The Song of Solomon also portrays wisdom as a woman, describing her beauty,

41

another word for *wisdom*, in erotic language. The Song of Solomon is found in the holy book of the Jews, the Torah, and is also located in the Old Testament of the Christian Bible.

In some sources, Isis is actually identified as Sophia and as the "Virgin of Wisdom" and appears among many different races and peoples (Hall, 1928, pp. 45, 48). Isis takes a great variety of forms and is multicolored, not unlike the stages of alchemy. She was known as the goddess with 10,000 appellations.

Isis personifies the mediator between God and human experience, between Earth and heaven. That is, she crosses boundaries and unites. Isis is not subject to fate and can overcome the destiny of all the goddesses and the ruling of the stars (Baring and Cashford, 1991, pp. 268–69). Like the archetype of the Wise Old Woman, Isis "is always there for us, strong and unyielding to obstacles in our way. She is the one who waits when all other methods fail us, when we feel utterly alone, when we have completely lost our way" (Zeta, 2007, p. 1).

Winged Isis adapted from the wall painting of Isis from the tomb of Seti I
(Photo: Susan Faron)

There is a story told about how Isis creates wind with her wings. The tale describes Isis as the one who greets us on the other side of life. It seems she hovers over the body, taking its last breath, and is there in the "Beyond" to provide the first breath of new life with her wings (Zeta, 2007, p. 1).

Isis was known as the "Crone of Death" as well as the "Mother of Life" (Goddess Gift, n.d.). She is described as the Egyptian goddess of rebirth who "remains one of the most familiar images of empowered and utter femininity." Isis, a "paragon of motherly virtues," gave birth to her son, Horus (Goddess Gift, n.d.). According to Jacobs (2015), "The spirit in its original form is always female and comes from the Great Mother."

There is much about the story of Isis, Osiris, and Horus, their son. My interest, however, lies in the mother-son images, Isis with Horus on her lap, not unlike the Mother Mary holding Jesus. Multiple comparisons of these mother-son sculptures are evidence of their shared symbolism. Importantly, giving birth to Horus symbolized a deep spiritual goal for Isis—the feminine giving birth to a new masculine spirit. This reflects a deeply religious aspect of Isis. It represents a sacred experience that cannot be articulated or fully understood. Jacobs (personal communication, 2018), who has studied these images for many years, recognizes that Isis's spiritual experience is a great mystery and not comprehendible in a lifetime.

Isis conceived Horus only after she had resurrected and reintegrated her husband and brother, Osiris, on a spiritual level (Hill, 2010, p. 2). In one version of the myth, when Isis was mourning as a widow of Osiris, she and her sister, Nephthys, had such depth of love and grief for their brother that it helped restore him to life.

Along with Isis's recitation of magic spells, speeches written by Isis in funerary texts at Osiris's death describe her multiple feelings: her sorrow, her sexual desire for him, her anger with his abandonment—all these were an important part of the healing. The power of these emotions played a role in his rebirth and was meant to evoke his natural agency (Pinch, 2006, pp. 79–80, 178–79). In other words, the energies of *eros*, the "wisdom acquired by feeling-experiences" (von Franz, 1996, p. 130), helped bring Osiris back to life. Moreover, Isis also assisted in restoring the souls to others who had died bringing them renewed wholeness like she had for Osiris ("Isis," 2016).

Isis's ways are totally different from the judgment and logic of *logos*, the opposite of *eros*. Instead of making something intellectual and masculine of the spirit, Isis promises ongoing life and forgiveness. According to Jacobs (2015), an orthodox belief in Russia holds that without wisdom, humanity is doomed. Isis has been a bearer of such wisdom from antiquity.

Isis brings a moral principle to ruling humankind, bringing men and women together, compelling men to love women (Jacobs, 2015). It is also written that she taught women how to "tame men enough to live with them" (Goddess Gift, n.d.). Importantly, Isis put an end to murder and cannibalism (Baring and Cashford, 1991, p. 269).

Isis distinguished herself from other goddesses by spending time among her people for their benefit. She taught reading and agriculture and was worshipped as the goddess of medicine. She taught Egyptians how to grind corn, make bread, spin, and weave cloth. Later images of Isis depicted her with a crown of wheat, symbolizing her role as an earth and fertility Goddess, not unlike Demeter (https://art.thewalters.org/detail/15040/isis-holding-a-cobra/).

Similar to Mary and again like Demeter, Isis has also known deep personal loss ("Isis," 2016). The snake and scorpion are associated with Isis, whereas the darker aspect of life is missing from the Christian Mary. Isis is a "terrestrial, water and air goddess rolled into one. She was considered as the complete female from which all life forms sprung" (Egyptian gods: Isis, n.d.).

Isis is often seen as a version of the Black Madonna, archaic and earthy with a natural wisdom, including absolute darkness and uncertainty and fear of death (Jacobs, 2015). Nevertheless, Isis in her black aspect is required for new light to come. The darkness is needed for the seed, the incubation, for rebirth, and is the ultimate mystery. From a symbolic perspective, darkness is not seen as a polarity, but solely as the absence of light, which refers psychologically to being totally unconscious. Paradoxically, "She is the light in the shadows," and has been referred to as a night-light essential for life. Isis is the dark goddess of clarity, truth, and reflection (Zeta, 2007, p. 1).

Ancient Roman statue of Isis, in the Collection of Greek and Roman Antiquities in the Kunsthistorisches Museum, Vienna. First half of the 2nd century, found in Naples, Italy. Made out of black-and-white marble. Isis, originally an Egyptian goddess, was increasingly popular among Romans, who made her one of their own, with Roman attire, features and dress. (Photo: Gryffindor, CC BY-SS 3.0 and CC BY 2.5)

Jacobs (2015) describes Isis as the creative feminine and natural spirit, whose expression, we have learned, comes through feeling. One of her attributes is playing a sistrum, a rattle with three strings that she made herself. It is a symbol of what is and what will be. Through her magic, Isis creates music with the sistrum, using this same creative feeling to drive away evil spirits and demons. In fact, her magical and creative powers are the distant origins of using noisemakers on the last morning of the year in Switzerland and on New Year's Eve in the United States.

Isis is the vessel for good and evil, but she longs for the good and shuns the evil—although she may do negative things in order to further consciousness, Jacobs explains. Isis does not destroy evil, but contains it. Under her influence, I would suggest, the feminine value of nonviolence is consciously lived out. That is, under the divine guidance of Isis, psychologically speaking, humanization of the drive for primitive violence could develop into a state of more natural aggression (Jung, 1980b, CW 18, para. 1660).

Jacobs describes the myth referred to by von Franz (1980, p. 61) in which Isis puts a poisonous snake in the father-god's path, having used his spittle to knit a holy snake. Originally having the greatest power, the sun god Re had become old and uncaring, and people were suffering under his reign. Hence, Isis places the serpent along his daily route, and he is bitten, its poisonous venom making the senile man very ill. Isis offers her magic powers of healing in exchange for his revealing his secret name, which carries *mana* or life power. Magic and healing go together in Isis. At the end, Isis succeeds and gains power equal to the godhead (von Franz, 1980, p. 61). This story depicts the underworld's poisonous energy, which, according to Jacobs (2015), "promotes good while still remaining allied to evil." In other words, Isis can "use that energy to promote good," and she "never kills."

From a psychological perspective, the alliance of good and evil could be felt, then consciously held, and allowed to live in our lives without angry destructiveness (Jacobs, 2015). This is not the same as being nice, but rather an experiencing of the urge of wanting good. "I ordained that the true should be thought good," Isis proclaims. Jacobs suggests we can experience the flow into life *with* dark energy.

It is difficult to face an expression of poisonous energy and avoid acting it out, which would be basically dishonest and represent only an extreme. How do you metabolize or dispose of toxic energy and be true to yourself and the other? Isis describes it above as an awareness of the urge or impulse toward good. She likens it to an inner sense of rightness, which allows a greater awareness for holding and living a more natural aggression.

The first challenge, I suggest, is to recognize or become aware of the poisonous or destructive influence inside—to pause—and then follow more consciously that impulse, maybe even to get away, whether it be a literal outward retreat or a symbolic inner detachment. One of the primary goals is to *not* identify with the destructive energy. This may take time and require a holding, delay of gratification and moments of not knowing. Remaining centered in yourself helps avoid escalation and a power conflict. Every individual surely struggles with this dilemma.

Maintaining boundaries, with the awareness of enduring both sides, yields a conscious aliveness, according to Jacobs (2015): "We try to achieve the middle way," she encourages, versus moving from "one extreme to the other." The drive to individuation requires the necessary balance between good and evil, not in the *logos* way, which would involve a rational process, but with a feeling sense of life energy.

The vessel often seen in Isis's left hand contains the water of life and the water of death; it is deadly and also revitalizing (Jacobs, 2015). Of Isis it is written, "The ancient Egyptian goddess Isis has many gifts to share with modern women. Isis embodies the strengths of the feminine, the capacity to feel deeply about relationships, the act of creation, and the source of sustenance and protection" (Goddess Gift, n.d.).

From Sophia to Isis to Mary, the development of the archetype of the feminine is seen. Russian icons, according to Jacobs, combine and go beyond traditional Christian mythology to broaden our perspective on the feminine divine. The icons depict salvation and healing. Jacobs says they appear "like an old wise woman" and suggests the viewer can feel in their faces a knowledge of darkness and death.

Wisdom has come through images since the beginning of life, according to Jacobs (2015). An unspeakable and often numinous experience of the wisdom archetype can be felt through the viewing or creation of art. This same experience likely occurred when the ancients first drew figures on the walls of caves.

The veneration of Isis as the goddess of wisdom lasted over 3,000 years, until the second century CE (Baring & Cashford, 1991, p. 225). She was worshipped from England to Afghanistan, originally spreading from Egypt throughout much of the Roman Empire and Mediterranean areas, including Greece (Tyldesley, n.d.).

CHAPTER 3
Circumambulating *Eros*

As titled, this chapter is a circumambulation of *eros*, not only by an articulation from the perspectives of Sibylle Birkhäuser-Oeri, Russell Lockhart, Marie-Louise von Franz, and C.G. Jung, but also through the lens of my own personal experiences of the Wise Old Woman spirit. By slowly spiraling around the motif in this way, we move increasingly closer to the mystery of *eros*, while remembering that an archetype can never be fully understood.

Birkhäuser-Oeri begins our circular path, explicating how the mother archetype works through humans. In her book, *The Mother: Archetypal Images in Fairytales* (1988), she begins by describing their influence via *eros*. Lockhart, author of *Words as Eggs: Psyche in Language and Clinic* (1983), is the next creative writer and expert on particularly unique and original ways of understanding and living *eros*. Von Franz's reflections on *eros* follow, including how she appraises American culture on *eros* functioning. Lastly, *eros* will be seen from the perspective of Jung, who recognized over time the development of *eros* and expanded it into a symbol of the source of life itself. Thus, I begin, appropriately, with the Mother.

Eros as the Wise Old Woman Spirit in the Archetype of the Mother

Just as the multitude of the feminine deities casts light on the aliveness of the Wise Old Woman archetype, so do the many forms of the Great Mother archetype. If the Wise Old Woman spirit is contained in the Great Mother archetype, then the mothering function could be considered a part of wisdom's makeup. The mother archetype is central to the feminine principle and *eros* is its foundation.

Birkhäuser-Oeri writes that images of the mother are eternal, not unlike the feminine deities, having subhuman or superhuman traits quite different from human mothers, yet expressing inner psychological realities (1988, p. 13). Grimms' fairy tales, in particular, are the "barebones of the psyche," and less distorted than personal associations (von Franz 1996, pp. 1, 26). In folk or fairy tales, qualities are portrayed in black-and-white abstractions—not as the complex mixtures that are part of being human—so inconsistencies between good and bad characters can be more easily identified. According to Birkhäuser-Oeri, the Earth Mother archetype as represented in fairy tales shows an endless diversity and, like all archetypes, is depicted in both good and evil forms.

For example, the mother, grand or otherwise, might be the good-enough mother who provides wise guidance that helps children learn to share or she might be a witch mother who initially kidnaps, and then imprisons, a beautiful maiden destined to be a queen. Whereas one provides helping *eros*, guidance, wisdom, and *emptiness*, the other is abandoned and abandoning, her despair turned desperate and her greed for power mistaken for self-control. These are very different expressions of the maternal archetype, one an example of an aspect of the Wise Old Woman spirit and the other more like a dark Sorceress.

An important distinction to be made is between the *eros* that refers to connection or relationship, whether loving or hating, versus the *eros* that pertains to a higher order love beyond mere preference or attraction, to the highest form of feeling: a "genuine interest in ... and being there for the other person" (Von Franz, 1999, p. 70). Ideally, connection and love breathe together, but relationship too often is absent of love. *Eros* as an unselfish love, the mother-father of all higher consciousness, is a creative force, an eros-love, if you will, and incomprehensible to the intellect.

Birkhäuser-Oeri affirms that nature and spirit can only maintain their "independence through continually experiencing the antithesis" of each other and by recognizing how one affects the other (Birkhäuser-Oeri, 1988, p. 18). She also observes that goddesses of early and classical religions from thousands of years ago have maintained an aliveness that continues to be seen in suprapersonal fairy tale images of "a female who never dies" (p. 18).

She reminds us of our conscious loss of this divine female power, the feminine principle, which was worshipped as a great goddess for thousands of years. Birkhäuser-Oeri notes that the Christian religion "possesses no goddesses, and for centuries [Western] culture has lacked a proper appreciation of *eros*" (1988, p. 85). As mentioned in Chapter 1, with few exceptions, religious culture worldwide is one-sidedly patriarchal in nature, both neglectful and hostile to *eros*, and thus, harmful to everyone.

This disparagement of *eros* was one of the accidental discoveries I made while reading many of the fairy tales, rather, parts I did not read. That is, important aspects of the Wise Old Woman *as eros* were missing. Not even alluded to, just missing. Important feminine experience, female or male, went unacknowledged. Consequently, and for example, vital periods of Rapunzel's life were absent but will be dreamed forward and come from active imaginations I had with the Wise Old Woman spirit. She guided the text toward a way of understanding the cultural implications of a feminine arrested, tested, and later redeemed to a royal Selfhood.

Eros: A Way of Discerning the Wise Old Woman Spirit

Examining the Great Mother archetype brings us psychologically closer to the ground of the Wise Old Woman spirit. You will read about the Healing Nature Mother, who resides among Birkhäuser-Oeri's fairy tale manifestations in the character of Granny Evergreen. She appears in natural timelessness, enhancing life beyond the evergreen, pointing toward the eternal harmony and solidarity of loving *eros*.

Make no mistake, it's the psychological qualities of *eros* and *emptiness* that we need to understand and live, that we require for balance and grounding. Now is a good time to invite you to reflect on your own inner experiences with a helping old woman, one who has entered your life in dreams, felt visions, active imaginations, or synchronicities in the outer world. This review of memories may be the most important thing you can do to begin to grasp the writings, ideas and feelings about the Wise Old Woman spirit's *eros* and *emptiness*.

As an example of my own remembering, I had a deeply felt dream in the early days of my analytic training. I required surgery in the spring of 2008, missing a *Blockcourse,* the two-week intensive lectures and study that the C.G. Jung and von Franz Centre held twice a year in Switzerland, when I had just begun the course in the fall of 2007.[2] After searching for an analytical home for so long, I was a bit distressed about missing classes so soon. In hindsight, the experience seems not so unusual. I felt the loss, nevertheless. I wrote the analyst supervising my first paper to explain its delay. Here is part of what I wrote to him of my fate and my dream:

DREAM AFTER BEING SLOWED BY SURGERY RE: FAIRYTALE WRITING (AUGUST 17, 2008)

Dear R.H.,
I confess, "ego" has had to accept the slower-than-anticipated progress, experiencing this reality with a bit of distress. I had a dream not long ago about my being ...
... in a group in which Jung, himself, was in attendance. He was tall and handsome and white-haired. Another woman in the group asked Jung, "Do you love me?" Jung arose, and without a word, went to her and gave her a hug. I cried silently when this happened. Then Jung came over to me, and again, without speaking, he embraced me and gave me a big hug.

Now apart from the personal meaning of the dream and the power and numinosity in which the old man himself embraces me, a closer look reveals the most important message of all, the one arising from Jung's own positive *eros* and feminine energy, the Wise Old Woman within.[3] It is just this feminine energy, this Wise Old Woman's *eros,* that resides

---

[2] The Centre was founded in 1994. This was twenty-ninth Blockcourse at that time.
[3] The Wise Old Woman seems potentiated here by making herself known through Jung in my dream—the woman within the man within the woman—that's me. This suggests that dream figures themselves may have an animus or anima (the language developed in a heterosexual context). Jung's non-verbal response of positive connection symbolizes eros, and as the foundation of the feminine, leaves no doubt that the feminine is a part of the man. It's no surprise that a mothering eros arises from Jung, emphasizing and distinguishing his greater integration of the feminine.

within every man and woman, offering the connectedness needed for unity, strength and peace.

In the dream, Jung heard and felt my unspoken words and responded with a gesture of warmth, acceptance, and reassurance. I could say that he treated me in a motherly way. This wondrous experience seemed to occur with Jung's Wise Old Woman spirit, within the image of the Wise Old Man he represented. This is a wonderful example of how the feminine divine enlivens a man, in this case, the Jung in me, and guides him invisibly toward a heartfelt relatedness.

What can fairy tales tell us now as we turn our attention to three questions of particular interest?

1) Knowing that the Wise Old Woman spirit is a part of the Great Mother, in what ways do the various maternal archetypes reflect the feminine uniqueness of the Wise Old Woman?

2) In what ways do the Wise Old Woman's maternal dimensions influence human experience of *eros*?

3) What role does *eros* play in distinguishing the archetype of the Wise Old Woman from the archetype of Wise Old Man?

The answers might allow us to search for and see the archetype of the Wise Old Woman by observing feminine energies manifest in all humans.

Birkhäuser-Oeri on Maternal Archetypes: Reflect, Influence, and Distinguish

Birkhäuser-Oeri wrote about how the *eros* of the archetype of the mother as seen in fairytales can influence humans. In addition, her observations may help us in distinguishing the archetype of the Wise Old Woman from that of the Wise Old Man.

She reminds us that all characters in fairy tales represent "different tendencies within a single psyche" (1988, p. 109), which not only echoes the archetypal divinities of Chaos, Eros, and Logos, but also bridges them to the archetype of the Great Mother and to the human mother. The same may be said of dreams; figures in a dream typically represent various energies within an individual.

Birkhäuser-Oeri recognizes that the "two chief principles of all existence" are the father and mother archetypes (1988, p. 14). "Eros, the connecting principle, is the basic principle of the mother," she states. Joining what is divided and reconciling the opposites are essential aspects of both the maternal archetype and the *eros* principle. The Great Mother is described as creating links among all things and life in the darkness of illusions (p. 122). A connection between the unconscious and conscious in a loving *eros* way provides a sense of purpose and has a stimulating effect (p. 124).

Birkhäuser-Oeri also observed that *eros* connects people with others as well as with themselves (1988, p. 134). Fairy tales show that the Earth Mother, among many names for the Great Mother archetype, is "a dangerous power of darkness. [They also show, however,] ... her positive functions of helping, healing and creating as the birthplace of a spirituality at one with nature and the body. She personifies the *eros* principle, which combines opposites, while logos divides them" (p. 19). Birkhäuser-Oeri continues:

In her life-enhancing aspect, nature mother is also the principle of love in its deepest sense. That is why the Great Mother in mythology is nearly always a goddess of love, not only in the sense of a destructive passion, but also in a relationship promoting wholeness ... and can free us from unbearable isolation. (p. 134)

Birkhäuser-Oeri equates the feminine principle to love, and the lack of a valid attitude to it as the source of great psychological suffering in our time (1988, p. 18). In all humans, the instinctual drives are affected by the mother complex and can interfere in the spiritual process (p. 16). On the other hand, the mother complex can also foster creative living in relationship with the Wise Old Woman spirit.

As the basic principle of the mother, *eros* "needs human beings to come to consciousness" (Birkhäuser-Oeri, 1988, p. 57). In psychological terms, the Great Mother helps people hold a protective, motherly attitude toward new and threatening unconscious material until it can be "taken in" and "warmed with emotion" (p. 70). This is one example of how the feminine *eros* function helps with daily dream work.

The symbolic mother, like Isis, Birkhäuser-Oeri notes, is the source of light to be found in the darkness. From a psychological perspective, going into this darkness, into the unconscious, is a prerequisite for increasing consciousness and, in this case, for freedom from possession by the symbolic mother (1988, p. 22). The archetype of the mother, she states, has its effects on human beings "in its destructive guise, ... as a shaper of destiny and ... as a force for change and renewal of life" (p. 25). She explains, "The highest form of *eros* is one which serves totality ... [and is] not controlled by the ego" (pp. 57, 76).

Circumambulating *Eros* in the Fairy Tale of Fledgling: The Fire Mother

In that light, our fairy tale adventure begins with Birkhäuser-Oeri's presentation of Grimms' fairytale *Fledgling*,[4] a tender story of two young children who are deeply loving and dear to one another. Most importantly, Fledgling, a child-hero, is connected by a deep emotional relationship to the feminine.

Here is Birkhäuser-Oeri's synopsis of the tale:

The hero of this story is a foundling discovered by a forester high up in a tree. A hawk had stolen him from his mother while she was asleep and taken him to the tree. The child, named Fledgling, is adopted by the man and grows up with his daughter Lenchen.

The children are very fond of one another. However, there is an evil cook in the house and one day she decides to cook Fledgling and eat him. Luckily Lenchen discovers the plan in time. First thing next morning she says to her brother, "Don't leave me, and I won't leave you," and Fledgling replies, "Never ever." Lenchen warns him not to forget, and they both run away.

The evil cook sends her scullion boys after them, and there follows a metamorphosis-chase. Before each important action Fledgling and Lenchen swear faithfulness and love, she saying,

---

[4] Also translated as *Foundling Bird*.

55

"Don't leave me, and I won't leave you," and he replying, "Never ever." In this way they succeed in escaping from the scullion boys and later the witch, and finally they destroy her. When Lenchen changes herself into a duck she pulls the witch into the water, where she drowns.

This unwavering emotional bond is the positive *eros* between them of mutual love and faithfulness, a kinship that goes beyond ego efforts. Although the children represent not yet developed parts within a human psyche, they are, nevertheless, a loving pair and not unlike sweethearts. This kind of youthful relationship may be seen psychologically as potential wholeness or "something coming into being" (Birkhäuser-Oeri, 1988, p. 76).

Always serving wholeness, *eros* in this brother-sister relationship symbolizes connection to the process of becoming united within, versus attachment to an outer object. She states that we only know ourselves through relationships or *eros*. To that end, we remember that a partnership with the Wise Old Woman spirit, as an emissary of the Self, offers connection with the Infinite, increasing self-knowledge and the capacity for genuine relationship.

This particular tale vitalizes the process of the masculine being guided by the feminine principle and enlivened by an emphasis on the Wise Old Woman spirit's qualities—*eros* and *emptiness*. This is the very transformation needed to break open the patriarchy's lopsided grip on the world today.

As stated, fairy tale figures comprise multiple energies within an individual. Therefore, according to Birkhäuser-Oeri, on a personal level, the forester's daughter, Lenchen, can be understood as the anima of Fledgling.

Fledgling is so named because as a young baby boy, he was taken to his destiny by a dark spiritual force, symbolized by a hawk. He was kidnapped by this divine darkness from his mother's arms as they lay sleeping on the ground below, then placed in the highest tree. Sadly, the mother's loss is disregarded, quite unseen in the story, and the *eros* in her grief is not written. This devaluation and void of *eros* will be noted again when learning about Rapunzel.

The babe is then found by a forester who adopts him. Fledgling, so named, grows up with the forester and his daughter, Lenchen, who loves Fledgling, as he loves her in return.

Thus, the auspicious beginning is the babe's divine theft that opens our story with sorrow and *emptiness*, an *emptiness* that holds the potential for eternal love unseen, yet in Fledgling's future. Seen as a dynamic within a single human, these three (forester, Lenchen, and Fledging) represent internal energies that fill three-fourths of the picture.

The fourth aspect is symbolized by the terrible mother, or *Fire Mother*, an old woman who is also the household cook. The witch-cook is readying the pot in which to boil Fledgling because she wants to eat him, like a devouring mother complex from which the hero struggles to achieve *separatio*.[5] Psychologically, being cooked is about being exposed to the intense heat of archetypal emotions and passions of the unconscious. This is similar to the archetypal hero's journey, which often includes encountering danger from the personal mother.

Lenchen, however, gets wind of the evil plot and warns Fledgling. Together they plan their escape. By seeing ahead, Lenchen functions as his intuition. Moreover, Lenchen serves as his inspiration and imagination, suggesting he change shapes with her when evading the wicked cook's pursuit: "Turn into a rose-bush and I'll be the rose upon it."

Thus, Fledgling is a fairy tale that anticipates the union of the opposites as he and Lenchen commit their hearts to one another, remaining faithful to each other and an unknown future. Lenchen turns to Fledgling saying, "Don't leave me and I won't leave you," and he replies, "Never ever." This echoes Jung's and von Franz's statements: "Protect me and

---

[5] *Separatio* is a stage in the alchemical process that psychologically has to do with review and rediscovery of formerly hidden parts within. It has to do with the breaking up and filtering of psychological material. Greater consciousness then helps us decide to discard or integrate this psychological material. D. W. Hauck (n.d.) writes, "Separation is letting go of the self-inflicted restraints to our true nature so we can shine through." Following the decision, one's essence can be reclaimed along with the "visionary gold" once rejected by the overly rationalistic masculine. Note that Jung was delighted to discover that the alchemical process could serve as a vessel for conveying psychological experiences; specifically, he compared the psychological stages of human development, or individuation, to the multiple stages found in alchemy.

I will protect you," and "Help me and I will help thee," both citing the invitation to partner with the unconscious (see Chapter 1). They repeat these words to each other before every act of escaping the witch-cook. By repeatedly pledging faithfulness and love to one another, promising eternal *eros*, they are able to overcome the destructive tendencies of the witch-cook. In other words, the person with a negative devouring mother complex can ward off her primitive aggression through *eros* with the opposite pole within (Birkhäuser-Oeri, 1988, p. 78). In this case, the psychological unity with the boy's own budding inner feminine is another influence of *eros* from the positive side of the mother archetype.

In the end, Lenchen, having imagined herself into a duck and swimming upon Fledgling as a lake, pulls the cook down under the water, drowning her. Birkhäuser-Oeri calls this thoughtful use of fantasy a "magic gift." The terrible mother had just laid down at the water's edge, preparing to drink it.

As seen by the outcome of the fairy tale, imagination provided by the anima is one way for a man to avoid an otherwise destructive complex (Birkhäuser-Oeri, 1988, p. 78). Clearly, imagination also works for a woman who has to wrestle with her own terrible mother inside. The agent of change within the culture appears to be the *eros* of the renewing youthful feminine, a helpful energy who can go beyond logic and strategizing to call up magical and creative solutions when there are otherwise none. When Birkhäuser-Oeri suggests that the real purpose of *eros* is true relationship between one individual and another, she is talking about *eros* as a vital healer within each individual and between each other throughout the world.

From a male standpoint, the loving and interdependent relationship that Fledgling has developed with his anima reveals the necessity of *eros* to life balance, inner unity, and integrity. It should be noted that multiple and ongoing assurances of love are a part of any lasting bond and could be said to be required for any serious and deepening connection. As Lockhart says, "Eros needs telling" (1983, p 129).

I maintain that the same applies in today's circumstances, culturally speaking, insomuch as the routine but conscious voicing of courteous regard for another—for example, "Thank you," "I appreciate it," "You're welcome," and "Excuse me"—is a vital step toward an authentic and healing community. Of course, the first step is really the step of courtesy toward the self.

It seems that Fledgling's destiny dictated the course of his life in which he would lose his Earth Mother only to discover renewal by developing a relationship with the youthful feminine. The faithful union of Fledgling and Lenchen reveals a loving alliance not unlike the one we can have with the Wise Old Woman spirit. From a collective perspective, this could be reflection of a working alliance within society between the feminine and masculine principles, inviting a balance that, in this case, is led by the wisdom of the maiden feminine. Lenchen's *eros* leads the way.

Circumambulating *Eros* in the Fairy Tale of Rapunzel: The Imprisoning Sorceress

In her book *The Mother: Archetypal Images in Fairy Tales,* Birkhäuser-Oeri turns to the fairy tale *Rapunzel* to show how knowledge of one's own shadow is required for healthy *eros* functioning.[6] In her work Birkhäuser-Oeri introduces us to this truth: only when we're able to accept and love ourselves, are we truly able to love another.

Eros depictions abound in this fairy tale; however, *eros* has also been left out of important parts. Because of this, Rapunzel's birth and early life will be dreamed forward and comes from the Wise Old Woman spirit during active imaginations. The Wise Old Woman thus directed my focus to important aspects of *eros* at four life stages: 1) Possibilities for *eros* in Rapunzel's early life, 2) Rapunzel's likely experiences of *eros* in the tower, 3) How *eros* could have served Rapunzel's survival in the desert, and 4) Ultimately how Rapunzel realizes a *coniunctio* and fulfillment of her destiny as a Queen.

These imaginations represent only one possible version of her life's beginnings. Dreaming the story on with the help of the Wise Old Woman is a unique and unpredictable event, a way of emerging through image and making meaning in the empty spaces of the tale.

---

[6] Here, I use Jung's later definition of the meaning of shadow as comprising all of what is unconscious in us. That includes unknown parts of our psyches—negative, positive, or neither, and parts of ourselves not yet discovered or developed.

Thus, the words I use to fill the unwritten spaces of this tale strive to connect Rapunzel's life experiences with her culmination as a Queen, the ruling cultural value. It is with humble recognition that this part of the tale speaks to us through the wisdom of the Wise Old Woman spirit.

Certainly all fairy tales can be divided into stages, but in this particular tale, Rapunzel lives through four conditions corresponding to these stages: 1) early life isolation *and* relationships in the walled-in garden; 2) locked up in the tower and relationship primarily within herself; 3) survival in the desert and relationships, again; and finally, 4) her ultimate *coniunctio* with the prince and her life as a Queen. The tale essentially ends with the feminine at a new beginning. In other words, change can be observed in the feminine collective unconscious over time that points to significant psychological development toward a greater wholeness.

Rapunzel, as a symbol of the dominant feminine unconscious, is uprooted, unloved, and lives with great loss and extraordinary isolation throughout her young life. Until she is visited by the prince, the only individual she has known is the enchantress-witch. Is this a part of the unconscious feminine's life right now? What rejected aspects of the feminine, conscious and unconscious, remain with us today?

Sadly, but also fortunately, it is Rapunzel's own dark feminine against whom she struggles. Is the old way of womanhood threatened by the new? All Rapunzel has known, in human terms, is the enchantress. Once she is found out, ejected from the tower, and sent into the desert, she confronts her own demons, withdrawing enough of her projections from the witch, working to be more conscious of what she's doing, and thereby discovering herself to become who she's meant to be.

First let me provide a synopsis of the tale combining both Birkhäuser-Oeri's and Grimms' renditions:

At the beginning of the story there is a man and his wife who have been childless for a long time. When the wife at last becomes pregnant she sees a plant called rapunzel, a type of lettuce, growing behind her house, in a garden that belongs to an enchantress. She has such a strong desire for it that she believes she will die if she does not get some. Her husband obtains it for her once, but when he tries a second time he is caught by the owner of the garden.

"Let mercy take the place of justice," he pleaded, "I only made up my mind to do it out of necessity," explaining how his beloved wife would die without the rampion. The sorceress softens and spares his life, but he can only escape her power if he promises her the child his wife is expecting. "It shall be well treated," says the witch, "and I will care for it like a mother." The man in his terror consents to everything.

When the child is born, the sorceress arrives. She names the child Rapunzel and "collects it." Rapunzel grows into the most beautiful child under the sun and has long golden hair. When she is twelve, the sorceress locks her up in a high tower in the forest. She is the only one who can reach her by calling "Rapunzel, Rapunzel, let down your hair" and climbing up the girl's long plaits.

A few years later a prince is riding through the forest and hears the girl's beautiful singing. He watches the witch's method of climbing up to the girl, imitates it when she is away, and so reaches Rapunzel. He immediately proposes to her, she accepts, and together they plan for her escape; he will bring her a length of silk each time he comes so they can create a ladder out of it for her to climb down the tower.

The prince climbs up to her every evening once the witch has gone for the day. On one occasion, however, Rapunzel gives herself away: she tells the witch how much heavier she is to pull up than the young prince. The witch is mad with rage at the deception, cuts off Rapunzel's hair, and takes her to a desert place where she lives in great misery.

Then the old woman waits until the prince comes that evening and pulls him up by the girl's plaits. She greets him with a poisonous look and says scornfully: "Oho, you've come for the love of your life, but the pretty bird's gone from the nest and won't sing any more. The cat's taken it, and it'll scratch your eyes out too, you've lost Rapunzel. You'll never see her again!"

Wild with despair, the prince throws himself off the tower.
He is not killed, but the thorns he falls into pierce his eyes. He
wanders around the forest blind for a number of years until he
finally reaches the desert place where Rapunzel and the twins, a
boy and a girl who have been born in the meantime, are leading
a miserable existence. He hears her song and finds her again
by following the sound. They embrace, and two of her tears that
wet his eyes restore his sight. Now he takes her back into his
kingdom to be his wife and they live happily ever after.

Rapunzel's story reflects the oppression and disdain the feminine has suffered, and her first opponent appears as a negative mother complex. The split-off and dark mother archetype for this fairy tale is referred to as "enchantress," "the owner," "sorceress," "witch," "the old woman," or according to Birkhäuser-Oeri, "Mother as Imprisoning Sorceress" (1988, pp. 82–94). When Rapunzel tries to escape, pregnant with twins, she is abandoned in the desert. Her prince, or the masculine of the time, is helpless and cannot save her.

Although there are no descriptions of how she faced her desert demons during this process of integration, her reunion with the masculine suggests its accomplishment. I now briefly offer possible themes of this process that are typical of the feminine's psychological task of becoming conscious, beginning with self-knowledge, self-forgiveness, and self-acceptance.

Possibilities for *Eros* in Rapunzel's Early Life

At first glance, Rapunzel, "the prettiest child under the sun," seems anything but loved by her parents, betrayed before she is even born, according to Birkhäuser-Oeri. Is Rapunzel more a witch's possession than a cherished and beloved daughter?

Rapunzel is born the daughter of a typical couple, though they are childless for many years. When her pregnancy was discovered, the mother surely fantasized about her future baby, holding expectations for all the best and feeling new life and movements within. Although unconscious and unknown, the mother's ideas about Rapunzel would likely have been in support of a royal life path.

Certainly, an *eros* connection existed between the mother and child even before Rapunzel's birth, so, of course, the mother grieved her sudden loss when she was born. Motherly feeling is not confined to the nearness of her child. In her moments of sorrow, could the mother have intuited, maybe even dreamed, that Rapunzel had a great destiny before her, that she was fated to become the queen?

Indeed, Rapunzel becomes the emerging dominant feminine. She represents a new *eros* and fresh emotional value, an arising feminine within the collective and opposed to *logos*. The birth of Rapunzel can be understood as the end of what has been a state of barrenness in the culture, a barrenness replaced by a heroic feminine. In this sense, her coming into being might be understood as symbolic of *eros* being reborn.

According to the fairy tale, Rapunzel's pregnant mother is seized by desire and thinks that she will die if she can't have the lettuce grown just beyond the neighbor's wall. That high wall is symbolic of the decades of injustice and degradation that the feminine has suffered and how such abandonment can result in the most negative of ways—the rejected feminine as expressed by the witch or sorceress. In other words, the wall itself creates the witch. The process of walling off, or rejecting one aspect of the maternal principle, separates it from the rest of psychic life, thus distorting the maternal.

However, the mother-to-be pines for the rampion (*rapunzel*), an earthy image of feminine wholeness—fresh, round, and leafy-green. Moreover, rampion is known to have white, thick, deep roots that can be eaten as well as the leaves. These roots can be understood as symbolizing "inner values rooted deep in existence" (Birkhäuser-Oeri, 1988, p. 86). Her yearning shows again how the mother and baby Rapunzel-in utero are connected through an *eros* already between them, something invisible, but surely real.

The mother accepts that it is forbidden, but her cravings increase every day, and she eventually begins to falter and look pale. Her husband inquires with alarm, "What ails you, dear wife?" (Grimms, 1972 p. 73). When he hears that his beloved fears dying without rapunzel, he rallies against his own risk of life, thinking, "let it cost what it will" (p. 73). On an individual level, his attitude reflects the courage needed to connect with the unconscious when called to the process of individuation, facing what's "behind the wall."

Indeed, the enchantress confronts the father the second time he climbs the wall and descends into the garden. When the father explains that his wife's life depends on the lettuce, the enchantress's anger is softened. To spare him from her powers, however, she demands Rapunzel when she is born in exchange for the lettuce. In his terror, the father agrees.

At length, having promised the father that the child will be well taken care of and receive her "motherly" care, the enchantress "collects" the baby as soon as she is born. No mention is made of the father telling the mother of his promise to the witch, suggesting that Rapunzel's kidnapping is not only a traumatic loss, but also a source of deeply felt guilt by the father. He had begged the witch for mercy, but his fear of death seemed to paralyze him.

The disparagement of *eros* was glaring at times. Exceedingly painful to read, or rather, not to read, the mother's loss is not even mentioned, nor is the father's. Where is *eros* in this part of the story? Important feminine experience, female or male, is unacknowledged. Why did the author leave it out? Isn't this omission the exact thing that happens in our lives when feminine *eros* isn't even conscious, not even given a second thought?

The missing *eros* seems replaced by the mother's cravings and the father's horror in facing the witch. Although each of them lacked ego strength, seemed helpless and feared for their lives, no mention is made in the tale to suggest they would have chosen to relinquish the long-expected little one.

We might ask, after waiting so long for new growth to emerge from their relationship, why did the parents seem to succumb so willingly? But then we remember the power of the unconscious and the grip of the complex. The Jungian term *complex* describes a more or less autonomous behavior—one with patterns and predictable outcomes and characterized by extreme emotion.[7] To be caught by a complex can feel dehumanizing

---

[7] Under Notes: "*Complex*, as has been said, is not to be taken only in a negative sense, but as a plexus of charged images in the mind surrounded by powerful emotions, a focus of mental energy, a fatefully significant core" (Birkhäuser-Oeri, 1988, p. 160).

and, at the same time, arise from the spiritual depths. *Autonomous* means unconscious or self-contained, existing independently, and having sway over us at times that we don't understand (Birkhäuser-Oeri, 1988, p.160). Once activated, the complex blinds us to all we can temporarily know and may put us at risk for losing our dignity in a way that means losing ourselves. In other words, we are beside ourselves. The wife's extraordinary craving for the forbidden lettuce depicts such an irrational wisdom coming from the complex. Why would she want the very thing that endangers her husband's life?

The secret of the complex is that it belies great value and bespeaks the *eros* we unconsciously experience with another. Birkhäuser-Oeri questions if there might be an invisible deeper source in the mother's psyche for her craving. Could the unborn Rapunzel require this particular lettuce for proper nourishment of her psyche's development, a kind of baptismal integration of the dark?

On the surface, *eros* appears nonexistent between the parents and the newborn. Nothing is written about it; it is simply not mentioned in the tale. That *eros* could be so out of mind, so not present, is tragic with a seriousness of the gravest sort.

This issue was addressed by the former Prime Minister of New Zealand, the Rt. Hon. Jacinda Ardern, who spoke of the problem of such omissions, remembering the importance of kindness, the significance of empathy and tone of communication. At the two-year memorial for the 2019 mosque attacks, Ardern asserted in an inspirational speech the importance of including certain words for building trust:

> Many of us will remember, or indeed have seen children being taught from a very young age to be stoic. That if they face the harsh words of others, they should adopt a stiff upper lip. Perhaps it has been our way of teaching children resilience in the face of those who might intend to cause harm. Of course, we want our children to be resilient, but surely no more than we want our children to be kind?
>
> And so we have to ask ourselves, what does it take to create a generation that is empathetic but strong. That is kind, but fair.

That is knowledgeable but curious. That knows the power of words, and uses them to challenge, defend, and empower …

We all own and hold the power of words. We use them, we hear them, we respond to them. How we choose to use this most powerful of tools is our choice.[8]

It is noteworthy that as of 2022 New Zealand has been named the second most peaceful country in the world (Iceland is number one), according to the Global Peace Index. The country is widely known as favoring inclusivity and diversity, both targets of white supremacy.

From a worldwide perspective, the conflict with *eros* is typically depicted as society's (unconscious) adhesion to the patriarchal status quo versus support for *eros* as an emerging and feminine newness. However, in much of the collective, *eros* is barely recognized at all. Certainly in Rapunzel's case, positive *eros* seems nearly obliterated at times, and this shows part of the state of the kind of world that lacks loving *eros*. It's just missing. Lost children are subject to the fates; the important rebalancing of societal functioning, stalled.

This stall or delay may have to do with Birkhäuser-Oeri's warning that what's new is dangerous simply because it *is* new and not yet known. Fear is born of not understanding, and fear begets violence. Specifically, the ever-changing melting pot here in the United States, with its new and diverse ethnicities and colors, poses what seems like an unending struggle with a powerful white supremacy and those identified with authoritarian dominance.

Returning to the tale, Rapunzel's upbringing could not have been all loss and fear. In fact, prior to being locked in the tower, her life with the enchantress likely allowed important development outdoors in nature where she could run freely and play among the plants and flowers, maybe even streams and rocks. Certainly she encountered a variety of creatures: squirrels, raccoons, possums, rabbits, snakes, and other animals that lived near the garden and became her friends. Their presence offered Rapunzel a direct experience of her basic physical instincts, so she could witness

---

[8] "Jacinda Ardern Marks the Second Anniversary of the Christchurch Massacre," *7News Australia,* March 14, 2021, https://www.youtube.com/watch?v=Obvteq2S3S4.

for herself their way of survival—scrounging for food and water, mating and birthing, building a home—learning by proxy the skills she would need later.

A more conscious and reciprocal relationship with the Wise Old Woman spirit often begins like this, with undisturbed early experiences in nature, particularly if the mother is absent or difficult. This is the kind of psychological development that grows within the individual, not only for Rapunzel's greater consciousness, but also as her deepening respect for Mother Earth.

Remembering Jung's childlike game of playing among the watery reeds and stones, we might imagine Rapunzel creating a personal village herself, with figures of pebbles or clay with imaginative lives of their own. While these are only possibilities, the course of the tale suggests that there were many hidden but enduring and positive *eros* experiences along Rapunzel's way.

The years between birth and age twelve are formative years, and for Rapunzel, they must have been years of creating relationships with every living and nonliving object of her affection, years symbolic of unconscious connection with the Wise Old Woman spirit. Couldn't the Wise Old Woman have provided such a compensation? This seems so, despite the hardships Rapunzel faced—or maybe even because of them.

Relationships of all types save Rapunzel despite her seeming to live a most solitary life. Although specifics are unknown, it appears that the love relationship Rapunzel developed with herself provided the strength and nourishment she needed to carry on. Perhaps the enchantress's mothering side was sufficient when it was just the two of them. Even occasional support during Rapunzel's early childhood could have served to reinforce her sense of self, bolstering her self-esteem.

This was likely a time of learning how to differentiate *eros* as a higher love from the hate, fear, or power drives that often contaminate *eros,* changing or distorting it, and distinguishing it from the helping *eros* of the Wise Old Woman. Dreams and a garden's variety of relationships with nature served as guides. Rapunzel surely experienced for herself the outcome of her choices, which later helped her face life-and-death situations. Rapunzel's early childhood was undoubtedly a significant time of preparation for the emerging youthful feminine she represented. That stage of growth, highlighted within the fairy tale, is a reality to consider in terms of how the culture needs or prepares for the transformation that lies ahead.

Rapunzel's Likely Experiences of *Eros* in the Tower

Looking at Rapunzel's tower life from the outside, we see little visible social experience—only abandonment and imprisonment. In truth, Rapunzel's new circumstances seem similar to those in the sorceress's walled-off fortress-home, only worse. Is she to live the very isolation, the split from the greater reality, that can lead to her demise? Jung would say that the more distant a part of us is, the more troublesome it often becomes. How can Rapunzel be spared becoming a witch? What is it we're not seeing, scripted as we are to perceive in a certain way?

The dark feminine sorceress intensifies Rapunzel's seclusion when the child turns twelve by locking her into an impenetrable tower. Her solitude is amplified and deepened. Living in this confinement, Rapunzel continues to live apart from ordinary outer life and, indeed, from the very ground itself. Where might she find *eros?*

A closer look allows for two significant exceptions, motifs that serve as 1) *eros* to the earth, her long golden locks reaching down to the ground; and as 2) *eros* with the air around her, her beautiful voice of song cast afloat upon the ether.

These two experiences of *eros*, I suggest, help solidify Rapunzel's psychological foundation. They become the basis of her continuing journey forward. With the symbolic connection to Mother Earth by way of her plaits and a bond to the heavens with her song, Rapunzel is centered and open to the healing powers of both nature and spirit.

To begin, the yellow tresses are a source of multiple differing types of *eros*, connecting Rapunzel with the earth, linking her with the witch, and eventually uniting her with the prince who immediately falls in love with her. Therefore, hair as *eros* in this story shows connection to and from various others—including to her inner self—which is sometimes needed, sometimes an imposed necessity, and sometimes a bridge to her destiny.

Birkhäuser-Oeri (1988) reminds us that hair has neither nerves nor pain when cut. She relates this to the autonomous parts of the psyche that also grow involuntarily. At first, she reasons that Rapunzel would be naive and idealistic about the separate world below.

However, hair growing out of the head has to do with imagination, fantasies, thoughts, and ideas. Maybe Rapunzel has visions and memories of the garden where she had played freely as a child. Perhaps she reflects as she brushes her hair, feeling comforted by the gentle tugging, the way it might feel if her hair were being softly pushed back from her face.

Even though the hair itself has no feeling, the roots to the scalp are sensitive to pressure and pulling. When stroked with tenderness or even massaged, the head can feel particularly soothed. Whereas a touch on the head in other cultures may be seen as rude or taboo, as in Korea or Fiji, a touch of the hair or the head in Western culture is meant as a personal but kindly gesture, extended with empathy to a child or beloved or to one who is ill or dying or sometimes as a romantic prelude.

Birkhäuser-Oeri observes that the extraordinary length of Rapunzel's hair suggests it is a symbol for profound thoughts. In this context, hair may refer to a greater awareness of reflections and ideas, sometimes phrased as "seeing the light" or "it dawned on me." Moreover, greater consciousness is often imaged in dreams as a blonde figure, not unlike Rapunzel.

Knowing our own thoughts can be considered a kind of *eros* with the self, and through self-knowledge, contribute to a growing sense of integrity and wholeness. Perhaps this is the beginning of shadow exploration. After coming to terms with the natural denial of her imprisonment and the inevitable making of promises for its reversal, Rapunzel might ask herself, "What did I do?" Along with other mistreated children worldwide, she may wonder for many years about this, struggling with a kind of negative inflation, a false self-blame.

However, inner work especially as a teen can be a time of discovery, often revealing unknown skills and new talents (Avila-White, Schneider, & Domhoff, 1999). For example, many songwriters at a very young age can testify to the serendipitous arrival of lyrics as well as the tunes themselves in their dreams. In addition, dreams being so often compensatory, Rapunzel may well dream of making new friends or even escaping.

Confinement in the tower also means no peer pressure or judgments by the collective. Memories, hopes, and what ifs surely fill the largest part of tower life. Rapunzel has time to think, reflect, and enter the soul-searching necessary for the unseen and harsh test ahead.

Here, in the soul-searching, hair can be related to the spiritual realm. Birkhäuser-Oeri observes that Rapunzel's long, silky, golden hair has special value and is a symbol of greater understanding. Samson in the Old Testament is known for the spiritual strength that his hair symbolized. Rapunzel's hair could likewise have been a source of spiritual strength, the head being closer to the heavens, psychologically speaking, and described as "enlightenment, like a halo" (Birkhäuser-Oeri, 1988, p. 88).

A second way that the Wise Old Woman's *eros* comes to life is in Rapunzel's beautiful singing. It is the unique nature of her voice that first catches the attention of the prince when he is out riding in the woods. Instead of going toward a more cheerful and familiar harmony, the prince is attracted to Rapunzel's poignant tone born of years of imprisonment and suffering.

The beauty's subtle notes make the prince listen carefully. Birkhäuser-Oeri asserts it is only with great suffering that the feminine can find *eros* with the inner masculine. In other words, despair creates the possibility for "an emotional relationship with the positive animus," a transformation happening in the world within to both feminine and masculine energies simultaneously (Birkhäuser-Oeri, 1988, p. 89).

I must add that firsthand suffering within the feminine is also requisite for the development of deep feeling between any two humans in the outer world, apart from their gender, remembering that both feminine and masculine aspects belong to every individual. We do not have to go looking for the suffering. It will come of its own. It is how we meet it that poses the lasting question.

So the prince follows the melodious sounds, drawn to their emotional character and beguiled by their notes. As an ancient and eternal form of emotional expression for both humans and animals, singing is a natural outlet for feelings, delivered at best in harmony with the tones of the universe and invisibly related to the sky and air of the world (Birkhäuser-Oeri, 1988, p. 88).

J.E. Cirlot asserts that "singing ... is a natural connection" and further that "... singing ... is an image of the natural connexion [connection] between all things, and, at the same time, the communication, the spreading and the exaltation of the inner relationship linking all things together" (Schneider, 1946; quoted in Cirlot 1962, p. 215). It seems that Rapunzel's singing unknowingly creates a link to her future love and life.

With music, *eros* can be experienced as a sacred and spiritual connection to the higher powers. Prayers and rituals may be offered up in song, often in tune with the Wise Old Woman spirit. In this sense, *eros* as Rapunzel's singing, unites her to all without and within, seen and unseen, and at the same time, creates a celebration of its very self. The maiden's *eros* toward herself could be a refrain crooned daily as a melodious source of nourishment.

These two experiences of *eros* serve as both an anchor and a bridge to the outer world and befit Rapunzel's conscious foundation for all that has yet to unfold. From another perspective, the outer reality connected to the inner world is this *eros* and the core of all we do and are.

Eros reveals itself in unlimited ways throughout the dimension of time. The number 12, corresponding to her age when she's locked in the tower, reminds us that Rapunzel is experiencing multiple levels of growth—emotionally, psychologically, physically, and spiritually. "The dynamism of the number 12 can be seen as a need or possibility to activate the inner center by all the aspects or qualities of time" (Abt, 2005, p. 156).

It's not difficult to imagine that upon entering the tower at age twelve, Rapunzel's psyche is indeed enlivened from the inside, the human biology of adolescent development starting to churn, her womanhood literally beginning. The instinct of reflection and the heart's urges toward creativity are also stirred. Note that all these instincts are in communication with the body and all an expression of unconscious *eros*.

Her body's remarkable shape-changing growth is matched by a reawakening of emotional life each day. I imagine this as a part of Rapunzel's psychological development, the whole of which is being similarly stirred. Quite naturally, she begins with the grieving of the deep and ongoing loss she has sustained, loss she has endured for her whole life. After years of abandonment by both of her parents and now the enchantress as well—for imprisonment is also an abandonment—mourning is surely a part of Rapunzel's suffering.

Being centered in herself, Rapunzel can allow the experience of a natural depression, especially after such an abrupt *separatio* from the enchantress's walled-off home. The walled-off home is all she had ever known and now she is separated even from that. It is like an *enantiodromia*, seemingly turning her life in reverse or bringing it to a standstill, as tower life cocoons her with all its unknown workings.

Thus, she has time to mourn, to reflect, to digest, and to embody. There is time for memories, feelings, and *eros*—all in the *emptiness* of the tower. Could she have felt the presence of the Wise Old Woman spirit *as the emptiness*?

Picture Rapunzel looking out the tower window. Does she see the life she missed? How could this be a part of her destiny—increased isolation and *emptiness* in the tower? How might the Wise Old Women reach out to her, despite her being bartered, abandoned, kidnapped, and locked up?

Perhaps the fates do have a healthier kind of experience in mind for Rapunzel. Securely attached to the earth and sky, Rapunzel can explore her rich inner life. What might lie ahead in her discovery of the Self? The forced introversion in the tower seems to encourage self-exploration and self-examination. How might Rapunzel's faithfulness to the Wise Old Woman's *eros* have sustained her? Could her connection to the Wise Old Woman provide for greater self-confidence and help prepare the way?

Is this not unlike the stay-in-place orders we have lived under during the COVID-19 pandemic? Jung would tell us that reflection is an instinct, a basic necessity of life, yet it is not necessarily valued in the extroverted United States. Although confining in terms of social discourse, staying inside—whether voluntary or mandatory—offers a similar invitation for thoughtful introspection, contemplation and self-discovery.

Perhaps Rapunzel stumbles or even adventures into her inner life of dreams. When the unconscious wants to be heard, often its message will break through to consciousness and be remembered. At other times, a residual vividness of feeling or image is created, lingering when we awaken. Could these nightly dream-visitors invite and help begin a daily conversation with the Wise Old Woman spirit?

The Wise Old Woman spirit as the *emptiness* in the tower serves as a kind of alchemical vessel, providing a sacred place for being, creating and ripening. The secured tower, symbolic of a phallus-container, holds the creative powers of insemination and incubation, almost a premonition of what is to come.

During her later time in the tower Rapunzel meets the prince and becomes pregnant. The significance of the pregnancy, with the later emergence of the twins as a double newness, accentuates the effects of time, *eros* enveloping the feminine and the masculine together.

Perhaps the freedom of Rapunzel's early life, together with her inner work and reflection in the tower guided by the spirit of the Wise Old Woman, help her establish a loving and helping *eros* toward herself. Perhaps this can be seen as an invitation that still stands for many of us today, offering a chance to continue and deepen our basic self-regard and *eros* with the Wise Old Woman spirit and ourselves.

How *Eros* Could Have Served Rapunzel's Survival in the Desert

Unfortunately, the first *coniunctio* with the prince is short-lived. While hefting the witch up the tower, Rapunzel slips and speaks of her heavier weight. Enraged, the witch viciously cuts off Rapunzel's beautiful hair and, with no remorse, banishes her to the desert.

Sadly, Rapunzel is heavy laden with no help from the masculine. Unsuspecting and horrified by the witch's cruel surprise, the prince throws himself from the tower in to the bushes below. Their thorns pierce his eyes, blinding him, and he wanders lost in the forest for years, a reference to the unseeing masculine of the time.

When Rapunzel is ejected from the tower, she sees the true colors of the sorceress. Rapunzel endures the witch's ruthless abandonment again, this time with her unborn twins. Together they huddle alone in their desert suffering. Rapunzel must completely rely on herself for the first time in her life. Stranded in the middle of nowhere, she faces survival in a hot and arid desert, a place of extremes. Concretely and symbolically, the searing, unrelenting heat of day requires a human living in the cold of night.

Psychologically speaking, night is the very place of unconscious process, a place from which our nocturnal dreams arise. We can imagine that Rapunzel's survival is likely championed by the Wise Old Woman herself, even if unconsciously in her dreams. Although the path of individuation is a solitary one, it is also one in which the Wise Old Woman may be found.

Nevertheless, Rapunzel's life is described as miserable. Her struggle for survival must have included a soulful tending to her loss and grief. Moreover, the desert often symbolizes a place of shadow's demons—in this case, the shadow of a culture in which the feminine is cast out or down and treated as inferior.

Rapunzel's experience of shadow is not described, but sources of unconscious aggression like anger, resentment, and self-blame often occur in a child who has been abused. Her story reflects the oppression and disparagement the feminine has suffered at the hands of the patriarchy, remembering her first opponent appeared as a negative, animus-possessed would-be mother. This archetype is depicted as the sorceress from whom she seeks release, just as the feminine in society strives for autonomy and liberation.

From the perspective of the unconscious feminine, the demons of the desert are the parts first projected onto the other, then necessarily faced in oneself when alone in the desert of the psyche. Rapunzel has no one to lean on except herself. Perhaps the graces of the Wise Old Woman spirit are nearby. Remember, it is when there is nowhere else to turn that the Wise Old Woman's help can appear.

Rapunzel's later reunion with the masculine suggests some degree of integration is accomplished. If Rapunzel faces up to seeing the worst in herself—the witch-like underside of grief, helplessness, and sometimes, self-destruction—she may feel greater self-understanding and completeness within herself.

A reckoning with other personal limits and weaknesses would be inevitable in the desert. When joined with the barebones facing of herself in the desert, Rapunzel's experience of shadow helps her rebalance and the three of them, herself and the twins, survive. Teenage Rapunzel seems destined to meet her limits again and again and to continue to live and learn from them.

Perhaps the inner witch becomes more humanized. Notwithstanding, Rapunzel's process may not be so much a self-effacement, based on the collective's judgment, but a discovery of her true worth, strength, and value. Could society's feminine be standing up for itself?

Yet surviving such an existence was Rapunzel's only recourse. What was it like? What did Rapunzel endure? How did she do it? Our clues to understanding the message of Rapunzel begin with a period of extreme isolation and abandonment for the feminine, living through a continuing separation from the world at large, followed by a forced removal from nature, to surviving the unsurvivable in the wild, bearing twins in the process, only to emerge as the dominant feminine and royal leader of feelings and values in the culture.

Jung writes in *The Red Book* about an active imagination in which he has an encounter with the desert and discloses, "Life leads me into the desert" (2009, p. 236). He uses words like "torment," "desolate," "uncanny," "unfruitful," and "endless infertility" (p. 236). It is in this desert that he finds his soul. This is the place of the soul, initially experienced by him as a "hot desert" (p. 236). Jung recognizes that when events, others, and personal thoughts are no longer, he can then be led into solitude or, as he describes, "be with oneself. ... Solitude is true only when the self is a desert" (p. 236). He writes. "I should also rise up above my thoughts to my own self" (p. 236). Then he asks, "My soul, what am I to do here? But my soul spoke to me and said, 'Wait'" (2009, p. 236).

"Wait" is exactly what the Wise Old Woman spirit said to me at this juncture in my writing with her nonverbal nod to both stillness and *emptiness*. Of course, the Wise Old Woman is the essence of "wait." Unsurprisingly, at fourteen months post-onset of a pandemic, respite was surely required.

During some of my waiting process, as I grappled with this unwritten account in the desert, I was gifted with two synchronistic events—a double synchronicity, if you will. First, Betty Smith, the leader of a seminar in June 2021, chose to read from the very same passage that I myself had been studying that week in *The Red Book* about Jung and the desert (2009, pp. 235–36; Smith, 2010). Second, in the course of our time, a group member told us about living in the Arizona desert for three years in a tent!

The woman spoke of her experience and how it developed over time, beginning with wearing tall boots and long pants meant to protect her from rattlesnakes, scorpions, tarantulas, coyotes, and all such dangers. Toward the end of the second year, however, the woman was wearing flipflops at night when she went out. What happened?

She got to know the creatures of the desert, became their friend, so to speak, and adapted to their needs as they did hers. They lived a peaceful co-existence. She also told of cacti that stored water for themselves, which humans could drink, and other sources of nourishment from the desert's seeming nothingness.

I thought of Rapunzel's early life and my active imagination with the Wise Old Woman spirit and how it was all about her many relationships, her *eros* with the wildlife near the garden. Among the new experiences that Rapunzel discovered in her totally unknown world, she likely also developed more relationships. How could she not have felt herself to be a changed person and brand-new mother to herself?

Her freedom and her twins gave her reason to live. Living itself was a success and helped her decide more consciously the best ways to keep the twins and herself alive. In other words, she continued building with positive *eros* as a means to greater wholeness and as a way of staying alive.

In contrast to her seemingly impossible displacement, Rapunzel carries new life, in fact, two new lives—twins—a girl and a boy. These new energies, masculine and feminine, are symbols of renewal, indeed, symbols of the Self, likely inspiring Rapunzel to prevail.[9] Her relationship with the children, highlighted by the *eros* and *emptiness* she experienced with the Wise Old Woman, must have helped Rapunzel keep going.

It is then, in this do-or-die situation, that she can accept and love herself, as the symbol of goodness that she is (Moore, 2018). In turn, she is able to love another—first, her babies. According to Faith Moore, "A fairy tale princess's outer beauty is *symbolic* of her inner goodness," and "Her inner goodness is *represented* by her outer beauty." She further explains, "The princess represents—the *ideal* of womanhood." This is a

---

[9] According to 2019 statistics, good-enough mothering by mothers and fathers is greater than 99 percent in the U.S. population (see https://americanspcc.org/child-abuse-statistics/.)

vital moment of courage for Rapunzel and a "coming to terms with the feminine principle of *eros*, with her own deeper self" (Birkhäuser-Oeri, 1988, p. 90).

Through the love for her babies, Rapunzel works to support them all, increasing her sense of self-worth and responsibility as a parent at the same time. Rapunzel psychologically transforms within her experience of motherhood. In the harshness and emergence of life, Rapunzel more consciously experiences aliveness and being, and through its acknowledgment, "love is not destroyed, but strengthened" (Birkhäuser-Oeri, 1988, p. 91). This is the invisible, but deeply felt love for humanity that the unconscious feminine carries in the culture, nourishing all those who would receive, and in this story, seeking to be reborn.

A certain freedom accompanies a connection with the Wise Old Woman spirit, apart from inner or outer realities. Might there not also be a part of Rapunzel that was challenged and comforted by the expanse of the space all around? Perhaps it is because Rapunzel's experience of *emptiness* is different now. With years of experiencing the benevolence of the Wise Old Woman, along with her own maturing, Rapunzel may have indeed begun to integrate a part of her shadow, simultaneously releasing energy to empower herself.

For example, when I was a teen mother, I learned very quickly what the real meaning of sharing was. Never did I take a bite of anything that my baby didn't insist on having it, too. I became immediately aware of my inherent self-focus and the very real need to expand my horizon.

From a Jungian perspective, conscious suffering, doing one's utmost, and knowing that one doesn't know, yet trusting the unknowable, is very different from an unconscious suffering in shadow. Ignoring the latter especially risks its destructive influence on emotional life.

Coniunctio and Fulfillment

The integration of Rapunzel's strengths and weaknesses built on her previous life stages now join her experience of life in the desert, a psychological holding of her feet to the fire in a test of ego functioning. Moreover, her experiences of aloneness extended her life into the mysteries of the psyche and gave her a way of seeing beyond the apparent.

This might be understood as a deepening of intuition, an unconscious, anticipatory knowing.

While the desert often symbolizes the site of shadow's demons, as Jung discovered, the desert seen here is also a place of the soul, open to renewal and creativity. At the beginning of his experience in the desert, Jung turns away from the collective, and indeed his own thoughts, to discover his soul as a virtual desert. However, and after being told by his soul to "Wait," a time nevertheless comes when he can direct his creative energy toward his desert soul. Later in this passage, Jung discovers through active imagination, the desert turning green and bearing the most "wonderful fruit" (2009, pp. 235–36).

In like style, Rapunzel creates her own wonderful fruit, her beautiful and melodic singing, drawing the stumbling blinded prince toward her as she once did before. Upon their reunion, two of her tears of joy fall upon his eyes and heal them. The *two* calls up Jung's tension of the opposites and likely has to do with Rapunzel's greater consciousness, acquired throughout her journey in the tale. The conflict of the two implies the possibility of a reconciling third. Perhaps it is that *third* that accounts for the redemption of them both.

Tears, long known to be healing, represent a link with the primordial seawater—the maternal matrix, including the Wise Old Woman spirit— and help soften humanity's callous parts. Alchemically speaking, this is descriptive of *solutio*,[10] an alchemical stage in the psychological process of transformation. Rapunzel's tears may very well affirm what our feminine cultural consciousness needs from the patriarchy today—*solutio*—its hardest parts softened, a calming and sometimes, a literal disarming. Von Franz describes salt, like sea salt, as a uniter and an opener—a paradox of the bitterness and the wisdom that arises from it (1996, p. 130).

---

[10] Oxford's dictionary defines *solutio* is as "the medieval forerunner of chemistry, based on the supposed transformation of matter. It was concerned particularly with attempts to convert base metals into gold or to find a universal elixir" (retrieved October 18, 2022). *Solutio* is primary among the seven operations in the alchemical process, often understood as its "root." *Solutio* is that which liquifies; all must be dissolved before any other operations may begin. The power of *solutio* is like the prima materia and requisite for rebirth ("Solutio," 2020).

Once released from the witch's spell, the prince and Rapunzel travel together to his kingdom where they marry and live happily ever after. Their union is a symbol of an eternal *coniunctio,* the alchemical pinnacle of the opus and humanity's goal for wholeness.

Circumambulating *Eros* in the Fairy Tale of The Three Spinners: Mother as Fate

Turning to the fairy tale *The Three Spinners,* Birkhäuser-Oeri highlights the *Mother as Fate.* The mother archetype, like the Wise Old Woman spirit, is known to fashion our destiny. She has a powerful and unique connection with predestination. Our attitude toward our destiny influences our fate as well as how that fate affects us. This underscores the importance of feeling positive *eros* toward our way of life, toward how we live: its pace and tone, warmth and empathy, how we unconditionally love ourselves. How else could we endure the harshness of living? Further, are we going in the direction we are meant to go? How do we know?

Perhaps this is when fate steps in, for better or worse, powerfully shaking up life. The experiential reality of the archetype of our fate can be deeply and abruptly felt. The archetype is autonomous, self-activating, and independent of ego functioning. Indeed, it shows up in our dreams. We may not recognize it, however, because feeling out of control can be unbearable or unacceptable. Of course, we are not in total control. Our not recognizing the effect of the archetype of fate doesn't mean it can't exert great influence on life. This is especially so when we remain unconscious of it.

Birkhäuser-Oeri writes that if we succeed in avoiding our destiny, our totality is sacrificed (1988, p. 115). Von Franz describes how sometimes we may barely evade our fate, like not quite succumbing to death, but this is greatly dependent on the circumstances and the attitude we are holding.

From a Jungian perspective, destiny will take us whether we want to go or not, with our support or without it, as we are dragged kicking and screaming. This has to do with the higher intelligence described earlier. Through relationship to it, we more consciously live our fate. The more we learn about our personal myth, the more we can experience our meaningful story with mindfulness and presence.

The Wise Old Woman spirit, a most needed form of this higher intelligence, is an important guide toward balance. With her guidance, we are increasingly faced with choosing how to proceed within our destiny. In this way, we may realize a greater sense of participation in a life that is exclusively our own.

It is helpful to remember that this tale of spinning women presents the image of a mandala that runs throughout the story, an image of totality and completeness. Let us now enter the realm of "The Three Spinners," the story of a feminine youth in distress and three grotesque and ugly women who represent superhuman powers and redemption. Here is a synopsis of the tale with both Grimms' (1972, p. 83) and Birkhäuser-Oeri's renditions combined:

There is a girl who is idle, refusing to spin in spite of her mother's incessant scolding. Filled with anger and impatience, the mother begins beating her and the girl wails. Synchronistically, the queen passes by at that very moment and hears the loud weeping from the road. Leaving her carriage, she enters the house to inquire what all the screaming is about.

Being ashamed of her "lazy" daughter, the mother says that she won't stop her spinning, that the girl wants to do nothing else, and that she is too poor to provide enough flax. Turns out the queen is happiest at the humming sound of spinning so she asks the mother if she can take the daughter with her. She has an abundance of flax at the castle where the girl can spin as much as she wants. The mother "heartily" agrees to give up her daughter.

At the castle, the queen shows the girl three rooms filled with the finest flax and tells her, "Now spin all this flax for me" (p. 124), promising her eldest son to be the girl's husband. The girl's industry, "... a willing hard worker" (p. 124), was more important to the queen than the girl's history of poverty or that she had no dowry.

Alone in the room, the poor girl is secretly terrified. There is no way she can spin all that flax, even if she were to live for hundreds of years, working from morning till night. She begins to cry, getting nothing done at all for three days when the queen then returns. She is surprised but understands when the girl offers the excuse of distress from leaving her mother's home.

Although the queen accepts this, she advises that the spinning should begin the next morning.

Alone again, the girl is without a solution and "in her distress, [goes] to the window" (Grimms, 1972, p. 84). *There she sees three strange women in outlandish costumes coming toward her. One of them has a broad flat foot, the next a great lower lip hanging below her chin, and the third a wide thumb. Standing before the window, the three women ask what might be amiss. The girl pours out her woes to the three strange women, and they offer to help her provided that she invites them to the wedding, is not ashamed of them, calls them "auntie," and lets them sit at her table.*

"With all my heart" (p. 84), *the girl promises, and in no time the spinners have spun all the flax most beautifully. One draws the thread and rocks the treadle back and forth, the second wets the thread with her lip and the third twists it with her left thumb. After the three rooms of flax are filled with beautiful thread, the women depart, reminding the girl not to forget how they had made her fortune possible.*

When the queen sees the rooms full of the finest yarn, she praises the girl mightily and prepares for the wedding. The girl keeps private that the women had helped her. The almost-groom is filled with joy, praising his bride-to-be for her diligence and ingenuity. The girl then asks if she can invite her three aunties, as they have been very kind to her, and she wants to share her good fortune with them. The three grotesque women come to the wedding. The prince, shocked, asks why they are so deformed, with a broad flat foot, a hanging lower lip, and a wide thumb? "Why?" he asked, and each answered in turn.

... a broad flat foot?

"By treading," the first one answered, "by treading,"

... a hanging lower lip?

"by licking" the second answered, "by licking," and

... a wide thumb?

"by twisting the thread," she answered, "by twisting the thread." (p. 86)

When he learns that all these oddities have been caused by spinning, the horrified prince forbids his bride ever to touch a spinning wheel again, and that is how she got out of spinning the horrid flax.

The Three Spinners, drawing by Susan Faron—"A Broad Flat Foot," "A Hanging Lower Lip" & "A Wide Thumb"

Similar to the Three Fates in mythology (Smith, 2010, p. 26), this triad of lady-spinners appears and decidedly participates in the young girl's destiny. Could these three maternal energies be a multiple expression of the Wise Old Woman spirit?

Four Perspectives

The tale's complexity and density merit a short introduction to four particularly helpful perspectives. These might also be considered the messages of the fairy tale.

First, this young girl, unaware of the winding path ahead, surprisingly discovers how feminine wiles can play a critical role. Indirectly and privately, the feminine has learned the value of the serpentine path. Without logic or deliberation, and quite unintentionally, the maiden's way is feeling and spontaneous. The way of helpful *eros* leads to one saving connection right after another. It seems that there can be a positive outcome in the worst of circumstances when *Mother as Fate* deems it, even when, as with the girl, the Fates are with us unconsciously.

Similarly, the Wise Old Woman may be expressed within the Fates so honored in the United States today—November 7, 2020—joined with a conscious and concerted effort by people for equal rights and balance. Perhaps the vote in 2020 to preserve democracy was a conscious participation of the American people with Fate. This day, Joseph Biden's election to the presidency, echoes how a destiny in sync with itself and in tune with our best humanity, is blessed by our partnership with grace.

Second, the tale conveys the vital importance of accepting the disreputable parts of ourselves. Becoming who we are meant to be not only involves integrating uncomfortable aspects of ourselves, but also allows a kind of freedom to be exactly who we are. Accepted by society or not, both are vital to wholeness.

This shadow work, unlike that previously shown in Rapunzel's harrowed journey for survival in the desert, is more about cultural pressures, but once again focused on the animus in the maternal. Identified with a patriarchal conformity, these limits come up against the natural feminine functioning in us all. Whereas the patriarchal collective depresses and denies the innate expression of the feminine, this youthful feminine does not betray her instincts. Going with destiny is accomplished by living it. And as seen, the Fates in this tale unfold and in time reveal in the damsel's favor.

A third message of "The Three Spinners" is the necessity of balance. One-sidedness is against life, and you have seen how repulsive the three spinners look. As discussed, going to extremes and wanting only the good risks the inevitable rebalancing—an enantiodromia or sudden reversal of direction. Jung reminds us that any addiction or repetitive behavioral extreme is bad, even if perceived as good.

Finally, the story encourages trust in the unconscious. Does this sound like *The Fledgling*? "Protect me and I will protect you." Not blind trust, nor blind faith, but a trust that's born of open-eyed experience, humility, and receptiveness to life. This young girl is inexperienced, and thus unconscious; she follows her instincts, open and humble before help from the queen. The Fates seem to carry her along. As Birkhäuser-Oeri writes, "The archetypes … are an experiential reality with the power of destiny," not merely theoretical constructs (Birkhäuser-Oeri, 1988, p. 114).

It seems that trust in the unconscious *becomes* as we relate to our dreams, ponder synchronicities, explore active imaginations, and pray. We do so to appreciate, listen, celebrate, disclose, and connect to the archetype of higher wisdom—to the qualities of the Wise Old Woman, specifically. Of course, the ways of connecting with the unconscious are unlimited and can also be initiated by the unconscious itself.

With these perspectives, or four eyes as witness to the tale, we see that "The Three Spinners" begins with a power struggle. There is conflict between the young girl and her shadow mother. Note that the girl, her mother, and the queen comprise three feminine figures, with the girl serving as the unlikely heroine of the story.

The daughter often represents the potential for renewal in a culture, a feminine *eros* that suggests futurity, spontaneity, irrationality, relationship and feeling. At the beginning of the tale, the masculine is notably absent. This is the extremism noted previously. However, the number 3, denoting directional and irreversible change in time, points toward something happening in the future in the tale. Could it be transformation? As I follow the events of the story, I ask myself, "How could that happen without Destiny?"

Images of Spinning: Fate, Fantasy, Wholeness, and Song

It is noteworthy that Birkhäuser-Oeri describes the theme of the spinning woman as the most frequent image of the fateful dimension of the mother. She likens a dream or a fairy tale—both "products spun by the same Great Mother"—to a wise and guiding power and "perhaps a feminine aspect of the divine" (Birkhäuser-Oeri, 1988, p. 116). This wise power is often an elderly woman symbolizing "an essential part of the Great Mother" (p. 116).

We return to Von Franz's explanation of the spindle as an attribute of the Wise Old Woman spirit and the witch, the latter associated with pointed remarks aimed at hurting another (1983, pp. 44–45). Thus, the spindle can be used in destruction or more positively function as a source of creative invention.

Another example is found in the story of "The Six Swans." A ball of yarn, an image related to spinning and a gift from a wise mother figure, helps the king find his way. The yarn ball has the ability to anticipate as the Wise Old Woman herself does. The yarn knows where the path is going because it carries the energy of the Wise Old Woman. She knows our fate.

Alongside the weaving of our destinies, spinning has many related qualities. Seen as a typical feminine activity, Birkhäuser-Oeri suggests that spinning symbolizes the unconscious activity of the mind and provides a creative outlet. "Spinning is putting together lots of separate bits to make a continuous whole, in the same way that images are connected in fantasy" (1988, p. 116). As she has stated, "Nothing becomes real without first being imagined" (p. 122).

She sees the human mother as the Great Spinner insomuch as she spins mostly positive fantasies about her baby and what she wishes for it. She helps the child become herself. If the mother's invisible thoughts are negative or not much there at all, then the child can have great difficulties and lose her way.

According to Birkhäuser-Oeri, the mother can make a difference with her belief in her child's (or spouse's) abilities and in her show of positive faith. On the other hand, if the spinning-woman energy is used as destructive wishful thinking, it can bring great harm. This direct influence is due to the psychological link the mother has with the child or anyone of emotional closeness.

Spinning can also be thought of as the healing that comes when singing or humming, creating a greater calm. This is when the queen tells us she's happiest, hearing the humming of the wheel. It recalls the story of the Swiss man who, confronted alone in the woods by a large-racked moose, kept his wits about him and lulled it with his humming. The huge animal was apparently soothed by the song and slowly sauntered away.

Another meaning of spinning we have seen is stirring in place, an *emptiness* of contemplation and pondering—and an image of the Wise Old Woman spirit in unbroken movement. Stirring is circular, the opposite of making progress in a linear way. Spinning is one way to create the circular mystery of reflection.

Nevertheless, spinning in this fairy tale is misused to exert personal power, which becomes the focus of a struggle for continued development of the feminine. It's really not about spinning, rather about decision making and freedom.

Here we see the traditional feminine creative, spinning, faced with outright rejection by the girl in the tale. She has turned the spindle's point upon the conventional feminine mold, not to criticize like a witch, but to protect herself and to choose more freely on her own behalf.

The tale reveals the distortion that occurs when the overload is on a singular expression. This is related to the absence of the masculine noted at the beginning of the tale and is a good example of how no matter which direction the imbalance is loaded, one-sidedness causes deformity and great harm.

Psychologically speaking, if spinning is understood as unconscious and conscious fantasy, and feminine expression is limited to that, then acting upon it is denied. As Birkhäuser-Oeri has stated, fantasizing is "necessary" for a while, but there comes a time when you can't make it a habit and go on fantasizing forever (1988, p. 126). Nothing can happen, and in this case, both fantasy and action suffer, as seen here in the feminine. Inaction becomes impotence in behavior when the woman is denied choice and movement through her own animus functioning.

Initially, the mother and the daughter in the tale each seem to live their own dark behaviors. The daughter is described as idle and the mother's actions are inappropriately aggressive, demanding instead of teaching, and speaking untruthfully to be seen in a favorable way.

This is reminiscent of an analysand of mine who suffered a harsh inner maternal critic, a relentless negative mother complex speaking sadistic lies and predicting his failure as a person. The thought of his mother evoked loss of every hope—his career would be ruined, and he would never find true love. The extremeness of this punitive expression describes the tremendous and destructive power of the maternal archetype isolated from the Wise Old Woman's wisdom.

Returning to the tale, the maternal's abuse of power, if seen within an individual, reflects the negative animus within the mother. Moreover, the fairy tale portrays a cultural complex against the natural feminine in men or in women. The society shown here is of a patriarchal nature

86

in which the perceived wrongs or less understood aspects of human behavior, particularly feminine behavior, are disconnected from collective consciousness. They are disparaged, disallowed and repressed.

In the context of strict role limits, the girl's idleness can be associated with the culture's denial of the feminine. The girl is depicted as these rejected and dissociated parts, *eros* being first among them. Feelings of genuine sadness, anger, or independent valuing are disallowed; honesty is silent. The cultural feminine is discouraged from creative endeavors or meaningful work suited to the individual. In spite of this, the girl represents a new and fertile feminine.

A denied creative urge can get quite loud, and the youth cries out. From the perspective of one psyche, there appear to be two different maternal energies: a destructive nature and a royal caring quality, perhaps as a spiritual compensation for the girl's suffering. Was the queen's arrival a precursor of help on its way from the Wise Old Woman spirit? It seems that her appearance at the girl's direst moment was a miraculous response to her call of need.

Indeed, she is in need. Her mother, or unconscious negative maternal part, abused the girl with verbal and physical violence. This is the very thing the Wise Old Woman spirit opposes. The collective's patriarchal authoritarian attitude has entered the psyche as a maternal critic. The dominant feminine aspect is thus depicted, both unconsciously and consciously, and represents the typical attitude toward the feminine of the time. The mother's tirade at the beginning of the fairy tale is no doubt born of the same frustration and helplessness she herself feels as a co-sufferer of feminine oppression. Positive *eros* has broken down; separation keeps happening.

In spite of this violent *separatio*, the daughter's great dislike of spinning and the traditional feminine role is clear. The girl tries to be faithful to her feelings. Being beaten, she suffers instead. Regardless of the history of women, the maiden appears to follow an emerging urge in the feminine to create in a new way. In other words, the essence of femininity as spinning is open to continuing development.

Could this openness be a kind of *emptiness* versus poverty of balance and flow? Is this an *emptiness* that's holding and still? Is the girl's need not to do this, a refusal to go against herself?

The queen driving by just as the girl screams out points to a synchronistic event, a meaningful coincidence, and portends a fateful meeting. The queen tells how she has heard the girl's cries from the road, and the embarrassed mother, thinking her daughter deficient, lies and says the girl wants only to spin. The maternal shadow wants to be seen as unable to keep up with her daughter's need for flax because she is poor.

The queen, whose presence anticipates the Wise Old Woman spirit, introduces much-needed positive *eros* to the girl's experience. When the queen arrives, *eros* moves away from violence and destruction and supports the girl's life. The queen as the ruling feminine is a saving grace for the girl, suggesting that the same saving grace may appear in the culture to promote a youthful and renewing feminine principle.

The maiden says nothing, keeping to herself the circumstances of her life, as it is private and deeply humiliating. Even today, it is well known that children often feel responsible and guilty when parents are troubled, controlling and abusive.

The queen asks the mother if she would allow her daughter to go with her to the castle where there will be plenty of flax, as she loves the hum of the spinning and is eager to help the child. The kindly queen can be thought of as offering the girl a life of abundance in every way, both emotionally and physically, a life of the royal road to wholeness through an eventual *coniunctio* with the prince. Understood psychologically, the youthful feminine is gifted with a fateful blessing that leads from abject misery and imbalance to a *coniunctio* with a noble animus and a life of becoming what she is meant to be.

The fairytale continues and the girl learns that if she spins well (three rooms full of flax), then she "shall have [the] eldest son to be [her] husband" (Birkhäuser-Oeri, 1988, p. 124). The queen won't hold her material poverty against her because she appreciates hard work—"dowry enough," she thinks (p. 124). However, from the girl's perspective, there is no hope of meeting her next task: spinning the rooms filled with flax; she doesn't even like spinning. She doesn't even know how to spin. How did she ever get into this mess? How do we ever get into our messes?

In front of her are three rooms of flax and three days in which to spin it. Here again, the number 3 continues to emphasize the directedness and dynamism of the story. Left alone in a room in the castle to perform this gargantuan task, the terrified young girl weeps for three days.

How can her crying help, the patriarchy would ask. As we have seen, the shedding of tears, or salty water, is known to be a healing *solutio*, the psychological process of softening. They are also associated with exertion or strenuous experience, such as in "blood, sweat, and tears." They can be symbols of jewels, life-giving rain or rays of sun.

Importantly, the maiden's crying seems to reveal a depth of sadness that comes with the violence and misery inflicted upon her by her personal mother. It is not merely her own mother in the tale, but the negative power aspect of the animus within the collective maternal at the time. Whether the inner feminine or masculine, or seen in an outer world man or woman, the negative masculine continues to dominate even today.

The maiden next finds herself at the window and sees three women approaching, the first having a very broad flat foot, the second with an underlip that hung way down over her chin, and the third having an exceedingly broad thumb. Approaching the window where she was standing, they offer empathy by asking the girl what was wrong.

The window, a symbolic view with a clear but protected distance, offers the girl some perspective. The three strange-looking women are remote to her, psychologically speaking. The women not only represent the odd feminine in the culture of the time, appearing in atypical or even unacceptable fashion, but they also display the deformation that results from abuse of power. Whether inner or outer figures, those who seek to control the girl's options cause repulsive distortions: the enormous foot, the baggy lip, and the bulging thumb.

The Foot, the Lip, and the Thumb

What message does the symbolism of each spinner's expertise and malady reveal? How does their meaning fit with the destiny, imagination and music of our lives? How is the potential for ego's rational action shown? Further examination of these three motifs offers insights.

According to Jung, the foot is associated with the reality of contact with the earth and is often a symbol of fertility and generation, with especially phallic qualities. He describes the traditional Pueblo people's dances of stomping with the feet on the ground in a way that is similar to a repeated reentry into the womb (1967, CW 5, paras. 356, 480–81).

The foot, important for balance and support, is also associated with a person's standpoint. The foot is seen as a symbol of the soul because it helps the individual stand, as in being upright, and connotes an understanding that comes with rightness (McVane, 2012). The ideas of putting your foot down or to finding your footing may describe such an understanding.

On a negative note, foot can also connote a swift kick in the pants, or refer to changing one's mind and getting cold feet. To drag your feet describes symbolic delay, and to be on one's "back foot" indicates a defensive posture. Jumping in with both feet can be good or bad, though surely a full commitment.

In this particular tale, the foot is that which creates the movement of the treadle when using the great spinning wheel, and it is the treadle that drives the wheel. It is not unlike a treadle sewing machine in design. Thus, the foot is used to turn the flax into thread, with the first aunt performing this function ceaselessly.

This might be a psychological way of expressing a continuity of action, the back-and-forthness, if you will, and steadfastness associated with developing a good-enough relationship or positive *eros* function. That is, ceaseless treading could be considered a requirement for ongoing connection.

Thus, the first motif of treading has to do with reality, fertility, generation, phallus, balance, support, rightness of soul, movement, drive, and continuity of action, connection, and commitment. It also has to do with assertion, position, kick, change, delay, and defense. Are they not all aspects of the *eros* and wholeness of the Self? Embracing the Self, birthing it, relating to it? Is the missing masculine bound up in the foot?

The second aunt's role is to lick the thread. This motif, the lip, is similarly ambivalent and, like the foot, has both a darker and a lighter side. Negatively speaking, lip can refer to giving someone lip, as when a person speaks defiantly or critically. The girl's refusals to spin were likely seen this way.

The independent thought of the girl, so unacceptable in the tale, is not out of the ordinary for a teen from today's perspective. Exploration and curiosity when safely expressed are encouraged, although girls and their efforts often continue to face devaluation and discrimination.

This is sadly so for all ages of women and the feminine in men. Here in the United States, for example, it is common knowledge that a man asking for directions when he is lost is discouraged and derided. If you're a man, any sign of not knowing is usually seen as weakness and is unacceptable, especially in the business or sports worlds. It's similar in politics. Politicians hardly ever admit they made a mistake or didn't know what they were talking about. A woman not knowing denotes vulnerability and inferiority, both characteristics historically associated on many surveys with that of the feminine ("Bem Sex Role Inventory," 2021).

Lip can also be understood in the context of keeping a stiff upper lip, a way of describing a stoic or courageous stance (see the discussion earlier in the chapter about the Rt. Hon. Jacinda Arden and stoicism). Moreover, the lip that licks is associated with spittle, which Jung refers to as "soul-substance" (1981b, CW 8, para. 411). Some Native Americans perform a ritual of spitting into their palms and holding them up to the sun upon its rising. Their belief is that doing so helps the sun continue to cross the sky in its daily journey.

In another reference to spittle, we recall that Isis also used Re's drool to mix with earth and knit a poisonous snake (von Franz, 1980, p. 61). The creation and power of the saliva-earth poison is revealed when the sun god is subsequently bitten and becomes very ill. He confesses his name, thereby sharing equal sovereignty with Isis. Re is made well with the help of Isis and, I would add, through the much-needed rebalancing of power.

The healing power of human and animal licking has been known since ancient times. Sacred dogs at Asclepius temple were known to lick the wounds of those who were diseased and came for healing. In fact, the word *lick,* as in *licking to wholeness,* is associated with wholeness and was defined as unwounded or unhurt.

The symbol of the thumb, a mobile part of the hand, is seen as just as essential to the human as the foot. The thumb, like the other symbols, can be positive or negative. A negative perspective reveals what can happen to the neglected feminine function when it's under the thumb of a culture that represses it.

In a more positive light, a thumbprint can denote the uniqueness of an individual. In this way, the thumb can symbolize the outer personality, relating to the outer world—including others, objects, and situations. The thumb and forefinger together can point to an outer object of interest. In this way, the symbol seems to have a more extroverted quality.

Looking closely at how the thumb is used offers an important context for understanding its meaning. The thumb twists the thread when using a spinning wheel, doing so in a counterclockwise direction or to the left. Left points in the direction of unconscious process, suggesting that this spinning woman has had an enduring and conscious bond with the feminine unconscious.

This could be seen as an alliance with the Wise Old Woman spirit in which we may experience her through dreams and attention to synchronicities, helping us discover and live our myth. In anyone, consciously connecting with the unconscious feminine through the twists and turns of fate also includes active imaginations, expressive art, and bodily mindfulness and movement. Like the twisting of the thread, all inward bound, it's a left-turning over of continuous movement.

Since the Wise Old Woman spirit is a shapeshifter, this triad seems a fitting symbol for the Mother as Fate, spinners *par excellence* creating ideas, images, and thoughts. The Axiom of Maria, a precept in alchemy, declares: "One becomes two, two becomes three, and out of the third comes the one as the fourth." It is attributed to third-century alchemist Maria Prophetissa ("Axiom of Maria," 2022). The Wise Old Woman spirit can be seen as the one that comes out of the third, symbolized by the Three Spinners of Fate.

These feminine helpers, these Three Spinners, not only reveal a miracle in spinning with divine perfection, but also undeniably show the downside of extremes lived out on a human level. Their deformities result from what they do—they are the image of solely spinning and of getting off center. Such extremes are a detriment to human feeling and life.

However, the first spinner's oversized foot contains the much-needed energies of both feminine and masculine qualities. Second, the way-down lip, with its undeniable licking toward wholeness, provides healing and unity. Together they work with the third, the thumb, which serves a conscious and enduring relationship with the unconscious.

Thus, all three promote a partnership with the Wise Old Woman spirit. In the outer reality of yarn spinning, these three functions—the treading, the licking and the twisting—work together to create the yarn. This collaboration symbolizes the Wise Old Woman's unity and enduring connectedness—her *eros*. The garish women at the window listen to the young girl's plight as she pours her heart out to them.

The Wise Old Woman spirit, as the trio of spinners, responds to the girl's pleas and comes to her aide. The three aunts offer their miraculous skills in exchange for being graciously accepted at the girl's wedding table. The youthful maiden is reminded that she would never have been able to marry the prince without the three aunts' help. Together, their appearance and supernatural talents evoke the young feminine's humility.

These three exaggerated features of the trinity of aunts—the Wise Old Woman—in dynamic form, visibly present the undesirable aspects that develop out of a repressed and disparaged feminine in the collective. Their appearance reflects a culture in which the feminine in its fullest sense is not allowed, neither in its perceived ugly or unpleasant aspects nor in its newly emerging creative impulses. Anything done to excess, in this case, the traditional feminine role, will get worn out, ugly, and rebel. This is similar to many cultures, not only the dominant Christian society of the time, but also in Jewish and other major traditions.

At the end of the tale, the queen's son, so disturbed by the effects of spinning as revealed by the aunts' appearance, vows to never have his bride touch a spinning wheel again. As the spinners remind the girl, the *coniunctio* and coming together of the bride and groom could only have happened with an acceptance of them by the bride. In other words, the girl has integrated the dark side of the feminine and knows it as her own.

It is these same undesirable aspects of the feminine that work together to evoke the transcendent function, and in unison, allow for the coming together of the feminine and the masculine. As Birkhäuser-Oeri reminds us, their service in spinning has facilitated a transformation so that spinning is no longer needed.

Spinning has accomplished its purpose: The girl incorporates the dark feminine, symbolized by the three spinner-aunts. Thus, cultural life becomes more open to the feminine principle *in toto* and shows *eros* more kindly received within the society.

Moreover, the *coniunctio* means that development moves toward greater freedom for both the feminine and the masculine, inside and out, and a more equal distribution of power between the two. As the masculine bows to the feminine, it experiences the feminine itself, which creates a more balanced and functional relationship. In other words, transformation and wholeness result.

The beautiful spinning of rooms of flax was a divine blessing. The girl married the prince, realizing a *coniunctio* with the masculine, and was also freed to become herself. The integration of her shadow feminine, together with the girl's conscious incorporation of her animus, introduces the needed balance to complete her life experience. In that sense, feminine regeneration, with its revelation of *eros*, is the central motif of the tale.

Circumambulating *Eros* in the Fairy Tale of Granny Evergreen: The Healing Nature Mother

Now I will turn to the fourth and last maternal archetype to be discussed—the *Healing Nature Mother*. It could be said that the Wise Old Woman spirit expresses herself as the fairy tale figure Granny Evergreen. An old German folktale,[11] the story of Granny Evergreen is "about living in peace instead of fighting" (Birkhäuser-Oeri, 1988, p. 134). This points to the European goddess-centered culture, circa 7000 BCE, that lived in unity and without violence for 4000 years.

The theme of this fairy tale is all about love, *eros,* and the much-needed feminine. The tale of Granny Evergreen reveals the face of love in its many appearances: strawberries, heart, mandala, roses, water, and tears. Below is a synopsis of the tale combining both Birkhäuser-Oeri's (1988) and MANANcigogne's (2011) renditions:

> *Two children are looking for strawberries in the woods for their sick mother because she pines at heart for strawberries. In the depth of the woods, they meet an old lady dressed in green, who*

---

[11] Folktale and fairytale are used interchangeably here.

94

*asks them for the strawberries they have picked. She tells them
how she could not bend to pick the berries and asks, "Might
you give me some of yours?"* (MANANcigongne, 2011).

*When they give them all to her, Granny Evergreen assures
them that she only needs a few to satisfy her hunger and returns
their present for their mother. In addition, she gives each child
a beautiful rose, one white and one blue, which will always stay
fresh. She simply adds that the children should not quarrel and
should water the flowers every day. "Let kindness guide in all
that you do," she reminds them (MANANcigongne, 2011).*

*"When the first strawberries touched their mother's lips,"
goes the story, "she recovered, and that was Granny Evergreen's
doing" (Birkhäuser-Oeri, 1988, p. 134).*

*Now the children water the flowers each morning,
and whenever they see how "fresh and pretty" they are they
remember the old lady's admonition. However, one evening
they do quarrel over a toy and go to bed without making it up,
and the next morning the flowers have wilted and turned black.
They do not regain their blue and white coloring again until the
children have shed many tears on them.*

*This has the effect of keeping the peace between them for
ever after. "So, the flowers became their great treasure, and
they remained fond of Granny Evergreen to their lives' end"
(p. 135).*

Birkhäuser-Oeri invites a deeper understanding of the tale's profound
meaning, one that belies what appears to be a simple childhood tale of
morality. As in the other fairy tales, I cannot fully explore all its many
meanings; instead, as before, I will focus on *eros*. Granny Evergreen
further reveals how *eros* works in our lives and how it might have been
born.

Here, again, is the two-mother situation, the human mother,
symbolizing society's ailing feminine and the suprapersonal nature
mother, who knows the ways of magic and healing. Indeed, healing is
what is needed by the heartsick mother who pines for strawberries. In

trying to help their personal mother, these two children serve as mediators between the two mothers.

In comes Granny Evergreen, the Wise Old Woman in green, all decked out in nature's duds—green through and through and living as ever green; she symbolizes eternity itself. The strawberry conveys its own sense of the eternal as a symbol of Venus, the goddess of love.

Growing naturally on the forest floor, all red and juicy and dotted with seeds, strawberries suggest fertility and possibly erotic qualities. Birkhäuser-Oeri continues telling how the children find them easily in patches in the woodlands, experiencing nature in her giving form. That same nature, yet unknown by the children, can also take away.

Perhaps the mother suffers without proper cherishing, receiving little affection and with no apparent partner. If strawberries are associated with love, maybe she longs for a lover, envisioning the red heart-shape of a strawberry when cut through its middle.

Birkhaüer-Oeri writes that in many cultures, the heart has to do with energy and is considered the seat of emotions. It was seen as the center of the body in classical times. In Native American tribes, the heart is often understood as the source of wisdom. Saint Hildegard of Bingen has referred to "the soul as the fire in the hearth of the heart" (Birkhäuser-Oeri, 1988, p. 135). According to Birkhäuser-Oeri, Pliny refers to the heart as the source and beginning of life: "Home is where the heart is." Thus, being sick at heart is suffering soul-sickness as well as feeling emotionally distraught and needy.

A cultural perspective reveals the condition of the feminine as quite ill, impoverished, often starving, and as of June 2022 with the *Dobbs v. Jackson Women's Health Organization* decision overturning *Roe v. Wade* and a women's right to abortion at the federal level in the United States, cruelly without the basics of support and autonomy. In this story, the depleted feminine represented by the mother figure is depending on new growth and the recent additions of the children to her psyche. Both are promising in nature, but inexperienced in the ways of human relationships and survival.

Children generally symbolize the future but can also represent the part of the mother that is naive. Birkhäuser-Oeri describes this as "unselfconsciously naive," suggesting the children are not yet aware of themselves as vulnerable and fully separate little human beings, as if their egos are still emerging. The two youths are still close to the mother's unconscious and live more by instinct and impulse, just learning the need for ego strength. Their gender is unknown in this fairy tale, but many tales depict a brother and sister as symbolizing renewal.

The children's relationship with their mother seems to be a positive one in that they want to help her. A mutual trust has been established. Perhaps that is why, when Granny Evergreen appears and approaches quite unexpectedly, the children not only recognize her but also, quite naturally, transfer their good feelings for their mother toward the Wise Old Woman as Granny Evergreen. Perchance, they were awed by her verdant numinosity?

The Wise Old Woman spirit as Granny Evergreen *initiates* the connection with the children. That she is hungry suggests an *emptiness* from which she emerges. She makes the first move, wisely asking for the favor of a few berries for herself, old as she is and not so able to bend over.

As commonly known, one of the best ways to strike up a friendship is to make a simple request. Even as the children recognize Granny Evergreen, her reaching out in this way eases their coming together with her and begins an intimate process of loving exchange.

The children's acceptance is without hesitation, and their regard for the Grand Mother is shown by a willingness to give all they have gathered. Imagine how gently she shows the children the importance of limit-setting, assuring them she only needs a few to satiate her hunger. The Wise Old Woman as Granny Evergreen demonstrates how to accomplish balance by taking only what is needed. The Wise Old Woman as *eros* gives meaning to measure—"a few to satisfy."

This living with limits, this taking solely the amount required, this modeling of sharing equitably with each other and the planet, has been all-too-slowly recognized as the remedy for our past overconsumption. Are we only now realizing that we have gone beyond the limits of world population for the resources and room that we have? Von Franz warned about the dangers of overpopulation decades ago. The problem stares us in the face when we go to the beach and see how trash is swarming the ocean and littering the sand with millions of small plastic pieces.

The use of resources has been amplified manyfold by the sheer abundance of affordable goods availed us by the fossil fuel industry and other related corporations. Until fairly recently, the consumer has unconsciously participated in the crisis levels of climate change. The fossil fuel industry is widely reported to have known for more than forty years of its products' great harm to the planet. Although disproportionately held, producers and consumers alike bear responsibility for their ignorance, thoughtlessness, or intentional greed and selfishness.

Birkhäuser-Oeri observes that in the mid-20th century, as now, many people in society falsely believed they could control and manipulate all their "psychic functions" as well as others and events. Whether then or today, sole focus on one's own desires, sexual or otherwise, is an incorrect attitude toward *eros*. Insisting exclusively on one's way should not be used for exerting power or control over another. It doesn't work anyway or it backfires.

Unfortunately, individuals who identify with their ego are vulnerable to inflation and distorted judgment. Birkhäuser-Oeri describes these people as psychologically immature and infantile. It is as if they never relinquished feeling entitled to have mom do whatever they want. This one-sided attitude toward *eros* leads to the degradation and poisoning of love. She writes about how an "incorrect attitude toward *eros*" can "lead to ego taking over the drives and keeping them down in its own profane sphere" (1988, p. 136).

Ego efforts have produced few answers on their own. Attempts failed, for example, on February 13, 2021, to convict a former president in spite of the large majority who agree that he incited a mob to riot at the United States Capitol on January 6, 2021. The Electoral College vote-count to certify Biden as president was being affirmed that day. Can we not confess we've met our limits?

In this folktale, Birkhäuser-Oeri points out that the berries the children had picked for their mother symbolize the very part—the naive, unselfconscious part—that needs to sacrifice its ego desires. When Granny Evergreen intervenes, she does not force the children; she asks them, and to their credit, they volitionally share what they have.

Granny Evergreen essentially expands the children's awareness so that the other's perspective comes into view alongside theirs—when two piles of strawberries are created from the one. This story depicts the children's first consciousness of self and other, that is, awareness of the aforementioned *separatio* and "twoness." Although *eros* is in focus for this fairytale, *logos* serves *eros* here and depicts the inherent cooperation between them when balance prevails.

Moreover, their trust in the Wise Old Woman as Granny Evergreen reveals the intuitive confidence of these children in the presence of a feminine deity. Indeed, their certitude is well placed as they witness Granny modeling limit-setting regarding the measure of things, first by differentiating the few from the rest. Then Granny Evergreen returns the many extra strawberries the children had given her and sends them as a gift for their mother.

Importantly, the Wise Old Woman as Granny begins the heartbeat of partnership, the *eros* of giving and receiving with grace. At that moment, a process of loving intimacy begins, a participation in the sharing and reciprocity of relationship. Also, this folktale of love appears unique among the many origin stories about the creation of *eros* (GreekBoston. com, n.d.): here, *eros* appears born from relationship with the feminine divine.

Here is the back-and-forthness of collaboration, even within a power balance of infinite inequity. Granny Evergreen models trustworthiness by taking only what she needs and returning the rest to the children. She does not take advantage of the children's naivete. Instead, she gives again, this time by her modeling and beginning the process of teaching the children about divvying things up and sharing.

This is particularly interesting because sharing is the children's problem in the second half of the tale in which their numinous flowers almost die. Although Granny Evergreen tells them not to quarrel and to live the kindness they want, the children are unable to stay conscious about their anger and almost lose their great treasure. Throughout history and continuing into the present day, sharing is one of the world's primary problems as there exists a grossly uneven distribution of resources and power to access them.

The strawberries sent to the mother by Granny Evergreen have been transformed into a curative gift. Their sweet red hearts instantly work like a miracle drug with the mother's first taste. Clearly this kind of love is healing to the neglected feminine.

When Granny Evergreen asks, the children give freely, forgoing their personal situation and postponing the task at hand. Indeed, it is their sacrifice that becomes the amazing source of healing when returned by Granny for their mother. The children's willingness to share reverberates, and like a stone dropped into a pool of water, creates ever-widening ripples of *eros*.

As Birkhäuser-Oeri notes, "The intervention of mother nature sets up a relationship with a mysterious, numinous power of *eros*, which can give a person who has sacrificed ego-wishes a comprehensive and integrating experience of love" (1988, p. 136). This experience is foundational for healthy psychological development.

After receiving Granny's loving guidance, the children are each bestowed a beautiful rose, one white and one blue, the light and the dark. She tells the children to water them daily, and the flowers will always stay fresh providing images of beauty and connectedness. As Jung writes, "The saving factor is the symbol, which embraces both conscious and unconscious and unites them" (1971, CW 6, paras. 446–47). The dark and light hues of the roses likewise show both a conscious and an unconscious aspect to love and wholeness.

Jung has noted an abundance of meanings for the rose, providing a helpful context for understanding the flower. "Rose mysticism," seemingly "penetrated into alchemy ... in the form of the red tincture ... the healing or whole-making effect of a certain kind of *Eros* ... which unifies the individual as well as the multitude in the sign of the rose and makes them whole" (1968g, CW 13, para. 390). "The 'rose garden of the philosophers' is one of alchemy's favorite symbols" (1968d, CW 12, para. 235). He writes that Arnaldus de Villanova authored the "*Rosarium cum figures,* where the rose is the symbol of relationship between king and queen" (1968g, CW 13, para. 387).

Jung also tells how alchemical texts called attention to the rose when alchemists first used "*Rosarium*" or "*Rosarius*" (rose gardener) as a title for several books. He describes how the rose, in a spiritual sense, is an allegory of Mary, "but in the worldly sense it is the beloved, the rose of the poets, the center of the earth ... the city ... the fortress ... the house of divine wisdom ...," with the rose having the significance of a mandala, "as is clear from the heavenly rose in Dante's *Paradiso*" (1968g, CW 13, paras. 387, 389).

Jung refers to the "Lamaic mandala" of Tibetan Buddhism as the "Rose" (1968d, CW 12, para. 139). He explains that a mandala often appears when an adult is confronting the problem of the opposites in human nature, when psychic dissociation or disorientation occurs. He observes that this is Nature's way of attempting self-healing and that it represents an instinctive impulse rather than self-reflection (Jung, 1959, pp. 3–4).

The mandala as a flower has been described as the epitome of the feminine, which Jung confirms when he writes that the rose is decidedly feminine (1968g, CW 13, para. 389). Von Franz declares the rose as the symbol of eternal life, "of life—that survives death," (1987, p. 34). In fact, a rose can be considered a symbol of the Self and source of love itself.

Expanding these amplifications, analyst Gary Toub offers that the rose may be understood as the feminine face of God, experiencing that bliss himself in a wondrous dream (Toub, 2019, Personal Communication, Note 3). It is interesting to contemplate the two roses as faces of the Feminine Divine, her countenance doubled and reminiscent of the yin and yang.

Would the face of the roses offer glimpses of a bright awareness of white or the lively mystery of blue? It appears that this double exposure of two roses in this tale, not only connects the opposites but seems to emphasize the urgency and need for faithful care. Could this be another petition for partnership with the Wise Old Woman spirit?

Von Franz writes about one medieval author who reiterates that the rose "belongs to the goddess Venus and means love." She suggests that "there is no love without thorns," referring to the inevitable "involuntary hurts that lovers always inflict upon each other" (1993, p. 54). The ambivalence ascribed to every archetype applies to the rose, as well, attesting to its wholeness.

Sadly, when the children succumb to their power instincts, evoked by desire for a particular toy, they awaken to find the roses black and nearly dead. The children had fought, going to bed angry. The watering, which was required every day, was apparently forgotten. This need for returning to tending appears to be decisive if we want to live peacefully. Failing to water the roses, the need for the feminine's inner child to do its part in its own development is emphasized.

The water that the roses require for life potentiates the symbol as another hallmark of love. Often, water is a metaphor for love itself. Like water, love stays with the woman or man who holds it loosely, as in an open cupped hand, yet the person who tries to grip the water finds that it flows away, and they are left with nothing.

Water like love, is essential to the life forces of fertility and creativity (Walker, 1983, p. 1066). From the I Ching: "Water comes as a heavenly gift from above. It is placed within the earth and gives rise to all life upon earth … The water of life is a feminine symbol and has its parallel in the aqua permanens of alchemy … and is extolled as 'vivifying'" (Jung, 1968c, CW 9i, para. 246).

In the *Women's Encyclopedia of Myths and Secrets*, water is described as "the first of the elements … the *Arché*, mother of all things … water gave birth to 'spirit,'" the masculine principle (Walker, 1983, p. 1066). The "Mother-letter M (Ma)" served as an ideogram for the "waves of water," and "water" and "mother" are universally tied (p. 1066). Thus, the Wise Old Woman spirit, as related to the mother archetype, may be visualized here as part of her unending flow.

Tears are also related to love. Extending my previous discussion, tears of joy, tears of worry, tears of sorrow—all relate to an inner or outer love. They might involve the love of work or joy of love, the loss of a beloved animal or the worry we have for children, but tears are relational at heart.

As we have discovered, tears vary depending on their meaning and source. Tears that come from peeling or slicing onions are not the same as tears of sadness, which release toxins specific to the one crying. In this way, tears offer physical and emotional cleansing.

Tears, adaptive to human existence, support life and are on the positive side of natural selection. For example, tears often elicit "an immediate response of help, empathy or comfort" from others (ARAS, 2010).

Hence, the children's tears become their saving grace. It is at this junction in the fairy tale, when they find the roses wilted, that the children begin to cry. They cry and cry and cry, repentant in their grief, shedding tear upon tear for the blackened roses. As a result of their genuine remorse and weeping, the flowers come back to life, fresh and beautiful as they have always been.

Solutio, the alchemical operation of softening and breaking up hardened psychic parts, had been evoked. A metamorphosis took place as the tears restored the roses, a transformation nothing short of redemption and a new beginning. The children's tears are experienced as liquid gold and are shed as liquid *eros.* Looking closely at this part of the tale, the roses' life was not only contingent on the children's sorrow and contrition, but also dependent upon a heartfelt recommitment to rose care.

Significantly, the children clearly know that the saving didn't happen by itself; they realize that their feelings of deep remorse made a difference. Moreover, the flowers could only stay alive with daily loving care, with daily watering-love. Suffering the loss of the roses meant unbearable separation from the Self.

In their deep sadness, they recommitted to live in peace and these new parts of the psyche took responsibility for their behavior. They worked to see their own part and suspend judgment, softening any disagreement before going unconscious again, that is, before going to bed. From a symbolic perspective, going to bed can be understood as going unconscious, and Granny Evergreen's advice was to not go to bed angry. Going unconscious can also include repression. Sometimes repression is a convenient defense that expresses itself as "I forgot."

Psychologically speaking, the Wise Old Woman spirit, appearing through Granny Evergreen, recommends staying conscious long enough to avoid a smoldering erosion of *eros*. Festering conflict is to be distinguished from typical disagreement and grows with neglect. The children, or the parts of renewal within each of us, must stay awake and alert; we must devote small, faithful, and routine energy to the peacekeeping task.

This folktale suggests that peacemaking happens in brief moments of time, in minutes that can be repeated and passed on to the next relationship—the mother in this case—in a continual building and rebuilding of peace. A daily ritual for peaceful living is offered here.

Conflict resolution in outer life includes a certain receptiveness and reciprocation, not unlike the sharing of strawberries, and not unlike the children's agreement to rose care. Many methods can help us manage hurt and anger, such as conscious counting, deep breathing, diplomacy, or redirecting one's attention.

Moreover, there are Jungian approaches for integrating issues of conflict at an archetypal level. Individuals can learn to recognize signals coming from the unconscious when they fight, which can help create a better relationship (Toub, 2021).

It is vital to remember that peacemaking is the primary goal versus being seen as right. This mindful intent determines how an individual might relate to a disagreeable situation so they can actually live that peace.

It seems that if an *eros* attitude can be upheld as a loving awareness of the twoness of relationship, then containment of the archetypal rumblings within allows it to still be heard and, therefore, known. Relating with positive *eros* means that expressing deep feelings and archetypal desires can occur without violence while also being a source of self- and other-knowledge. When one feels right with oneself, increased energy is released and made available.

Most importantly, Granny Evergreen teaches us to live the peace we want and need. From a psychological perspective, the tale of Granny Evergreen depicts an inner reality with an openness to collaboration with the Wise Old Woman spirit. This is a peacemaking effort in and of itself. It bears repeating—open collaboration through attention to dreams or active imaginations is primary and helps develop an inner unity as the back-and-forthness of *eros*-intimacy occurs.

The tale of Granny Evergreen, as with any partnership, shows that both sides must want a relationship and be willing to work to create and continue it. If there is little honesty or accountability on either side, then there is no partnership and no positive *eros*. One way that violence can be met is with nonviolent resistance, according to the individual's situation, whatever form that may take. Sometimes the thing to do is to walk with others in peaceful protest. At other times, whether a survivor of domestic violence or an innocent on the street, the most conscious way to go is to run.

As a staff psychologist for a state hospital many years ago, I discovered the importance of running. I wore special shoes—flat, thin black-leather tie shoes, short boots, but professional looking, in which I could run fast. This was before women wore sneakers to work. The hospital population consisted of the developmentally disabled, psychiatrically disordered, and penal code offenders in a locked facility. The patients included murderers and rapists. I carried keys to get in and out of the unit where my office was located.

One day I happened to have a raspy throat, a touch of a cold, on a day when the staff and other psychologists met briefly to discuss patient needs. There were three psych techs, one unit supervisor, two other psychologists, and me. Silently standing close by was the patient whose needs we were quietly discussing. When I spoke for the first time, emitting a gravely and lower tone than usual, my patient was apparently triggered, instantly attacking me.

Her fingernails tore down my face, neck, and chest, leaving scratches down my front. My shirt was torn, and chunks of hair pulled out. The attack only lasted seconds. As I struggled to get away, the three psych techs pulled her off me. This particular patient had a reputation for jumping the same person over and over again, and she was tall and strong. After that, I went around in my suit and boots, shadow boxing for weeks when alone, and I never turned my back to her again.

Sometimes your very best is to continually make peace within. In this tale of Granny Evergreen, it seems that *eros* has everything to do with peace keeping. A ritual to peace is revealed in this story and can be seen as a four-step process.

Giving and Receiving—Partnership

Eros is initially portrayed as Granny Evergreen's initiating and modestly requesting some of the fruits of love. Granny Evergreen as the Wise Old Woman spirit begins an intervention with the children in order to instill a new attitude of relationship. When Granny Evergreen makes a request, the children respond with enthusiastic generosity.

Willing Separatio Inspires Magical Healing

Granny takes what is needed, however, only enough "to satisfy," and teaches the children about *separatio*. They watch as she models a dividing up that leaves room for sharing. They show receptiveness to learning, tolerance for appropriate division, and receptiveness again when the sharing actually occurs. Because of their friendly sacrifice, Granny Evergreen returns the remaining berries for the children to take home to their ill mother. Once home, they discover that their sacrifice has been magically transformed into soulful and healing berries for their mother.

Share, Care, and Be Kind

When the children first leave Granny to continue home, she gives each of them a beautiful rose, a white rose and a blue one. Her only instructions are to water them daily and not to quarrel. Granny alludes to not going to bed angry. Behaving kindly is emphasized.

Failure, Ownership, and Solutio

When the children do quarrel and get stuck, they discover for themselves why it's important to never enter the night with madness. When they succumb to an everyday power struggle, they disturb the peace they had promised to keep.

The children suffer how natural aggression deteriorates into primitive violence. They themselves actually live the peace disrupted. Feminine wholeness has wilted without the water of love, forgotten in the heat of anger.

In the shock of loss, the children are penitent and filled with grief. When they see that they have failed the roses, an avalanche of tears pours forth. This is *eros*. They cry with deepest despair and buckets of salty primordial substance fall upon the flowers. As they shed their tears, the depth and taste of salt naturally combine bitterness with wisdom—the salt holding the tension of its opposites. With faithful watering, attention, and recommitment to keeping the peace, the children witness the beauty of the flowers and fullness of life revived.

Psychological development may be seen in these four steps, like alchemical stages, and may be imaged as a spiral. This circling process is like living a mandala of peacemaking. This is not a strict up and down movement, but rather a sideways growth, written horizontally, here: A) *Giving and Receiving—Partnership; B) Willing Separatio Inspires Magical Healing; C) Share, Care, and Be Kind; D) Failure, Ownership, and Solutio; and A) ongoing through D) and continuing* ...

The thinking part as the four steps is, indeed, an important human guide. However, Emma Jung and Marie-Louise von Franz would remind us that what is essential for a realization of the Self, for a sense of unity and peace, or a world without war, depends on one's *psychic attitude* and the use to which efforts and talents are placed. Bearing the tension of the opposites seems to be a part of it, at least, much of the time. Peace may be hard to measure but is, nevertheless, profoundly felt.

That is, attitude considers value, orientation, and openness. Such perspective points us to what is important, in which direction to go, and how feeling helps make sense of it. What begins as Granny Evergreen's friendly request deepens among the children and herself as the birth of an *eros* of intimacy, felt balance, and partnership.

It seems that psychological posture is more than the behaviors that define it. It's one of those things that is difficult to articulate. Mostly unseen, stance is nevertheless the "how" of living and the tone of relating. As mentioned, attitude is felt, and when expressing the notes of the Wise Old Woman's *eros*, is friendly and typically apparent from the get-go.

So, as it is written in the tale of Granny Evergreen, the flowers, symbol of the feminine divine, quintessential symbol of the Wise Old Woman as *eros*, "became their great treasure." Perhaps the two roses together reveal a peacekeeping attitude, a poise that held the children's relationship with the Wise Old Woman spirit, here as Granny Evergreen, in love and peace unto the end of their lives.

To continue my circumambulation of the quality of *eros,* one of the two unique characteristics of the feminine principle of which Jung wrote, I move to more contemporary writings from Lockhart, von Franz, and Jung, himself.

Lockhart's Remarkable Thoughts on *Eros*

A brief review of Russell Lockhart's work continues to reveal more about *eros*. He writes that "Eros, as lapis" is of the highest value (1983, p. 183) and suggests that *eros* begins with remembering.

He breaks down the word to re *member*: *re*, meaning *again*, reminding us of the again-ness of relationship; and *member* from the Latin *memor*, meaning to be mindful. He suggests that the mind full of images that come again and again could be the start of an active imagination (1983, p. 187). From within the Latin word *memor*, another Indo-European root word comes forth: *smer*, in one form meaning *grease* and *fat*. Memory is "what sticks," and fat adheres and leaves traces. Therefore, memory is the "fat of the mind" (p. 188).

So *eros* has to do with memory and remembering, connecting what happened to what is being re-imaged, if not re-experienced. In this way, *eros* is a kind of waking up of the psyche to that which demands attention. Following Jung's idea that *eros* "thrives only when spirit and instinct are in right harmony" (1969d, CW 7, para. 32), Lockhart agrees: "Eros is essential to any regeneration of the spirit and personality" and is the "principle of creative connection" (1983, p. 126).

Lockhart also describes one of many myths about the birth of *Eros*: "*Eros comes into being at the first utterance of creation,*" being born from the mouth of Chaos (1983, p. 125). This image suggests that *eros* needs telling, according to Lockhart, which is itself a creative connection. He reminds us that "One tells all at great risk" (p. 128), and that "Conscious love requires telling" (p. 132).

Maybe it is because *eros* is also burden, a suffering that undergoes or "goes under," or is "going to the underground of things" (Lockhart, 1983, pp. 115–16). He suggests that there is need for *eros* with words and that words are the living carrier and expression of spirit (p. 121).

Word originally meant *logos*, Lockhart observes. Perhaps *logos*, as "the speech by which the inner thought is expressed" (1983, p. 122), is birthed by *eros*. It might be said that the inner world is connected to the outer one by *logos* through *eros*. In other words, *eros* penetrates the surface of things and "requires developing a relationship to the inner process ..." (pp. 140, 173). In fact, Lockhart states, "an imaginal relationship with one's own psyche may be the very essence of eros." It is "essential for relationship with others" (p. 139). *Eros* is a principle beyond the four functions in Jung's typology, he continues, but it connects all of the functions together (p. 192). Lastly, Lockhart reminds us of how the alchemists stressed the importance of relationship to their work and held *"Eros"* and its opposite "Chaos" as "prominent images in their experience" (1983, p. 123).

Von Franz—Notable Reflections on *Eros*

Von Franz offers lively accounts of *eros* from a number of perspectives, recognizing that the presence of positive *eros* is central for good health and vitality. In alchemy, we remember how von Franz writes, "Salt is praised as the *Eros* principle, and is called an 'opener and a uniter'" (1996, p. 130). Furthermore, "Salt symbolizes the wisdom of eros, its bitterness together with its life-giving power—the wisdom acquired by feeling-experiences." She asserts that *eros* requires spontaneity to be fully alive (1993, p. 95).

For example, an analysand of mine, who thought of life as work, was distracted one day by his dog who had gotten in the mud. He spontaneously began washing the dog with the hose, forgoing his usual following-the-list routine, and felt the better for it. For my analysand, this was *eros* and a small step for becoming totally herself.

In fact, von Franz refers to *eros* as the "feeling side of life" (1982, p. 144); she relates the *"Eros* style" or feeling style in a society to the central God-image of the time and the "emotions, feelings and irrational attachments" to it. The God-image of a society has to do with the dominant conscious religious realm—the ruling religious attitude—and may or may not be a balance of feminine and masculine. Symbolically speaking, the intellectual or rule-oriented *logos* side is often represented in fairy tales as the king, and is related to holding certain philosophical views apart from the cultural feelings or values of the queen.

Here in the United States, society currently suffers extreme divisiveness and fragmentation, and the God-image is likewise fractured with the largest pieces comprised of the darkest masculine. The positive *eros* in the culture continues to be shunned or harmed by those in power.

This other side of the divide demands equality, including a sense of belonging, relationship, and a healthy *eros*. Many on this other side are young people who no longer look to the church, which formerly offered acceptance, guidance, and community. When God is the dollar, however, no container, and certainly no church, is big enough.

The one-sidedness of the masculine has come to emphasize as values having power over, over-production, and making money, even if the product harms. When the God-image is seen as the almighty dollar, accumulation of it and greed are not only accepted but also embraced. The bottom line holds sway at the expense of *eros*, the unifying function of the feminine.

Whether it be immigrants seeking asylum, forcibly separated from their children and incarcerated as are the children themselves, or climate denial directing money to the fossil fuel industry, or cuts to healthcare and social programs for the impoverished and elderly, or rejection of sensible gun reform, or lack of equal opportunity for minorities, or removal of woman's rights, or tax cuts for the rich, the dominant ruling principle now in the United States is ruthless and without positive *eros*. True at the time this part was initially written in 2018 and, unfortunately, still too true today in 2023.

In contrast, von Franz considers *eros* to be of the highest value. She asserts that the need for relatedness is the essence of feminine nature. Loving *eros* has to do with the way people relate to one another, von Franz reminds us (1999, p. 54). It means "genuine interest in the other person and in establishing relationship—being there for the other person." It "weaves connections between us and others but the connections can also be internal" (p. 70).

Notwithstanding, von Franz writes about *eros* that becomes too dependent and needy. It is then, I suggest, that it isn't loving *eros* anymore, but *eros* distorted by the power urge. Perhaps it is more accurate to say that *eros* as used here may signify relationship or connection, but not *eros* as defined by its highest value.

According to von Franz, not unlike the patriarchy's degradation of the feminine function (1993, p. 92), men tend to be neglectful in *eros* matters. She compares the Western attitude toward *eros* to the women in South India, who have a more differentiated manner. She describes the toughness, vulgarity, and lack of differentiation of the *eros* level in the West where *logos* development is far greater (p. 26). Lacking feeling analysis, *eros* is unrefined and relegated to simply good or bad, absent subtlety and detail. The facts may be correctly stated, but overlook or distort the feeling circumstances or emotional message. Expression is more primitive, revealing a poverty of reflection. Ego and feeling development are deficient and quality of relationship is wanting; again, *eros* itself is falsified and no longer a genuine interest in the other person, nor a basis for fair and just decision making.

A horrible and clear example is the US Supreme Court appointment of Brett Kavanaugh in October 2018. Women who had been sexually assaulted by the appointee came forward with great courage to protest the nomination, knowing the risks of a historically *eros*-deficient Senate. In spite of the evidence, and forgoing additional collaborative testimony, the Senate confirmed the nominee. The vote revealed the nation's split. One half believed the victims, validating their feelings and supporting their right not only to speak the truth, but also that the act of speaking truth would prevent someone from sitting on the highest court in the land who raged with bias, had a history of a serious drinking problem, who was alleged to have attempted rape and exposed himself another time, and was identified as a participant in other abuses toward women (Hauser, 2018).

Conversely, von Franz writes that the woman can have an educative and transformative effect on a man's *eros* (1993, p. 2). In the film, *Defending Your Life,* Julia had such an influence on Daniel, the other protagonist. They chance to meet in Judgment City, each faced with life after death and the prospect of going forward to the next step or redoing the life each lived. That decision was based on whether or not each had conquered their fear.

Throughout the movie their relationship blossoms, but it becomes apparent that Julia has done well enough and Daniel has not. Yet through their relationship—their growing *eros*—Daniel's deepening love for her leads to risking his life, a confirmation that he has overcome his fear. He is advanced to the next step to go forward with Julia, whose gentle effect on him effected a transformation. According to von Franz, a good-enough balance like this is difficult, but required, and includes "great tact and attentiveness" (pp. 211–12).

Balance in a relationship is needed in a multiplicity of ways—but the balance of power is most importantly held by positive *eros* or, said another way, *eros*-love. Von Franz states that it is the *eros* or love principle that represents a counter-principle to power, "against the drive of domination." She suggests that the "one who has eros instead of a power attitude wins against the other party" (1983, p. 252).

An analysand knew he had a problem with anger, for example, and came to therapy to deal with this. He was a big fellow and realized his explosive disorder physically threatened his family, whom he cherished. When he lost his temper, he would leave the house until he was in control. His wife and child knew he was working on his anger and loved him, standing alongside this shadow part of him as long as a safe plan was intact. A structure was developed regarding his departure, making it predictable and more conscious among his family members. Over time positive *eros* among them consciously deepened, simultaneous to his relationship with himself.

The relationship we establish with the Wise Old Woman spirit, and the *eros* experienced together, serves similarly as a key means of facilitating balance and living according to the middle way. Von Franz considers it one of woman's tasks to create "the human atmosphere of eros," and says that includes not looking at shadowy things too deeply, which she calls the "impersonal, cold cruelty of nature" (1993, p. 190). I would add that living in positive *eros* is one of man's tasks as well.

Looking too deeply is likened to "destructive inquisitiveness" and "infantile curiosity," ways that von Franz warns us about human nature's limits of knowing. At times Mother Nature or the unconscious needs to be shown a quiet respect and absence of intrusiveness. Avoiding evil or delaying the full force of our darkest moments can sometimes be a "deep saving instinct," von Franz writes (1993, pp. 190-195).

For instance, when 9/11 occurred a woman was spellbound, as were many of us, to the repeating television footage of the plane hitting the Twin Towers. She watched throughout the day until her three-year-old daughter walked up to the TV, quietly turned it off, and said matter-of-factly, "Too much TV, Mama." Even at the age of three, the little girl felt the instinctive need to end a curiosity that had gone too far and was having a negative effect.

In another instance, an analysand, who was a researcher by profession, learned that some areas she researched had invisible barriers. The unconscious warned her through her dreams about where and when to avoid certain topics. Sometimes she could do the research, but stopped at a certain point when her dreams indicated she should.

To look at evil, von Franz explains, means we become infected by it (1993, p. 195). She writes, "If I cannot do the human thing of turning away, then by looking at it, I act out myself the cruelty of nature." Looking away is one way of protecting and maintaining a loving *eros*.

From my perspective, this does not mean we ignore all evil acts or deal with them in a passive way. At an archetypal level, however, direct connection with evil is not only unbearable, but also invariably evokes our personal complex of evil, as in the case when the witch cuts off Rapunzel's hair. This means that a pattern, or automatic way of behaving, occurs with extreme emotion. Judgment is often impaired with omissions in differentiated feeling. When we face the autonomy of a complex, we need to pause, get centered, and return to balance in order to function effectively. Needless to say, it's much easier to write about needing to pause, than to actually do it at the onset of a complex. Catching yourself, becoming aware of its presence, seems to be half the battle.

It is not to say that we shouldn't protest or use nonviolent behaviors to resist evil policy in the country or another organization. It is not to say that evil shouldn't be dealt with, but rather to avoid overexposure. Protest the evil, but don't participate in it by acting with harmful intent. Resist without relinquishing your dignity. Recoil and withdraw from evil versus witnessing it.

This was the case in Roman times when people were entertained in the Coliseum by gladiators fighting to the death or slaves forced to wrestle with lions. Today, looking at gory images can be similar, whether watching violence online or imbibing in ghastly films as entertainment. Even football, a favorite national sport in the US, is coming under scrutiny as more and more concussions, serious injuries, and even deaths have come to light. As von Franz would say, we risk being infected or, in this day and age, desensitized to such cruelty and more apt to be cruel ourselves. Evil is beyond natural aggression.

Perhaps we have to recognize evil before we turn our gaze upon it and actually look. Evil can be dangerous, and there is something to be said for not escalating even during everyday experience. For example, experience has shown us that a coworker's critical remark typically goes no further when ignored. As an anonymous source observed, when tempted to fight fire with fire, remember that the fire department usually uses water.

Although what we can stand and our responses are individually determined, our instincts as well as our felt inner sense of right or wrong may be the best guide for how to respond—as long as we are more or less centered. Of course, mixed feelings may occur, particularly when the evil is attached to someone we love. All of this affirms why it is so necessary to study our dreams for guidance. Archetypes come to us in dreams through a natural spontaneity that guides us, perhaps through a wisdom figure such as the Wise Old Woman. By staying in touch with the positive human side, we may avoid getting sucked into infantile behavior and destructive curiosity. Von Franz suggests that a human atmosphere of *eros* can be created by holding to the personal and staying with the unique and human side of life.

Meaningful guidance can be found in a connection to the Wise Old Woman spirit. Maybe we could shift our emphasis. Is it not so much about dealing with evil as it is developing a relationship with the Wise Old Woman spirit? Then evil can be better contained or the individual properly armored for whatever evil may appear. The problem of evil versus *eros* is not new, but the goddess-centered culture that lived in unity and peace for 4000 prehistoric years shows us that our contemporary tribalism and warfare has a very real and positive alternative.

Jung—Unparalleled Descriptions of *Eros*

In response to the question, "In what ways are the various maternal archetypes uniquely feminine?" Jung provides an answer when he writes of women, "Eros is an expression of their true nature" (Jung, 1968, CW 9ii, para. 29). In the old philosophical sense of a Pan-*Eros*, in which *pan* means all, *eros* "permeates all nature as a creative and procreative force." Jung refers here to the life force throughout nature (Jung, 1968j, CW 10, para. 5). Speaking of women again, he posits, "Her real being is Eros" (1984, p. 14), and he defines *eros* as the "principle of relatedness through feeling" (p. 374). Although Jung is writing about women, it is vital to remember that the feminine function is a part of men's psyches, as well.

Furthermore, Jung writes that *eros* is "absolutely identical" with woman's conscious principle (1984, p. 487), and that women's psychology is chiefly characterized by *eros*, "no matter what type she is" (p. 659). Even more, "the highest form of feeling in a woman coincides with *Eros*" (p. 697). Addressing women's psychology, Jung states, "It's a question of getting her own *Eros* principle into its rightful place as the ruler of life" (p. 380).

Jung describes *eros* as residing in the realm of the irrational (1984, p. 553), "in which rational understanding and rational modes of representation find scarcely anything they are able to grasp" (p. 353). Jung regards both concepts—*eros* and *logos*—"as intuitive ideas which cannot be defined accurately or exhaustively ... and equivalents of the archetypal images of Sol and Luna" (1970, CW 14, paras. 224, 226). The activity of *eros*, Jung explains, "extends from the endless spaces of the heavens to the dark abysses of hell" (1965, p. 353).

"Love has to do with *Eros*," observes Jung (1984, p. 699), and accordingly, *eros* comprises the "incalculable paradoxes of love" (1965, p. 353), although "no language is adequate to this paradox" (p. 354). Love is a feeling and, like *eros,* love is relatedness. *Eros* is not the same as feeling, however. "The principle of *Eros* is not necessarily loving," he explains, " ... it can be hating too" (1984, p. 698). It seems that the use of *eros* here is meant solely as connection or relatedness, contaminated with the feelings of hate and abuse of power. Through *Eros*," Jung notes, "one learns the truth" (p. 329). In "Woman in Europe," from *Civilization in Transition*, Jung writes:

> But today religion leads back to the Middle Ages, back to that soul-destroying unrelatedness from which came all the fearful barbarities of war. Too much soul is reserved for God, too little for man. But God himself cannot flourish if a man's soul is starved. The feminine psyche responds to this hunger, for it is the function of *Eros* to unite what *Logos* has sundered. (1968m, CW 10, para. 275)

Clearly *eros* is meant to be positive here; hating is not implied in this union.

In later life, Jung expanded his understanding of *eros* by citing it as the mother-father of all higher consciousness (1965, p. 353). Considering our current understanding, the Wise Old Woman spirit herself can be understood as the mother-father of all higher consciousness. Jung recognized that loving relationship, *eros,* creates all of life. Whether within ourselves or amid outer-life relationships, positive connection is the source of a cherished creativity. In other words, *eros* is understood as a *kosmogonos*—source of all higher consciousness—of creation itself, the Wise Old Woman spirit, a vital expression of that source.

This is reminiscent of the higher intelligence previously discussed, that which knows what we don't and arises from the unconscious. Although beyond full comprehension, this knowledge can be helpful and tries to compensate for the ups and downs of outer life. From the perspective of *eros* as the mother-father of all higher consciousness, the feminine and masculine together, connected and in relationship, give birth to new experience. Balance and implicit guidance comes from each principle.

Eros, as symbolic parents, might be considered as an inner couple where opposites are not oppositional and who work in concert as a creative source. They may be imaged as Mother Earth and Father Sky, or as Nature and Spirit. This bespeaks the *hieros gamos,* sacred marriage, of the *pleroma* (Purrington, 2020).

So, of course, Jung related *eros* to love and in connection to that relationship, he quoted Corinthians 1:13 on love: "Love bears all things … endures all things … Love ceases not" (p. 354). He writes that love is "something superior to the individual, a unified and undivided whole" (Jung, 1965, p. 354) above the human ego sense of desiring or preferring. Thus, love, or positive *eros*, is not always easy and not easily understood or suffered, and not always even wanted.

One example that might offer a glimpse of Jung's understanding of what we might experience when approaching such a moment of higher consciousness is his description in *Symbols of Transformation* (1967, CW 5, paras. 523–24), specifically:

> The onslaught of instinct then becomes an experience of divinity, provided that man does not succumb to it and follow it blindly, but defends his humanity against the animal nature of the divine power.

This "onslaught of instinct" might be said to describe the psycho-logical state of mind when one is confronted with a complex or captured by a complex. To reiterate, the complex manifests as an autonomous cluster of charged images, following a predictable pattern and leading to a predictable outcome. It can be a positive or a negative complex in terms of the extremes of feeling attached to it. The complex can affect all that one temporarily knows and effectively puts blinders on the individual. Colloquially speaking, the individual is beside him- or herself.

A person may later ask, "What got into me?" recognizing that something different or weird happened, which often feels atypical to their way of being. Independent and autonomous, the complex has nearly complete control, if not totally complete. Complexes are ubiquitous, their frequency and intensity often depending on old tender places or wounds suffered in life and the degree of ego strength while enduring them, among other things. An example of the worst kind of complex may be found when reading in the morning news that someone has shot and killed their entire family and then themselves. That is, once a complex is activated, we lose almost all influence over ourselves, just as the word *onslaught* implies.

Defending your humanity—yourself—against your own urges and instincts by not following them blindly to succumb without thought or struggle, can lead, amazingly, to an experience of divinity. The Wise Old Woman's presence is found here, as part of that divinity. Remember, Jung called them "divine instincts" or the "animal nature of the divine power" (1967, CW 5, paras. 523–24). As in other writings, Jung stresses the symbol as the healing factor that allows the person to go beyond ego functioning and confront the inner demon. But how does this work and how can a mere human do battle with the God-energy within?

This is reminiscent of Jung's *Answer to Job*, in which God must fight against God, Nature against Nature (1969a, CW 11). Jung illustrates such a wrestling match by drawing from a Native American myth. Hiawatha moves through a process of transformation in which he must wrestle with an inner "assailant," in his case, Mondamin, the corn god and symbol of the nourishment he seeks. Jung states, "Hiawatha wrestles with himself in order to create himself" (1967, CW 5, para. 523). He accomplishes this by gaining access to the "equivalent" symbol of nourishment that he needs (para. 522), thus acquiring the strength and creative power to go beyond himself. Through the encounter, even the corn god himself is changed for the benefit of all humans.

Our personal struggle, however, is to not change the Wise Old Woman spirit, but to contain the blitz of our complexes, and the Wise Old Woman spirit can help. When aiding in our defense against the fierceness or passion of the instincts, the Wise Old Woman spirit can align with us as a partner and give us might to withstand the attack.

Eros, as the Wise Old Woman spirit or feminine wisdom figure, can be understood as the healing symbol for our personal wrestling matches, appearing in our dreams and birthing creative energy. "A balance between the opposites must be found ... [and as] this is not possible through logic, one is dependent on symbols which make the irrational union of opposites possible" (Jung, 1969, CW 11, para. 757). This includes how a relationship between a person and the Wise Old Woman spirit may be experienced as a felt vision of the intimacy between them or take form in writing, sculpture, painting or dance—any creative expression of that sacred wholeness.

My focus on *eros* raises the possibility that in today's context, it is particularly in connection and partnership with the Wise Old Woman spirit that we may find help in coming to grips with a complex. This is not to say it will be extinguished. Although beyond this discussion, the complex in essence often hides a deeper value which triggers it. However, the synergy between us, the Wise Old Woman and ourselves, meets or suffers the instincts as needed, helping us not succumb to its animal nature.

Instead, we do our best in relating to the feeling and experience of the complex as the Wise Old Woman spirit would! That's when its value may be discovered—in its meaning. At the same time, this partnership makes great efforts to pause, interrupt, distract, or slow the complex down—even to live it out more consciously without acting it out.

As you have read, the seizure of the complex has the potential to become an experience of Divine Power.

Surely the Wise Old Woman can be a helper in many ways, yet the possibility of prevailing with these most difficult energies is the heart of the matter and most significant. Impulse control seems often nonexistent amid our current societal turmoil.

When Jung and von Franz describe the complexes, they note that we need the help of the Self to effect real change (von Franz, 1982, p. 82). The Wise Old Woman spirit is just such a helping self, and as *eros* and emissary, could well lead our peacemaking efforts within as well as in our outer life.

CHAPTER 4
The Great Feminine Secret: *Emptiness*

C.G. Jung was early to champion the feminine principle as well as women themselves. It is a matter of record that women flocked to see him in Switzerland and began to follow him faithfully from his first entry into private practice (Bair, 2003, p. 169). It is also true that Jung's writings about the tension of the opposites occupied a central place in his thinking. As we have read, he considered the ability of humans to bear that tension as a necessity for avoiding World War III.

In presenting how the archetype of the Wise Old Woman might be differentiated from the Wise Old Man spirit, and considering the duality of an archetype, I seek to single out and emphasize the Wise Old Woman spirit, the helping side of the feminine divine of which we are in greatest need. Specifically, Jung's concept of the "great feminine secret ... *emptiness,*" (1968h, CW 9i, para. 183), so misunderstood and misshapen by the current view, virtually defines, along with *eros*, the Wise Old Woman spirit. *Emptiness* is an essential part of all she has to offer.

Generally speaking, *emptiness* is not well thought of in American culture. It is used as an example of negativity, e.g., a glass half empty, or unwanted nothingness. The "tank running on empty" suggests being out of fuel, and feeling "a pit in one's stomach" can mean bad news or a sense of dread. Emptiness can refer to boredom or nothing going on, a void of interest or pleasure. When depression occurs, life can feel empty and reflect the loss associated with despair.

One may empty the trash in order to dispose of, or remove, what is unwanted. Emptiness can signify something desolate, ravaged or barren and is often associated with loneliness and a life not lived. Moreover, emptiness may connote that something is missing, e.g., a cupboard being bare or having empty pockets when broke. Emptiness may also be described as just a waste of time, as if not being filled means life is frittered away. Even Jung himself disparages feminine emptiness as a nothingness to be pitied. The latter could be understood as born from the patriarchy of his day. These one-sided descriptions allude to the alien nature of emptiness that Jung describes.

On the other hand, Jung depicts the mystery of the feminine as the sacredness of "Yin." This refers to the helpful side of the feminine principle, including the Wise Old Woman spirit. In "Psychological Aspects of the Mother Archetype," originally written in 1938, Jung's writing is not a contradiction but an acknowledgment of the paradox of opposing positions. As offensive as it might seem today, particularly on the darker side, it is altogether consistent with his recognition of the *complexio oppositorum*.

Jung describes this emptiness as the "chasm, unplumbed depths, the yin" and, as mentioned, "absolutely alien to man." He ventures to describe it as the "whole 'mystery' of woman," thus relating it to the Great Mother archetype and to the Wise Old Woman spirit, in particular (1968h, CW 9i, para. 183).

Jung writes that the secret of "such a female is fate itself," and speaking "as a man" takes pity on this "vacuous nonentity" (para. 183). Jung was likely aware of what he was writing when he chose these words, which reflected the prejudice against the feminine of his time. In this way, he seems to speak from the male perspective of a more negative experience of the feminine and reveals some bias on Jung's part, even when promoting the feminine.

Whether for or against it or both, man is described as necessarily confronting this mystery. Jung dramatically writes, "He falls absurdly happy into this pit," the pit as symbolic of his relationship to the feminine, or "if he doesn't, he has missed and bungled his only chance of making a man of himself" (para. 183). Jung observes here that avoiding the feminine, whether the outer woman or the anima, results in arrested growth of the masculine. Without further entry into the discussion about how to achieve manhood, suffice it to say that what Jung describes as a pitiable "non-entity," he also acknowledges as having a great influence on male development.

Only two other references for *emptiness* are listed in the index of Jung's *Collected Works*. Both are found in his "Commentary on 'The Secret of the Golden Flower.'" He writes of the ultimate undivided unity, the "centre of emptiness" and goal of the yogi who seeks to "disentangle" consciousness from the "daemonic forces of life" (1968a, CW 13, para. 56). It is here, quoting from "The Secret of the Golden Flower," where the "god of utmost emptiness and life" exists, an ideal place free of the contents and illusions of consciousness, a state realized only in death (para. 56). Jung describes such emptiness as "identical in form with the primal beginning" (para. 57).

He observes that it is only through a humble recognition or personification of this primal beginning, this most powerful autonomous energy—a god or goddess—that a relationship with emptiness can be established. The Wise Old Woman spirit can manifest as such a personification and through relationship with her, healing can occur for both the individual as well as in the world.

Moreover, a proper *eros* connection with this spiritual personification allows a certain assimilation of it, and indeed, a depotentiation of its force can then be achieved (1968a, CW 13, para. 55). Thus, the *mystery* of the woman and the yoga concept of emptiness seem to relate to one another, each seen as a source of life and offering a place of beingness that can well occur through an experience with the Wise Old Woman spirit.

Emptiness can also be seen as a characteristic of the woman's physical being as literally her uterus or womb. This is the dark place from which new life can germinate, develop, and emerge. Extending this emptiness symbolically, Jung offers a multiplicity of descriptions— symbols representing physical, psychological, and spiritual meaning for the feminine uterus: *vas, vessel, womb, bath,* and *temenos* are among the names for this emptiness (1970, CW 14, para. 75; 1971, CW 6, para. 394; 1968d, CW 12, para. 257). *Stone, lapis,* and *illumination* are still other alchemical descriptors (1968l, CW 13, para. 112) as are *water, fire,* and the "arcane substance itself" para. 113). About the *prima materia* in its feminine aspect, Jung writes:

... it is the moon, the mother of all things, the vessel, it consists of opposites, has a thousand names, is an old woman, and a

121

whore, as Mater Alchimia it is *wisdom* and teaches wisdom, it contains the elixir of life in potentia and is the mother of the Saviour and of the filius Macrocosmi, it is the earth and the serpent hidden in the earth, the blackness and the dew and the miraculous water which brings together all that is divided. (1970, CW 14, para. 15; italics added)

Surely this is apt description of the Wise Old Woman spirit. In another place Jung writes about "The 'house of the sphere,' the '*vas rotundum*,' whose roundness represents the cosmos and, at the same time, the world-soul ..." (para. 373). In addition, he writes about the vessel as the head, the soul, the glass vessel (1968l, CW 13, paras. 113–15), the egg, and the dragon (para. 109). The vessel is that which must be made "by a kind of squaring of the circle," and the "vas pellicanicum" and Christ's body, called the "vessel of the spirit," are still other of its forms (paras. 115–116). Over four dozen page numbers are listed for "vessel" in one volume alone (1970, CW 14, p. 693).

Although the scope of this chapter allows only a brief overview of the symbol of *emptiness* and its variants, Jung himself wrote more than usual about the meanings of the *vessel* symbol. He explained that he wanted to "elucidate the psychology of relations between the worship of woman and the legend of the Grail," as seen in the early Middle Ages. He writes that the "holy vessel" is the central religious idea in the legend and calls it a "genuine relic of Gnosticism" (1971, CW 6, para. 401). It was a "medieval element ... that presided over the birth of modern individualism," he states. "It began ... with the worship of woman, which strengthened the man's soul very considerably as a psychological factor, since the worship of woman meant worship of the soul" (para. 376).

Jung notes that the survival of the vessel symbolism "must be interpreted as a spiritualization of the eroticism aroused by the worship of woman," spiritualization meaning "retention of a certain amount of libido" (para. 401). Vessel symbols are depicted in dream images as compensation, often for the overly active masculine, emphasizing again the need for relationship with the Wise Old Woman spirit. Jung suggests that the Grail symbol is beyond comprehension and critical analysis, and maintains its appealing aesthetic form and subsequent vitality.

Quoting Gerhard Dorn, a sixteenth-century philosopher and alchemist, he says, "The vessel is like the work of God in the vessel of divine germination" (1968d, CW 12, p. 237, n16), noting that the "'germinal vesicle' refers to a quasi-alchemical process of refining and ennobling." *Temenos*, another word for vessel, means "sacred precinct" (1968a, CW 13, paras. 34–36). Describing a vision of Zosimos, Jung cites a "bowl-shaped alter" and relates it to the "*krater* of Poimandres, ... a wonder-working vessel, a font or piscine, in which the immersion takes place and transformation into a spiritual being is effected" (1968l, CW 13, paras. 96–97).

In this regard he also mentions the symbolic attributes of the Virgin Mother seen in the "Litany of Loreto" as "a vessel of devotion, a source of wisdom and renewal." According to Jung, these attributes "show how the soul-image (anima) effects the conscious attitude (1971, CW 6, para. 380). The impact of the Wise Old Woman spirit can indeed affect the conscious attitude, but emptiness, for many here in the US, may feel distant and difficult to integrate, especially for the more common extroverted psyches.

Nevertheless, the 2020 COVID-19 pandemic, resulting in stay-at-home orders in many states, has tested this very situation. For all the current methods of meditation and relaxation, emptiness remains a frequent trigger for vilification. The quality of emptiness is often neglected or disparaged, but this forced introversion may lead to unexpected, even positive changes within the individual, perhaps more time for reflection or dreamwork. On an outer concrete level, 2020 reports and photos show clear skies in places that were typically polluted and wild animals making their appearance in empty streets all over the world, not to mention sea creatures seen thriving in the people-less oceans (Bar, 2021).

Jung describes how in later alchemy, the vessel was called the "*vas Hermetic*," which "too, is a uterus of spiritual renewal or rebirth" (1968l, CW 13, para. 97). Thus, *vas* is interpreted as the womb. The "stainless womb of this divine font" is another symbol Jung cites (p. 68, n8). He also describes the small vessel filled with "divine water of the art" that is brought to Isis by an angel (para. 97). In addition, Jung notes that St. Augustine likened the bridal chamber to the "virginal womb."

All these characteristics dovetail with the "almost infinite variety of aspects" of the mother archetype, such as the baptismal font or "vessel-shaped flowers like the rose or the lotus" (Jung, 1968h, CW 9i, para. 156). As previously noted, these are seen in mandala symbolism, insomuch as the rose is the Western equivalent of the lotus, which is interpreted as the womb by Tantrists. That is, the rose represents the maternal womb (Jung, 1968b, CW 9i, para. 652).

The "primitive notion of the uterus" is the root of vessel symbolism, according to Jung (1971, CW 6, para. 406). He also cites Mylius (1583–1642), a composer and alchemist, who "calls the vessel the 'root and principle of our art'" (1968l, CW 13, para. 113). Thus, the symbol of the vessel has a secular origin, having realized its inception in the third or fourth century (1971, CW 6, para. 395). According to Jung, the vessel is likely a pagan relic "adaptable to Christianity," especially in the worship of Mary, through which all mother goddesses were then related: "The image of the *vas Sapientiae,* vessel of wisdom, likewise recalls its Gnostic prototype, Sophia" (para. 398).

Associations to the mother archetype include "hollow objects such as oven and cooking vessels," as are "the uterus, *yoni,* and anything of a like shape" (Jung, 1968h, CW 9i, para. 156). These particular symbols relate to the uterine quality of the woman, but many other symbols apply to the mother archetype from other perspectives—"things arousing devotion or feelings of awe," for example, the deep woods (para. 156). Jung states that "the womb ... frequently symbolizes the creative aspect of the unconscious" (1967, CW 5, para. 182). When the feminine principle operates as the womb, psychologically speaking, it can give birth from its *emptiness,* with creativity arising out of apparent nothingness.

This process is reminiscent of the autonomous nature of the psyche, which introduces new ideas that seem to come from nowhere. Of course, the womb is fertile, protective, and meant to hold or incubate new life, and the phallus or spirit is needed to penetrate and fertilize the womb.

Moreover, Jung refers to the "regenerating womb," the "chalice," and the "'krater' of rebirth" (1967, CW 5, para. 626). He describes a woman's dream in which "The uterus is the centre [of her drawing], the life-giving vessel. ... The stone, like the Grail, is itself the creative vessel, the *elixir vitae*" (1968d, CW 12, p. 179, n124). In addition, Jung wrote of the uterine symbolism of rain and fertility charms of the early twentieth century in southern Egypt, and how the uterus of a woman was still considered magical and sometimes sacrificed (with the woman) in rituals performed by "natives in the bush" (1971, CW 6, para. 397).

Jung also offers examples of negative or evil meanings of the uterus such as the grave, darkness, death, secretive, a prison, the abyss, and having an ambivalent nature. Of a patient's dream, Jung notes, "The dark cave corresponds to the vessel containing the warring opposites" (1968d, CW 12, para. 259), and he describes a man's anima in another dream as "the dark and dreaded maternal womb ... which is of an essentially ambivalent nature" (para. 192). In Jung's discussion of "The Myth of the Hero," Beya's womb is interpreted as a prison in the Rosarium's version of the "Visio" (1968i, CW 12, para. 437).[12]

Nevertheless, the alchemists considered the vessel as "something truly marvelous," and according to the alchemist Maria Prophetissa, "the whole secret lies in knowing about the Hermetic vessel" (Jung, 1968i, CW 12, para. 338). Substances that were to be transformed were in retorts or melting furnaces, typical symbols for the Hermetic vessel. The statement "The vessel is one," or *emptiness* is unity, is repeatedly emphasized in alchemical writings, according to Jung, and can be understood as an "imitation of the spherical cosmos" (para. 338).

In a note citing Philalethes, Jung describes the vessel as the "Philosophical Garden in which our sun rises and ascends" (p. 238, n20).[13] He states, it is "a kind of matrix or uterus from which the *filius philosophorum*, the miraculous stone, is to be born." In other words, *emptiness* is the birthmother of the stone. The earth, as *prima materia*, is itself a womb, sheltering all the living things within it (para. 444). He describes the vessel as a "mystical idea, a true symbol like all the central ideas of alchemy" (para. 338).

Von Franz writes about "simply stepping back into the inner *emptiness* of the Self" as the "inner way of not fighting or getting involved

---

[12] In the "Visio" version of the Rosarium, Beya is the daughter of the King who is rejuvenated in the form of a youth. His death is "the result of his complete disappearance into the body of Beya during coitus." Death in this myth symbolizes "the completion of the spiritual descent into matter" (Jung, 1968i, CW 12, para. 436; see also para. 437).
[13] Most likely Eirenaeus Philalethes, the pseudonym for George Starkey, a seventeenth-century alchemist from Colonial America. Jung cites the "Metallorum metamorphosis" from *Museum Hermeticum,* a compendium of alchemical texts first published in 1625.

in [evil's] emotional or other effect" (1974, p. 246). Retreating into the Self, into the inner retort, or retiring into "the innermost nucleus of one's personality" is the sole way of protecting oneself from the attacks of evil. Thus, holding to the introverted way is "the only hiding place when evil tries to involve one in its powers" (p. 246).

A regular time of introverting, being in the *emptiness* or the vessel inside, also provides a place of focus for active imagination with the Wise Old Woman spirit, or for relating to the inner life of one's dreams, examining what the unconscious may be pointing to or supporting (p. 82). Von Franz also describes emptiness as sometimes related to depression, when "nothing is going on," and suggests that the unconscious accumulates an enormous amount of energy when the depression is long-lasting. "For something important to come up, you need this period of nothing happening, so to speak, in consciousness" (1999, p. 27). The need for nothingness inevitably precedes creativity.

Von Franz also tells us that the vessel is "one of the greatest inventions of all [humankind]," nearly as important as discovering fire, and that it serves as "a symbol of man's capacity to imprison, by his wit and intelligence, things which normally escape him" (1982, p. 79). Von Franz adds that Jung was always looking for some form in which to convey his experiences, and it was only when he discovered alchemy that he found it. She quotes Jung, "Alchemy. That's the vessel in which I can convey them" (1999, p. 96). Note that the ship is a feminine vessel (p. 33). Thus, it might be said that the ship of alchemy, as a symbol of the vessel and *emptiness*, first received, then held, carried and expressed Jung's ideas, feelings, and discoveries very well.

Von Franz writes of the "cryptic riddle," describing the dreams of long-term analysands whose material is so "difficult and complicated" that the dreams are virtually "useless" (1999, p. 107). Yet, after penetrating such dreams, it seems that they have much more to do with being than with insight. She suggests that the unconscious may be teaching people, not to realize or have great thoughts, but to learn "just how to be." She explains that "just being" is a Taoist form of uselessness; she sees such uselessness as a "higher achievement than the [developmental] stages before" (pp. 107–8). Perhaps *emptiness*, when well-developed consciously, could be described as this higher form of Taoist uselessness.

In discussing the feminine in her book, *The Mother*, Birkhäuser-Oeri offers additional perspectives on the womb—a physical manifestation of *emptiness*—declaring that the "mother image … symbolizes not only the psychological but also the physical foundation of human existence …" (1988, p. 14). She further notes, "The missing element in trinitarian thinking is bodily reality" or the "completing One" (p. 20). In fairy tales, the Earth Mother "often joins opposites into a new unity"; she is body, nature and "also spirit, a spirit-nature which includes material reality" (p. 20).

There is a spirit mother and a nature mother who can be said to coincide with the physical drives or instincts. Stating that the mother archetype, and her maternal aspects in particular, are analogous to the unconscious, Birkhäuser-Oeri asserts that the archetype "involv[es] the body and the mystery of matter in general" (p. 14). In this way, the mother image encompasses the concept of *emptiness*.

From a Western perspective, it could be said that the quintessential *emptiness* is the Grail in *The Grail Legend* (1970), about which Emma Jung and Marie-Louise von Franz have written. Much could be offered from what Emma Jung and von Franz wrote about *emptiness*. However, I will reduce their material to a few quotations, which are most important, taken from their chapter "The Central Symbol of the Legend: The Grail as Vessel":

> … the individual human being serves as a vessel, for only when the opposites are reconciled in the single individual can they be united. … So the vessel also becomes a uterus for the spiritual renewal or rebirth of the individual. … The vessel, therefore, also appears to represent an inner readiness for relating to the archetype of the Self. (E. Jung & von Franz, 1970, p. 112, pp. 143–44)

According to the alchemistic view, to be dead and buried—an incomprehensible state of existence—is looked upon as the primary condition and as the starting point for the *opus*, in contrast to the general view that death and burial come at the close of life (p. 132).

It is natural to suppose that things buried or hidden merely refer to something unconscious which only needs to be dug up or uncovered, like a treasure raised to the light of day. The concept of an empty grave, however, seems to point further. It could be a question here of something so concealed and invisible that it is as if it had never existed at all, something which did not merely need to be uncovered, but which to some extent had to come into existence first (p. 132).

We are reminded of the thousands of years of neglect and rejection of the feminine principle, as if it had never existed, as if it were invisible. Yet it is this very invisibility, this *emptiness*, that offers the potential—indeed, it is a requirement—for an encounter with the Self.

For example, in the dreams and fantasy pictures of modern people, this hidden, invisible something is occasionally depicted as a meaningful and numinous void. There is one dream image in which an egg-shaped void, from which rays stream forth, forms the middle of a world or mandala with an empty center. The words of Meister Eckhart beautifully express what is meant by this image:

> "Everything must be lost, the soul must exist in unhampered nothingness," or "Whosoever would come to God must come as nothing." Or, expressed in Eastern imagery: "In the purple hall of the city of jade dwells the God of Utmost Emptiness and Life." The Confucians call it, "the centre of the void." A nothingness, a void, is therefore the inescapable condition for the emergence of the Self. The Self is not already present from the beginning in a comprehensible form, but manifests itself only through the outer and inner realizations of a life lived to its end. (E. Jung & von Franz, 1970, p. 133)

Emma Jung and von Franz explain that the Self is not invariably realized, despite our biological unfolding. They also state that having dream images of the Self in symbolic form is not the same as a realization of the Self, nor is the Self manifest with merely a high degree of clarity and differentiation of consciousness. For it does not depend so very greatly on knowledge and ability or some degree of intelligence, but rather upon the use that is made of these attributes and, above all, on the psychic attitude a person adopts in the face of the various circumstances of life and fate (p. 134).

Questions abound, invoking curiosity, inviting reflection, and followed by even more questions. If *emptiness* is present from the beginning, as Jung suggests (1969a, CW 11, para. 609), then perhaps it is this same kind of emptiness from which all else is born—*eros* being created by its very birth, born out relationship with the feminine divine, becoming itself and giving life to all that follows.

CHAPTER 5
Emma Jung: Quintessential Expression
of the Wise Old Woman Spirit

Jung family home from the water (Photo: Susan Faron)

My hope is that this chapter about Emma Maria Jung-Rauschenbach might offer a beginning portrait of the Wise Old Woman spirit—so sorely needed today—as painted by the contours of Emma's life.[14] Thus, Emma Jung serves as an example of the Wise Old Woman spirit that I have been talking about in the previous chapters. The question that shaped the

---

[14] This note acknowledges the conundrum of how to refer to Emma Jung respectfully throughout this chapter. With her grandson's blessing, she will be referred to as Emma, Emma Rauschenbach, Emma Jung-Rauschenbach, Emma Jung, or Mrs. Jung. Referring to Jung, likewise, will be written as Jung or C.G.

development of this chapter is, "How might Emma Jung have developed a relationship with the Wise Old Woman spirit in her own way?" Although I don't know if Emma had an image of a female figure with whom she engaged in active imaginations, as C.G. Jung did with Philemon, I will nevertheless provide a glimpse of how the Wise Old Woman spirit might have been visible in her life in a multitude of ways.

Just as collective projections of the Wise Old Man spirit were placed onto Jung, projections of the Wise Old Woman spirit also likely occurred with Emma. Whether reality or projection, Emma seems to come alive through the grace of the Wise Old Woman spirit.

The material I select is very personal, unlike the more impersonal, objective, and more scholarly presentation of the Wise Old Woman spirit in the previous chapters.

Emma Jung: Living a Relationship with the Wise Old Woman Spirit

Walkway to Jung family home (Photo: Susan Faron)

My journey to Switzerland in the spring of 2013 to attend the Research and Training Centre's eighteenth Blockcourse and to conduct an interview about Emma Jung is of the highest value to me. Indeed, on the afternoon of March 13, 2013, I was honored to interview Andreas Jung privately about his grandmother. Andreas Jung is the fifteenth grandchild and one of the youngest grandchildren in the C.G. and Emma Jung family. Through Andreas, I experienced his grandmother more directly. Hearing about Emma from a family member seemed to honor a process about someone whose life was informed by the Wise Old Woman spirit. The interview seemed also to be honoring the directions I received from the unconscious, which, in turn, helped me get a better feel for her. I got a sense of her personality and was often moved through this close contact with Andreas Jung. Because of the interview, I heard and felt the *eros* within Emma.

Andreas Jung (Photo: Susan Faron)

Moreover, and much to my amazement, very little had been written about Emma Jung as of 2011 when I first began researching the Wise Old Woman spirit and writing about Emma, although I did find useful references to her in more than thirty-two books: informative phrases, lines, sentences, or excerpts about her, by her, and about C.G.'s relationship to her. Of course, more has since been published about Emma, including a play by Elizabeth Clark-Stern, *Out of the Shadows: A Story of Toni Wolff and Emma Jung*; and books *Love and Sacrifice: The Life of Emma Jung*, by Imelda Gaudissart (2014); and Catrine Clay's *Labyrinths: Emma Jung, Her Marriage to Carl, and the Early Years of Psychoanalysis* (2016). My writing about Emma has come primarily from the source: visiting Andreas and Vreni Jung in the Jung family home, my interview with Andreas Jung, my relationship with my Swiss analyst who was good friends with another grandson, and the many contributors who wrote from personal experience in *C.G. Jung, Emma Jung, and Toni Wolff: A Collection of Remembrances* (Jensen & Mullen, 1982). I have also considered people's dreams of Emma in my thinking about her, including my own. In other words, my account of Emma seems closer (or as close) to a genuine account of Emma's life from the perspective of the ways of the Wise Old Woman spirit.

I discovered that more than 90 percent of the writings about Emma described her in a positive light. One biographer wrote in an unfavorable tone about some of Emma's behaviors. For example, when Emma sat painting at the side of a grassy area in which C.G. and their children would play, she was criticized for not actively engaging with them (Bair, 2003, p. 320).

All of Emma Jung's years are of interest to us, especially when the archetype of the Wise Old Woman's energy might be evident. Nevertheless, it seems likely that the *old* part of the Wise Old Woman spirit's name means just that—*old*. This seems to point to a human kind of oldness and aging that could perhaps offer the best chance of becoming conscious of wise and insightful ways. This is one of the reasons why the interview with Andreas Jung on Emma's later years was so valuable.

I have selected several episodes in Emma Jung's life descriptive of times in which the archetype of the Wise Old Woman could likely have been constellated. By selecting among what others have said, I endeavor to present what is most relevant in relationship to the Wise Old Woman spirit. Keep in mind, the archetype of the Wise Old Woman, being eternal, may accompany us our whole lives, even if we do not notice.

A biography of Emma begins in the next section, followed by a few vignettes, beginning with her birth and concluding with her older years. Following each, a psychological commentary addresses the possibilities for constellation of the Wise Old Woman spirit.

The Life Story of Emma Maria Jung-Rauschenbach

This biographical summary begins with Emma's birth, March 30, 1882. She "grew up in three different houses," the first being *The Rose Garden House*, belonging to one of the wealthiest industrial families in northeastern Switzerland at the time (Ganz, Jung, Michael, Rohrer, & Ruegg, 2009, p. 18). Emma was very close to her younger sister, Marguerite, who arrived the next year in 1883. Along with a nearby cousin, Gertrud, Emma and Marguerite were "always doing everything together" (A. Jung, personal communication, March 13, 2013[15]).

Emma and her little sister, circa 1887
(Courtesy of Lorena Homberger's sister Bernice)

---

[15] After the first instance, personal communications will be indicated by name and date only.

Emma seemed to have an inner calm and was more modest, quiet, and introverted than her sister. Both girls were bright. Emma seemed to have a natural curiosity for learning about many topics and did well in school. Marguerite "had more temper," "was more playing [playful]," and had a more extroverted style. As an adult, Marguerite was elegant and went to famous places, whereas Emma preferred a "small ... little, tiny village" for getaways and was more down-to-earth (A. Jung, March 13, 2013).

Emma lived her first fifteen years with her family in a big house on the Rhine (*Rosengarten*) and also had a cooler, more rural summer home, *The Mount of Olives*, which later became their full-time residence when it was taken down and replaced with a new structure (Ganz et al., 2009, pp. 18–19; A. Jung, March 13, 2013, and February 13, 2014). There were servants in the house, and when the girls went out, a coach would transport them.

When Emma was eleven (in 1893), the time in Switzerland for finishing primary school, her father decided that she could not attend the gymnasium, which was approximate to an American high school. One author wrote that Emma's not being able to go further in school was related somehow to an illness her father suffered and the loss of his sight (Anthony, 1990, p. 15). The memorial service curriculum vitae written about Emma is translated as follows: "Thus the suffering of the father became an affliction for the whole family that they found hard to bear" (Hu F. Etter, personal communications, March 11, 2014).

Although Emma, who suffered great hardship far beyond her eleven years, had to forgo the opportunity to study at this higher level, she went to finishing school, as did her sister, as suited the girls of wealthy families. It seems her father wanted to guide or direct her into a certain class of society that befit her status in preparation for marriage, children and home. Being very traditional, and considering the realities of the time (women had no vote, work opportunities were meager, and so on), he may have felt that was the best way to assure her a secure future. Even so, Emma was very sad and sorry because "she would have liked to study, to do something of her own. She was gifted. She was very good in school" (A. Jung, March 13, 2013).

Of particular interest is that Emma's mother, Bertha, invited international orchestras to play in their home and sometimes invited them to stay for a few days while they performed in town. It seems that Emma played the piano a little (A. Jung, March 13, 2013), and even though she felt she could not sing, music was of great value to her. She was to later write:

> Music can be understood as an objectification of the spirit; it does not express knowledge in the usual logical, intellectual sense, nor does it shape matter; instead, it gives sensuous representation to our deepest associations and more immutable laws ... music admits us to the depths where spirit and nature are still one—or have again become one. ... it may mean a genuine religious experience and then ... it is of the highest value. (E. Jung, 1985, pp. 36, 37)

Nevertheless, Emma's father died earlier than expected, tragically at about age sixty-six, when Emma was only twenty-three and married just two years. However, Emma's mother seemed to manage the big household and extended family successfully as a widow on her own. She herself had a modest but generous nature, gave to the poor, helped the up-and-coming, and was very much liked by all (A. Jung, March 13, 2013).

Bertha's family, including Emma, is said to have "adored" her. Bertha—kindly, bright, and clever too—"lived the life of a great lady ... and [did] it so well." It is noteworthy that it was Bertha, as a young girl, who took Jung on walks in nature when he was just a toddler. Bertha, the daughter of a parishioner of Jung's father, helped with little Jung when his mother was hospitalized. Later, it was said of Bertha, "She was the one to understand Jung," and became one of Jung's analysands (A. Jung, March 13, 2013).

Jung first beheld Emma, age fourteen, as she stood at the top of a staircase. He was described as falling in love with Emma at first sight (Jaffé, 1979, p. 132). Apparently, Emma and Jung were silent in those few moments. However, Jung did not see her again for three years, even though he was "deeply shaken" at the time; he told a friend that he "knew in a flash, beyond all doubt," that Emma would be his future wife (Wher, 1989, p. 25; McLynn, 1996, p. 77; Hannah, 1976, p. 83).

Emma as a bride (Copyright Jung Family Archive)

It is unknown how Emma perceived him on that day. Later, her good friend Barbara Hannah said that becoming a "Frau Professor" was a disgusting thought to Emma (1976, p. 84). I wonder if she considered the possibility of the handsome young man, Jung, as a future suitor, or how his work might intrude or maybe even beckon.

One thing we do know is that Jung returned and proposed to Emma, who at first said, "No" (Hannah, 1976, p. 84, A. Jung, March 13, 2013, Brome, 2001, p. 77). Emma may have struggled with the idea of marrying a brilliant man who would be devoted to his work (Hannah, 1975, p. 84; Brome, 2001, p. 800.) Perhaps she also considered that he could offer the imaginative stimulus she missed when further schooling for her was denied (Anthony, 1990, p. 15). Hannah's impression was that their marriage was "fateful" and "meant to be" (1976, p. 84). By 1902, Emma and Jung were engaged. Jung did a painting for Emma during his semester of study in Paris just before their marriage, inscribing it, "Seine Landscape with clouds, for my dearest fiancée at Christmas, 1902" (Jaffé, 1979, p. 43).

Emma and Carl engagement picture (Copyright Jung Family Archive)

The two married on Valentine's Day, February 14, 1903. "A long acquaintance with this attractive girl blossomed into full-scale romantic love, and Gerhard Adler, who has read the love letters that has passed between them, testifies to their color and beauty" (Brome, 1977, p. 77).

Emma became a mother of five children. It seems that her children meant everything to her and, indeed, filled her life until they were all in school and growing up. As she wrote to Freud, children were "the only true joy" (McGuire, 1974, p. 456). She seemed to hold great feeling for each of her children and grandchildren. Certainly, Andreas Jung affirmed that all the grandchildren loved her deeply, of course including him, and held her in the highest regard (A. Jung, September 19, 2013).

Emma as a young mother (Courtesy of Jung Family Archive)

Von Graevenitz writes of visiting their home at Seestrasse 228, in Küsnacht, once when Jung was gone: "A swarm of grandchildren roared around the usually so quiet house. When I asked how many there were now, Mrs. Jung looked a little embarrassed. 'Nineteen,' she said" (1982, p. 30). In another story, I heard about Emma visiting one of the younger grandchildren when he was sick, taking him a toy, a wonderful merry-go-round with four horses and enchanting colors (A. Jung, March 13, 2013).

Throughout her life, from many perspectives, Emma appeared to be her own woman. For example, she lived the experience of mothering—organizing, managing, and caring for—five lively, very active children, much of the time without her husband being present. Indeed, she was seen as "the very foundation of the family" (Anthony, 1990, p. 17) and described as "an exceptional woman, and extremely capable mother ..." (Ellenberger, 1970, p. 79; cited in Brome).

Family picture Château d'Oex (Copyright Jung Family Archive)

Emma's advanced level of animus development—in particular, intellect and initiative—was evident when the Nazis threatened and Emma hastily gathered her family together, children and grandchildren, to drive to a hideaway location in the mountains. Hannah helped by driving two of their grandchildren. Emma was concerned that Carl wouldn't leave his practice, but he accompanied them for a few days to get them settled. He usually stayed long weekends, after that commuting back to Küsnacht several days of the week to see patients (Hannah, 1976, pp. 268–270).

There were many other ways that suggest how Emma Jung experienced and developed a creative animus. Sometimes this occurred in everyday situations, such as when she first learned to drive a car as a forty-seven-year-old grandmother (p. 198). Other times, her animus functioning was extraordinary. For example, in 1925, her skills as woman of the house included expanding the veranda, "doubling its volume" (Ganz & Rohrer, in Stiftung C.G Jung, Küsnacht, 2009, p. 119). Emma coordinated independently with the architect and workers while Jung was traveling in Africa for eleven months. The remodeling was finished when he returned (Etter, June 18, 2013).

Veranda of Jung family home (Photo: Susan Faron)

Emma seemed to have many dimensions and could be separate and silent, remaining in the background when Jung was in group discussion (Lynn, 1982, p. 41), or just as easily welcoming and conversing with the many distinguished visitors who came to their home, such as Sigmond Freud, Edward (E.A.) Bennet, Laurens van der Post, Fr. Victor White, Nils Bohr, and Richard Wilhelm. Along with her husband, she befriended Freud, and maintained a lively correspondence with him until he and Jung separated. Astonishingly enough, at the age of twenty-nine, Emma wrote: "I am following the voice of my unconscious" in a letter to Freud (McGuire, 1974, p. 452). Emma and Freud's relationship appeared vital, genuine, and warm. For example, Freud referred to Emma in a letter to Jung: "… your dear wife, well known to me as a solver of riddles" (p. 441). At other times, Emma encouraged Freud to discuss discrepant views with Jung. One example is how she wrote to Freud, "I think it would do you both so much good if you got down to a thorough discussion of it"

(p. 452). During this period, it seems like she functioned as a peacemaker between these two men.

In a time right for her, Emma developed herself and her own ideas about analytical psychology based on personal experience and her openness to learn, especially from her husband. Waiting until the children were developing well on their own, and with Jung's encouragement, Emma studied Latin, Greek, French, mathematics, chemistry, and, of course, analytical psychology (Anthony, 1990, p. 17).

Emma continued to further her animus development in many ways. For example, Emma was the first president of the Zürich Analytical Psychology Club and later became chairwoman of the curatorium for the newly formed C.G. Jung Institute of Küsnacht. A student in the early years describes Emma as "always warm and cordial" whether she was teaching at the Institute or in her home. She showed an "open and receptive attitude, very much her own person, who seemed to take the complexities and difficulties of life rather as a matter of course" (Lynn, 1982, p. 41).

Emma was seen as a peacemaker at the Institute as well as in other situations and as one who provided a continuity unique to her leadership; she was experienced as of "irreplaceable value" (Hannah, 1976, pp. 193–194, 299). Furthermore, the extraordinary animus development that Emma's life revealed appears to be joined with an equally mature sense of *eros*. Emma wrote: "… the sharpness of ethical discrimination is modified into an attitude of understanding Eros" (E. Jung & von Franz, 1970, p. 101).

Therefore, it is no surprise that positive *eros* functioning appeared in a number of ways in Emma's life; she was much liked by nearly everyone. Her colleagues, analysands, and friends all appeared to hold her in highest esteem. She accepted extroverted positions of teaching and leadership in spite of her natural introversion, winning the admiration and gratitude of those she guided along the way.

Emma Jung wrote two books. The first is *Animus and Anima* (1985). She was often recognized as an insightful, innovative, and independent thinker, "the first to strongly rework, elaborate, and expand on C.G. Jung's descriptions of the animus …" (Douglas, 2000, p. 152). Lyn Cowen echoed these thoughts:

Emma and Carl at Eranos (Courtesy of the Jung Family Archive)

Emma Jung ... wrote the first comprehensive statement on the animus from a female point of view. ... Her contribution is all the greater considering the times and context in which it appeared. She sees the "animus" as capable of progressive development in a woman. Her solution to the negativity of the animus ... is to emphasize the positive qualities: spiritual strength, intellectual focus, and creativity. (2003, pp. 25–26)

Emma wrote that what women have to overcome in their relationship to the animus is not pride, but lack of self-confidence and the resistance of inertia (1985, pp. 25–26).

Emma's second book, coauthored with Marie-Louise von Franz, is *The Grail Legend*, a voluminous and scholarly work of 452 pages. Emma devoted thirty years of research, study, and writing to it, but died before its completion. Her work on the *Grail* in later life might be considered as another child, born out of the continuing renewal of her creative *logos* development. Von Franz finished it at the request of Emma shortly before she died.

"Over the years, Emma developed herself independently as a psychoanalyst experienced in both theory and practice" (Wehr, 1989, p. 25) and was seen as a woman "with lively interests" who became Jung's collaborator, applying herself to the psychotherapeutic methods of analytical psychology (Ellenberger, 2001, p. 80; cited in Brome). In fact, Emma Jung was, "of all the wives of the early psychoanalysts, … the only one to become an analyst, herself" (Douglas, 2000, p. 35; Ellenberger, 1970, p. 681).

Emma and Toni with group of professionals at Eranos
(Courtesy of the Jung Family Archive)

Sheila Moon wrote of knowing Emma "as a person, an analyst, as a strong and quiet feminine being with her own ideas, her Swiss humor, her graciousness, and her quiet sensitivity" (1982, p. 43). It is noteworthy that Moon used the word *wisdom* four times in her written remembrance. Many have observed that Emma's warmth and sense of humor were a very real part of her brilliance and balance. Frank McLynn described her as follows:

Emma was an attractive, educated young woman, quiet, warm, independent, charming, and gracious. The personality that emerges from her letters and other writings is delightful: no nasty or malicious rumours have ever surfaced about her, and Jungians who remember her speak, in the inevitable jargon, of a "fine balance of creative animus and feminine functioning." (1996, p. 77)

Part of Emma's experiences as Jung's wife, however, included the triangular relationship they had with Toni Wolff. Toni was an analyst and writer who began as an analysand with Jung and became an intimate companion at the beginning of his confrontation with the unconscious. In the unpublished part of *Memories, Dreams, Reflections*, Jung described warning dreams referring to his relationship to Toni Wolff (passed on from Lorenz Jung to Hu Etter, September 13, 2013). Consulting such dreams, including active imaginations, was part of the deep thought and soul-searching Jung experienced at that time.

Although no one truly knows the circumstances beyond these three individuals, one account told of Jung's encounter in a life and death situation in which his decision regarding Toni Wolff was critical. A severe cramp overtook him while swimming in the lake outside his home, his life in grave danger, drowning imminent. When Jung recognized the cramp as a message from the unconscious and understood it as a symbol of going against his destiny, he redecided and returned to seeing Toni (L. Jung to Etter, September 13, 2013). As a result, after having previously chosen to terminate as Toni's analyst, Jung decided to return to that role, subsequently becoming intimately involved with her.

It became an extraordinary relationship for many reasons, but was outstandingly significant to the public because the three of them did not talk about it; they simply, and consciously, lived it out. They did not try to hide that Jung spent time with each of them, but all three contained their relationship as a private matter among them. This was particularly counterculture behavior during that era, occurring in a monogamous Swiss culture, where a man having a mistress was perhaps not so uncommon, but rarely lived out loud. In other words, relationships outside the marriage were typically held in secret.

Yet Jung's relationship was not that of simply having an extramarital affair. Coming at a crucial time of Jung's confrontation with the unconscious, following his break from Freud, it is widely acknowledged that Toni played a key role in developing analytical psychology along with Jung and Emma. Moreover, these events occurred in the context of an affluent, upper-class Swiss life at a time when feelings were to be expressed with reserve and subtlety, especially if you were a woman. Feelings were not conveyed through casual hugs and kisses, for example.

One writer told how she was deeply moved and impressed with Emma's "astonishing courage" (Douglas, 2000, p. 179). Another writer referred to Emma's and Toni's "heroic efforts" to make it work (Anthony, 1990, p. 35). Furthermore, it seems that Emma's and Toni's relationship deepened when Jung moved toward alchemical studies, Toni declining this part of Jung's journey. It is noteworthy that Emma continued to welcome Toni into the family home at that time (A. Jung, March 13, 2013). Perhaps Emma's own containment reflected the *emptiness* she came to understand, at the same time realizing the Grail-like *emptiness* of Toni's loss.

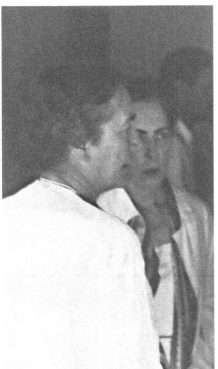

Emma and Toni at Eranos (Courtesy of the Jung Family Archive)

Some have described Emma's and Toni's relationship as understandably difficult at the beginning. Emma, in particular, suffered deeply (I. Gaudissart, personal communication, 2016). It is widely recognized, however, that Emma and Toni became friends over the years (A. Jung, March 13, 2013).

Part of their relationship development included regularly meeting together with another analyst, Carl A. Meier, in order to better understand one another and struggle through their mutual difficulties (Brome, 2001, p. 205). Indeed, the impression is that a remarkable relationship evolved between Emma and Toni.

Jung, as well as Emma and Toni, suffered in this situation, his misery somehow supportive of the hearts of each woman. This unpopular "solution," this triad, could be an example of the very aim that Jung pioneered: that is, as an individual, to consciously consider dreams, synchronistic events, and other messages from the unconscious, and together with this material, and despite the collective and the patriarchy, in particular, stand by the values of the positive feminine.

Standing by the values of the positive feminine is not about having two women (or men) in your life; rather, it is about listening to your anima the way that Jung did. Jung held to the positive feminine by attending to and analyzing his dreams and worked out his own path with heart. By following his own individual way, he was enabled to move forward with Toni and his work. It seems that Jung had been called by the Self. Henderson's observations about this dynamic relationship offer additional perspective on the *eros*-love in Emma's life: "It depended on a form of consciousness that totally transcended the ordinary worldly model ..." (Henderson, 1982, p. 33).

My impression is that each woman was so connected to her own unconscious that each provided a vital element in the experiential

Emma in the flower garden (Courtesy of the Jung Family Archive)

evolution of Jung's analytical psychology. I can imagine Emma, as one of this triad, consciously living out her part, personally experiencing this rejected feminine still so despised by the collective today. Was this not equally so for Toni? Moreover, Emma endured many emotions and feelings of abandonment, jealousy, and sadness. Were not all these feeling-experiences a part of Emma's integrating the whole *eros* principle about which she learned and wrote?

According to Hannah, a close friend of Emma's, "What saved the situation was that there was no 'lack of love' in any of the three" (1976, p. 175). Years later, Hannah tells of Emma's "amazing insight" when she disclosed that "he never took anything from me to give to Toni, but the more he gave her, the more he seemed able to give to me" (pp. 119–20). By all accounts, what seemed inconceivable had been transformed with the help of Emma's and Toni's great generosity, dignity, and courage. Indeed, an astonishing change occurred between these two women.

In 1947, four years after his heart attack, Jung himself acknowledged his own transformation. He wrote in a first-edition gift of his *Psychology of the Transference*, "*Ipse vulnerat et medtur*," meaning, "Also hurt and healed." At the beginning of the same volume, he dedicates the work, "To my wife" (Etter, November 19, 2013).

Emma and Carl in Bollingen (Courtesy of the Jung Family Archive)

In 1953 the Jungs celebrated their fiftieth wedding anniversary. This was two years before Emma's death. In the spring of 1955 Emma became very ill and had surgery, and Jung remained in Küsnacht to be near her. A particularly happy summer followed with Jung's eightieth birthday celebration and the Jungs staying together in Bollingen afterward. When the cancer recurred in the fall, Emma was hospitalized for only a short time before she returned home (Hannah, 1976, p. 324). Little is known about her death, although one focus in her dying days seemed to be on how nature continues to grow and provide what is needed, even in the harshest of climates (A. Jung, March 13, 2013).

From the perspective of an entire lifetime, only a few episodes are presented from an unlimited number of circumstances in which the Wise Old Woman spirit could have been constellated in Emma's life. Describing how Emma's extraordinary selfhood unfolded shows us how the Wise Old Woman spirit seemed to be present in so many parts of Emma's life. The Wise Old Woman spirit helped Emma especially through hard times, not only guiding her as a mother and analyst, but also through a great deal of suffering in her life. These situations vividly reflect what the Wise Old Woman spirit can provide—protection, nurturance, love, and guidance—and further inform our image of Emma and the archetype of the Wise Old Woman.

Emma portrait (with broach in front of leaves)
(Courtesy of the Jung Family Archive)

148

Although Emma as a woman is to be differentiated from the Wise Old Woman spirit, I hypothesize that as Emma approached wholeness, and the more complete a woman she became, she did so while working through a relationship with the Wise Old Woman spirit. Perhaps these glimpses of the Wise Old Woman *imago* in Emma's life can create a hopefulness in us. The four moments in Emma's life described next are an invitation to the reader to imagine being present with a Wise Old Woman energy and to recognize, feel, and experience her firsthand.

Emma Jung-Rauschenbach and Her Discovery of the Unconscious

Before Emma Rauschenbach had met C.G. Jung (who years later discovered the anima and animus), she experienced what she later knew as the "negative animus." It seems that Emma cleaned her own room when she was a teen, forgoing the help that a wealthy family invariably employed, so that she could take special care of a beautiful washbowl and jug that were of great value to her. Alas, she dropped and broke the jug one day, realizing "accidentally" on her own, that "something *in herself* worked *against* and not *for* her" (Hannah, 1976, pp. 123–24).

Psychological Commentary: Emma was apparently in touch with some deeper wisdom beyond her chronological age. It is as if she had discovered personality "Number Two," just as Jung called the unconscious in *Memories, Dreams, Reflections* (1965, p. 45). This second personality is a counter-power and not controlled by the ego. It is as if Emma both held the vessel and was the vessel at that moment. When this symbol of *emptiness* broke, a synchronicity occurred in which Emma first experienced consciously the power of the unconscious, likely including the archetype of the Wise Old Woman. To realize there is a power that goes beyond the ego is exactly what Jung defines as a religious experience (Jung, 1968j, CW 10, para. 8).

Emma and C.G. Jung's Relationship

Many authors offer observations of Emma's and Jung's ways of positive relating. For example, Moon reminiscences in her article, "Memory of Emma Jung," and ends by writing a memory of Dr. Jung, presenting a unique perspective on his relationship with Emma.

... he [C.G. Jung] had walked along the lake to a hotel where Mrs. Jung was to join us to sit outside and talk. I said, "Shall I go for Mrs. Jung?" Dr. Jung turned to me and said, "I don't send for my wife to come to me, I go to her." ... and he left to get her. (1982, p. 43)

Psychological Commentary: Emma's husband, being an important, internationally known person, nevertheless reveals a very human side to him—a humble attitude and great respect for Emma and for the feminine. It is hypothesized that the Wise Old Woman spirit, and *eros* in particular, contributed to their mutual regard for one another and attunement to a wise feminine aspect underlying their relationship.

Emma Jung-Rauschenbach's Death

It is hypothesized that the spirit of the Wise Old Woman was there with Emma and helped her throughout her dying process. For example, one of Emma's grandchildren went to see her late in her grandmother's life, not realizing how close she was to death. Without disclosing privileged information, I heard about how they talked, and looked together, at material about one of life's amazing natural phenomena (A. Jung, March 13, 2013).

Psychological Commentary: Although the details of this exchange are private and only abstracted here, Emma seemed to send the message that nature *wants* to keep it all going, but sometimes, maybe often, it takes extraordinary measures on the part of us humans. In my interpretation, Emma felt that life would continue, notwithstanding the coldness that living could be, despite the most desolate conditions, in secret and amazing ways, hidden and there to be discovered. At heart, it was a deeply felt visit in which Emma appeared to offer reassurance and hope to her young grandchild, even as she faced the greatest transition of all.

Bennet writes that Jung told him that when he disclosed to Emma the grave news of her prognosis four days before her death, Emma was "quite undisturbed," saying she felt "in a way relieved," having been preparing for her death since her operation the previous spring. Emma told her husband "she felt she was going to die" (1985, p. 60). The day Emma died Jung wrote in a letter:

The sea of divine mercy had swept over her end and spared her of all the horrors of long and terrible suffering. In miraculous fashion it heard my prayer for a quick and painless end. I am as shaken by that as by her death. (Jung, cited in Jaffé, 1979, p. 136)

It is noteworthy that Jung had visions and dreams of Emma before and after her death, one of them coming only two days before she died. He had a sudden flash, an unspeakable insight, "a great illumination" that "lit up a centuries-old secret that was embodied in her and had exerted an unfathomable influence on my life" (Adler, 1975, vol. 2, p. 284). Convinced it came from Emma as she lay dying in a coma, Jung felt that a profound knowledge had entered his psyche—as if Emma were gifting him, at the same time releasing herself. Jung speculated that Emma's "painless and royal death" was in part due to this amazing and silent transmission (p. 284).

Jung family tombstone with lavender flowers (Photo: Susan Faron)

Psychological Commentary: Note that Emma's relationship to Jung began and ended with a flash: One at first sight—the very birth of their bond—and the second, as far as we know, as she lay dying. These illuminations or insights could suggest the presence of the Wise Old Woman spirit. Surely Jung suffered the loss of Emma and, in doing so, would have experienced both the *emptiness* and *eros* required for receiving such ancient wisdom.

Emma Jung as Leader, Analyst, and Teacher

The Leader

A beginning student, Elined Kotschnig, told how in the newly organized institute in Küsnacht, there was high tension and "mutual criticism to be observed," but not directed at Emma Jung. Kotschnig wondered, "What was wrong with Mrs. Jung?" who was chairwoman of the curatorium at the time. It seems that Kotschnig felt it was just a matter of time before Mrs. Jung would disappoint her. Kotschnig wrote:

Until in the course of several months at the Institute, it became clear that everything was so right with Mrs. Jung that nobody felt the need to find fault. She was admired, respected, beloved, and she moved quietly through that first difficult year, a truly healing and helpful presence. (1982, p. 40)

It was Kotschnig's experience of Emma that inspired her to say, "the really individuated partner in the Jung couple was *Mrs.* Jung!" (p. 40).

The Analyst

From a different perspective, an analysand wrote about Emma: I found Mrs. Jung the most integrated person in Zürich. ... I found myself deeply moved by a woman who had so obviously found herself and her own authenticity in the midst of so many collective pressures ... an individuality separate from his [Jung's]. ... Also she became a *wise* and sensitive analyst. ... She was a joy to work with. ... a fine balance of creative animus and feminine functioning. (Howes, 1982, p. 34; italics added)

The Teacher

Sallie Nichols shares another story when attending Emma's class on *The Grail Legend*. Emma typically "fielded all questions from the most erudite and challenging ones to those that were more pedantic, or even naïve." This time she responded with silence (Nichols, 1982, p. 50). Apparently, this was quite unusual, given that Emma most often answered questions in her "simple, but knowledgeable way. ... Then she said quite simply, 'I don't know the answer to that. I just never thought of this question before'" (p. 50). Nichols goes on to say that she herself was "dumbfounded," imagining Emma's embarrassment, but Emma didn't actually seem embarrassed at all. Nichols writes:

Mrs. Jung, far from feeling embarrassed, humiliated, chagrined, guilty, ignorant, or anything of the sort, was enjoying the situation immensely! She was laughing in the most spontaneous and free way imaginable.

Oh, how I wish I could find the words to convey the essence of that laugh! Its quality was so unusual, that I can perhaps more readily define it in terms of what it was not. It was not "apologetic," "self-depreciatory," or "ingratiating." It wasn't "disarming" because Mrs. Jung obviously didn't feel threatened or on the defensive. I can't even call it "charming," because to do so would imply that her laughter was, at least partly, intended as a form of communication (i.e., to "charm" us). But the fact is, it wasn't intended for us at all.

That never-to-be-forgotten laughter was quite simply Mrs. Jung's spontaneous reaction to the outer situation, which she accepted as a humorous, "just-so-story"—involving no moral judgments, no guilt feeling, and no broken images of perfectionism or omniscience.

It was the musical laughter of a young girl—or rather, of a carefree and wise woman, an individual human being, stripped of the tremendous burden of false notions that most of us carry about and arrived full circle to recapture the spontaneity of youth, the innocence of those golden days before our natural harmony got buried under tons of garbage. (pp. 50–51)

Psychological Commentary: According to Jung, "Individuation means becoming an 'in-dividual,' and in so far as 'individuality' embraces our *innermost*, last, and incomparable uniqueness, it also implies becoming one's own self ... that is, a separate, in-divisible unity or whole ..." (Jaffé, 1979, p. 228). These depictions of Emma Jung confirm that she was, indeed, her own person. Might this reveal some ways in which she lived out the presence of the Wise Old Woman energy within her? Couldn't the Wise Old Woman spirit be seen through some of the ways that Emma led the Institute and modeled for her students? Emma appears to be among the very best models of a life relationship with the Wise Old Woman spirit, maybe even the model of our time (Howes, 1982, p. 34).

The return to "natural harmony" portrayed in this last example seems like the kind of androgyny we understand as the archetype of the Wise Old Woman. Don't both "young girl" and "carefree and wise woman" rekindle the spirit of the Wise Old Woman and the balance that she contains? This story seems an illuminating example of Emma's *logos* and *eros* working together. As I read the last episode, I imagine how she laughed and feel a sense of being there, too—that image of Emma teaching seems to show a friendly relatedness to the students while remaining simultaneously connected to the Wise Old Woman spirit.

Emma Jung lived numerous expressions of the Wise Old Woman archetype. Perhaps she could be among the best examples of the Wise Old Woman spirit in action *and* in non-action. Perhaps we could consider Emma as the actual missing "*Mother* of Jungian Psychology," as Jung has been its Father (Cowen, 2003, p. 3), or, as Sheila Moon has written, referring to Emma Jung, as "that incomparable Swiss 'godmother'" (1982, p. 42).

Portrait Emma, 1905
(Courtesy Jung Family Archive)

CHAPTER 6
Astonishing Visits in Dreams Worldwide—More Images of the Wise Old Woman Spirit

The Wise Old Woman spirit is upon us. She exists, consciously in waking fantasies and unconsciously in dreams around the world. I'm writing this amid the never-ending Coronavirus pandemic and as the earth faces an ever-more looming climate crisis. The fate of the human race is in question. The scales seemed tipped to eradicate us all. Balance is lost. Although there is much yet to be learned about the Wise Old Woman spirit, her qualities of *eros* and *emptiness*, so depreciated and disparaged today, are needed more than ever.

In keeping with *emptiness* as a prerequisite for receptivity, and *eros* as relationship itself, the Wise Old Woman spirit invites us, by her very presence, into active and consistent contact. The Wise Old Woman spirit has a partnership in mind, whether as a vigorous participant or in dignified and quiet stillness. She makes herself known; she is present here and now. She can be seen, heard, and felt.

The wisdom figure of the Wise Old Woman may come on her own in dreams or make surprise visits during active imaginations. At other times, she may use attention-getting imagery, deeply felt emotional shifts, and meaningful coincidences. Frequently, her presence is a numinous experience.

Images, sounds, or other unconscious manifestations may be met internally in dreams or in the outer world as synchronicities. Visions apparently occur in either realm. Although ancient records have revealed processes similar to active imagination ("Active Imagination," 2022), Jung is known to have consciously discovered and developed it. Active imaginations can be experienced in limitless ways, through dancing, drawing, singing, sculpting, writing, and so on.

Significantly we, too, need to actively seek a connection to the Wise Old Woman and *consciously* enter the relationship. The gods may be the only source of creativity, but they require human help.

The following stories about individual encounters with the Wise Old Woman spirit come from around the world: Norway, Texas, Canada, India, Great Britain, Switzerland, Arkansas, California, Spain, Brazil, and Australia. Going beyond Emma Jung, these dreams and active imaginations carry forward to contemporary times.

The experiences are amazing accounts that reveal, like all archetypes, the Wise Old Woman's presence throughout place and time. Several were first remembered many years ago. Some of the dreams show the healing influence of the Wise Old Woman spirit in the moment; other encounters are felt more deeply later, after the meeting itself. Either way, effects seem to last throughout life, these experiences with the Wise Old Woman spirit frequently remaining in the person's psyche.

My focus is on the archetypal level of the private accounts I discuss. I use as little personal material as possible for offering a context. My attention in the stories that follow emphasizes the two unique qualities of the WOW spirit—*eros* and *emptiness*—and how they reveal themselves in life. Through the circumambulation of her qualities, rather than offering a traditional interpretation, I seek to concentrate on what is most important and of highest value now.

These particular dreams and active imaginations are wonderful manifestations of the Wise Old Woman spirit, descriptions of images and encounters with her that we can use for our own observations, hypotheses, or personal musings. As seen by her worldly presence, this feminine wisdom guide, so diverse in helping ways, gets around and has been making visits for a quite a long time! Indeed, she makes herself known, quite dramatically sometimes, and often arrives during auspicious times.

California, Woman, 84—Drawing Us Closer to the Wise Old Woman Spirit

An eighty-four-year-old friend first inspired me to write about others' encounters with the Wise Old Woman spirit. When the woman told me her own powerful active imagination, it quite naturally became a stepping-stone to the WOW world. I was so moved that in my next day's active imagination, the WOW spirit extended the idea and introduced me to the notion of a worldwide exploration. Thus, the *eros* of our friendship was the beginning context for an international bridging of WOW dreams and active imaginations.

This particular active imagination was also an expression of another *eros*; my friend was exceedingly worried about her husband's poor health. They had been married for over sixty years. Quite naturally and because of her love for him, she made a great effort to avoid being critical.

And because she also loved herself, she sought relief from the burden of carrying fear for his risk. For example, she found herself aghast when he would eat pancakes and syrup in spite of being a diabetic with heart problems. No reasoning with him made any difference and the woman felt helpless, suffering an invisible anxiety much of the time.

Without solution or resolution, the woman felt depleted and empty. However, that same *emptiness* was the Wise Old Woman spirit, present and supporting the woman's openness and receptiveness. Upon my friend's learning about the Wise Old Woman spirit at a presentation I gave (Faron, 2019), she decided to have a talk with the Wise Old Woman about her distress. After waiting years for help, waiting in the *emptiness*, they met in the following active imagination.

Shortly after I attended your talk for the APC and when I was in bed half awake, I allowed room for the Wise Old Woman to help with my anxiety concerning my husband's health and his unhealthy choices. ... The fact is I'm really worried about him.

So when I tried to open myself for help from the Wise Old Woman there was an image of what seemed to be a simple cloth doll coming toward me in the distance. I never did see it close up, but it appeared to be made from a front and back stitched together and stuffed.

I thought of it as a Granny doll. Its shape reminded me of a clay figure I sculptured during your last workshop.

She initially came to me [in the outer world] as the doll given to me by my mother. It had been her sister's; she had crocheted the doll's clothing and put little spectacles on her nose so that she resembled a little old lady.

She floated toward me as I lay in bed, and I had an immediate sensation of letting go of my worry. I cannot accurately describe the feeling it gave me except to call it peace with a sense of letting go.

I don't understand why she came to me in that form, but she did help, as I don't feel so responsible for my husband's health and am able to back away. That sense of peace and release is still with me.

Here is what the woman said about the doll that came to her that day:

I'm trying hard to remember. What I saw was a doll made of just two pieces of fabric—the back and front sewn together. The Granny doll has a plastic head, legs, and hands. The Granny doll [given to me as an adult] and the cloth doll, [received] when I was around seven, both have attached movable arms. I'm pretty sure it wasn't the cloth doll. It seems it was more of a Raggedy Ann doll wearing the clothes my aunt crocheted for the Granny doll.

My aunt was honest and direct. People came to her for advice, and she didn't mince words. She said what was on her mind. She had a sense of humor even after an event when she was in her fifties that left her wheelchair bound for the rest of her life. It was rare to hear her complain.

She lived and worked hard all her life on farms. She raised six children, trained to be a nurse, and taught in a one-room schoolhouse. She was the strong one in her family.

I wish could remember more about the doll. At first she was just a dot of color against a black background coming toward me quite rapidly. My feeling at first was disbelief. Then awe and then peace.

Psychological Commentary

The unconscious seems to have joined the woman's first doll (A), a simple cloth doll, transformed into a childlike "Raggedy Ann," so completely huggable and lovable, with the other end of the spectrum, the more differentiated wisdom doll (B), an image of older age and having special seeing devices called glasses. Together they become the wholeness of the Wise Old Woman spirit. This family doll brings a heritage and long history of vitality, creativity, strong work ethic, dedication to teaching and service, deep valuing of relationships, fierce independence, perseverance, hardship, sacrifice, and a life close to nature.

(A) Cloth doll and (B) Granny doll

These photos are of two different dolls (A & B), the first being the cloth doll (A) that the woman received when she was about age seven. The next picture is of the Granny doll (B), the one that was passed down from her maternal aunt to her mother who then passed it down to my friend. She has them both to this day. As mentioned, her unconscious seemed to combine A & B in a unique way.

It is also noteworthy that the woman sculpted other Wise Old Woman figures at different times throughout her life. Two are the "Fisherwoman, [from] years ago" (C), and another, "Waterfall woman" (D), created during my presentation at the San Francisco Analytical Psychology Club. That bright yellow sculpture—the color of gold—appears to show the Wise Old Woman spirit emerging from the clay.

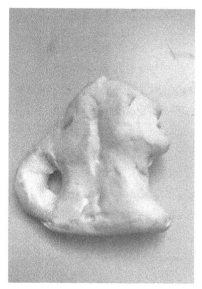

(C) Fisherwoman, sculpted by dreamer [from] years ago and
(D) Waterfall woman, beginning of sculpture by dreamer

Lastly, in September 2019, the woman found this doll (E) "lying in the street in front of my house."

Appearing unpredictably, the Wise Old Woman, even a bit "scuffed up," reassures her.

This is a beautiful story. So much coming out of a simple, heartfelt request. Certainly she was of another world, saying nigh a word and floating toward the woman. An encounter with the Wise Old Woman began for this woman in her active imagination as at first a dot, a mandala, and symbol of wholeness. Jung has observed that such circular symbols are more likely to appear when an individual is troubled or off-balance. They come as reassurance, in this case, "a dot of color ...

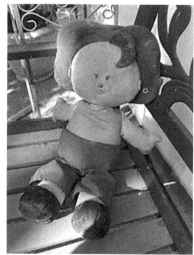

Doll found lying in the street—
"scuffy doll"

coming toward me," a mandala of feeling and *eros* (Jung, 1968b, CW 9i, paras. 713, 714). She knew immediately, felt it right away, almost as if the Wise Old Woman's reassuring appearance was all that was required.

When the woman had "an immediate sensation of letting go of my worry," she told of the great conscious effort required to do her part— what she called "letting go." This suggests slower breathing, relaxing of the muscles, and overall calming and a mustering together of both humble and hopeful feelings within. "I allowed room for the Wise Old Woman to help," she wrote. Perhaps the "letting go" becomes a "giving over," in this case to the Wise Old Woman spirit, who comes as a cuddly cloth doll reminiscent of the woman's mother and her childhood.

Von Franz explains that a doll can be considered the maternal essence, often experienced with a child's first doll who represents her baby or her own human development. She speaks the words of her own mother to the doll. In that way, the doll is also symbolic of the personal mother.

In Grimms' fairy tale *Vasalissa*, for example, the dying mother gives a magic doll to her child to keep secretly in her pocket at all times, to comfort and guide her along the way (von Franz, 1974, p. 158). These are two examples of the maternal feminine, which the doll can represent, but they also point to another possibility. Viewing this woman's active imagination from a psychological perspective, the doll can be seen as a figure of the Self—the center and circumference of all that we are here and beyond.

As an emissary of the Self, the Wise Old Woman spirit, a shape-shifter by nature, has responded in a most lovable form, a love you can hold and carry and nourish, a doll that is a source of wisdom and positive *eros* toward the self. The WOW spirit has approached in the most gentle and least threatening of ways—as the beloved doll of her childhood. Even from a distance, she immediately recognized her.

Following this miraculous happening, my friend was no longer bothered by the urge to plead with her husband, nor did she feel weighed down any longer with worry. In fact, she felt a lightness, the sense of caring presence, which has accompanied her since that time.

Indeed, from a spiritual perspective, the WOW can be seen as a soft, human-like sacred vessel. Moreover, the doll as the WOW takes on a human shape, allowing for easier integration into the human experience.

This is especially so since the doll is similar to the one she's had from childhood. In fact, at the WOW presentation, the woman sculpted a figure reminiscent of the cloth doll in her active imagination.

The doll's back and front appeared to be stitched together, suggesting a wholeness made from joining the unconscious to consciousness. Each time she talks to the WOW, paints her, sculpts her, dances her, sings her, whatever way she chooses, she is relating to, getting to know, and living in partnership with the WOW.

According to my friend, the lifting of the burden was immediate from those first moments. Remarkably, the WOW as a granny doll responded that instant to her plea, bringing a sense of release and inner peace. As previously mentioned, Jeff Raff, an analyst in the Denver area, describes this kind of experience as a "felt vision" (1997, p. 79). The vision need not be visual and may be experienced, instead, as an astonishing shift throughout the body, a divine intervention and powerful experience of the Wise Old Woman spirit.

The Wise Old Woman's visit as a doll inspired me to reach around the world for further discoveries about the WOW. It was the Wise Old Woman spirit in my own active imagination that elaborated on the idea of writing about other dreams, collecting them from all around the world.

Individual Experiences of the Wise Old Woman Spirit Worldwide

Norway, Man, 66

A man from Norway sent me three dreams, the first from 2006.

2006 Dream

I walk down the stairs from the first floor in my own house. I am a little dizzy as if I have just wakened up from a nap. It is daylight outside.

Approaching the ground floor I have the entrance door ahead of me. The door is closed. My two daughters stand, one at each side of the door, pointing as if to the outside of the door, and giving me all the hints in the world that there is something very numinous outside. I can also spot an expression of joy on their faces, as if they are about to present me with glorious news. It seems to me that they take on efforts not to make any sounds of any kind, urging me to be silent too. I can now hear a deep voice murmuring outside the door, and it strikes me that it comes from an older woman (not unlike my mother's voice). I feel a mixture of expectations and unnameable fear and wake up with a strong heartbeat.

The dreamer writes about the dream:

I found the first dream in a notebook of 2006, so it is quite some time before I started training. But the thought of taking Jungian training was very present even then, as it had been for several years already. The major event in my life at this time was the change of work, from a public psychiatric clinic to my own private practice. Indeed, an event to celebrate with a big dream!

This is one of a few dreams that keep coming back to me (as conscious memories) and I hold to be a diamond in my dream collection. I have always thought of it as an "introductory dream" to anima subjects and the subject of the WOW, in particular. She is invisible, unknown at the time, but now knocking on the entrance door of my everyday life and consciousness. And my two daughters (at this time, and in the dream in their teens) are her guiding agents into my life. I can feel some trembling at recollecting this dream even now.

Psychological Commentary

This dream is all about the feminine. Not only does the Wise Old Woman come "knocking" at the door, but also the dreamer's two young animas appear as grounding figures and joyful guides to a most propitious sound and sense and feeling. Expectations, numinosity, fear, strong heartbeat … WOW!

The Wise Old Woman spirit is recognized here by her role, her stature, her mystery, her sound, and her power. Visual absence may be necessary

THE WISE OLD WOMAN SPIRIT

as an initial protection from being overwhelmed. As a shapeshifter the WOW appears in different ways, and indirect contact can express her *eros* while emphasizing her power at the same time. Listening is surely part of the dreamer's partnership with this wisdom figure.

The WOW spirit clearly arrived at a threshold of the dreamer's life when he was beginning a career as a sole practitioner. The dream does seem like an introduction to the conscious world of the anima, "an older woman" in this case, whom the dreamer never actually sees, at least not with his eyes, but surely feels.

What stands out in this dream is the immense and numinous power the Wise Old Woman spirit exudes. Even the dreamer's recollection brings a flash of tremulous experience. It begins with his descent to the base floor of his home, a symbol of himself, on which he is then grounded. His return from a darker place of the unconscious in his dream is followed by the "daylight," which has a brief disorienting effect.

From an archetypal perspective, this first dream shows the dreamer coming to consciousness (he's just waking into daylight) and is very much focused on the WOW spirit. This is reminiscent of Jung's observations of a second consciousness—a consciousness within the unconscious.

The Wise Old Woman spirit comes when he's beginning his private practice, which even by itself is of great importance. She's always been there and likely has appeared at other points of his life like this one. Nevertheless, the light of consciousness is upon him as he approaches the entryway, guided by two youthful animas that are psychologically dear to him.

The "twoness" of the girls calls up the tension of the opposites and the number 2 as potential consciousness. In other words, the number 2 seems to underscore the greater consciousness ahead of him. These young harbingers of the future and joyful potentials of growth point to the feminine divine, conveying the numinous quality of what is behind the door. The dreamer senses the glory of the occasion and maintains the silence modeled by his guides, instinctively honoring the solemnity of the meeting.

At last, he hears deep sounds of murmuring on the other side of the door, which reveal the ancient quality of the old woman's voice. The dreamer is filled with anticipation and "unnameable fear." The Wise Old Woman spirit's visual absence may be protective of the dreamer, but it does offer sound and hearing. Perhaps the nonverbal aspect of this introduction reveals the power of an *eros* more deeply felt within the silence.

Note that after thirteen years, the numinosity of this experience continues and the dreamer's feelings, although brief, remain to this day.

2009 Dream

The dreamer wrote about a second dream in 2009:

Going through my dream notes, I did in fact find a similar, very short dream from 2009, the year I started [formal training]. It also contains this motif of presence-in-absence, and even in a mandala image. It was before [the actual] starting ... but at the time when I considered sending an application. ...

I am in a big hall. It is empty with the exception of an old woman that I never see. I only know vaguely about her. I walk around and look for her and become aware of the fact that the area is a kind of insula, a locked-up big room with four high walls, inside another more spacious quadrat room. The emotion I felt at waking up was comfortable.

Psychological Commentary

This dream begins in a "big hall" that is empty except for "an old woman." Emptiness, you recall, is what Jung called the "great feminine secret" and is particularly identified as unique to the Wise Old Woman spirit. The dreamer has some sense of her presence and "vaguely" knows about her, having become more conscious of her since his initial and powerful introduction to her three years before in 2006.

Again, the Wise Old Woman spirit's visual absence may be protective of the dreamer in these first two powerful dreams or perhaps the unconscious wants to emphasize sound and felt-sense, more intuitive receptors. As the dreamer has written, the "motif of presence-in-absence" reoccurs.

At the beginning, the dreamer walks, going of his own volition on his own two feet as he searches for her, suggesting a certain initiative and groundedness. As he looks for the old woman, his awareness of the space itself increases. The place is spacious and has two 4×4 dimensions, that is, an "insula" inside a "quadrat."

The dreamer's knowledge of being "locked-in" provides secure containment. His feeling is one of comfort or naturalness. In fact, by using the intriguing motif of a place within a place, or a room within a room, the dream appears to emphasize a double containment, perhaps as an alchemical holder for the dreamer's possible transformation.

Four, the number for wholeness, is potentiated as 4×4, an alchemical *mutiplicatio* of the very structure of consciousness. Because four can be considered a limit beyond which something new begins, perhaps it anticipates that change by strengthening the ego-Self axis or by deepening the relationship between the dreamer and the Wise Old Woman spirit. The promise of a new *eros* between them is exactly what the WOW spirit offers, a more complete and balanced *eros*.

2013 Dream

The same Norwegian dreamer was attending analytical training when he had this dream in 2013:

I am inside a big spacious hall, a kind of Production site. A lot of people, myself included, are busy with creative activities. I think we are about to make something out of glass, perhaps some paintings on glass.

At one point I am led into another room, smaller and in a way more "essential." But busy people around me here too. Suddenly I find myself face to face with an old woman of huge dimensions, sitting suddenly on some kind of a throne in front of me. She is very old, has a lot of grey hair, and Mongolian/Oriental [Asian] looks. She does not say anything, but looks at me. Her appearance is very surprising to me, but I feel impressed and comfortable, as if she adds some motherly quality to the things we are working with, in the production hall.

Psychological Commentary

Note that each of the three dreams begins with stairs, a doorway, big hall or "spacious" training site, and seems to convey a bridge from one place to another or to a surrounding vastness, in other words, connection or emptiness. Here, the Wise Old Woman spirit is seen visually, so we're turning away from the exclusivity of sound and hearing.

But to actually see her is a true blessing, and she emanates a particularly maternal quality in the third dream. As she sits on a throne it leaves no question as to her royalty, and her huge size speaks volumes, no pun intended. She is literally larger than life here, as she truly is, of course.

Her appearance is surprising to the dreamer, with her mass of gray hair and agedness. As far as her Asian countenance is concerned, it likely reflects greater depth in the psyche, mysterious or perhaps a bit more distant, psychologically speaking.

The Wise Old Woman spirit looks directly at the dreamer, providing *eros* as compensation for the overly logos training. Both halls are filled with creative activity. At first there is quite a large open space and then the dreamer is taken down to the smaller and more essential place. It is here that a confrontation with the Wise Old Woman spirit occurs, face to face, without words, and followed by the dreamer's feelings of support and comfort from her presence.

Fittingly, the unconscious sees the school as a "Production site" for creativity, but note how the smaller room is reserved for special and integral creative works. Glass is an interesting motif, not only because it's transparent, but also as sometimes connoting intellectual or psychological distance. It is hard, but breakable, fragile, yet protective and strong.

To paint on it suggests, however, that it is not so much to see through, but to provide a place for expressing creative energies. Painting suggests color and color suggests feeling and feeling suggests *eros*. With the addition of feminine *eros*, the glass then anchors the artistic creation and, together with the paint, becomes whole.

Original watercolor painting by Norwegian dreamer—*"I am led into a … more essential room … face to face with an old woman of huge dimensions."*

The Wise Old Woman spirit looks directly at the dreamer, providing *eros*.

Texas, Man, 76

A man from Texas sent me two dreams.

First Dream (about August 28, 2015)

The ADT people installed a new alarm system. Our old system was really old. This new system protects us at night. It took almost all day to install the new system. I worked on the introduction to my thesis almost all day. I need to add a couple of things and finish the conclusion. … Yes, I had heard about the New Jerusalem before I had the dream.

The dreamer had, indeed, heard about the New Jerusalem. Dreams of meeting with von Franz followed, presenting the Wise Old Woman spirit in her finest form. In one of the first dreams with von Franz, although not presented here in full, *eros* is highlighted and exquisitely described.

I had a dream in which Marie-Louise von Franz appears and instructs me on how to write a paper on the New Jerusalem. She asks me about my creative work, and I mention The New Jerusalem.

The dreamer continues his discussion with von Franz:

... the New Jerusalem is not out there. It is inside me. I tell her I am unsure about how to proceed with the creative. She assures me that I have the right attitude. I look at her, and she seems to anticipate my question. "Humility, gentleness, and tenderness; these are the qualities of Eros." Approach whatever I do from an Eros standpoint.

This dream seems to announce the big dream that follows.

Return of von Franz, August 29, 2015

The dream takes place in a dungeon underneath the earth where von Franz has come out of her tomb. She motions me to sit in a chair to her left. I turn my chair to face her. She has her glasses on and is looking at me intently. She looks at me over the top of her glasses. She says, "I know why you are here. Speak." I say, "I understand the New Jerusalem to be part of me—part of us. It is not out there; it is in here." And I point to my heart. She says, "Remember the symbolic! And don't forget the psychological! There are twelve precious stones and twelve gates in the New Jerusalem. Connect all of that to the lapis, to the philosopher's stone. Then ask yourself what this all means psychologically? What does it mean psychologically to you? This is your journey, and this is your connection to immortality." She looks me in the eye, and we shake hands. I leave the dungeon and climb up the old staircase.

Psychological Commentary

An auspicious dream, indeed! It is no surprise that the WOW spirit was a living part of von Franz's life. Indeed, the Wise Old Woman spirit expresses the gravity of her message by appearing through von Franz, who is surely one of the quintessential women of our time, having lived a life of creativity, wisdom, and devotion to Jung's ideas. That her life expressed and symbolized the Wise Old Woman spirit confirms that she's a guide in the dream.

Von Franz first listens and then helps, giving explicit instructions related to the dreamer's creative work. Deeply engaged with the dreamer, von Franz relates to him as a unique individual. As in the earlier dream, von Franz begins and ends their meeting with *eros*—literally articulated as "humility, gentleness, and tenderness." Likewise, she insists that both the psychological and the symbolic aspects of the New Jerusalem be remembered in a personally meaningful way. This is *eros*—personal connection ... perhaps *eros* in its double meaning.

Von Franz comes from the underworld, leaving her tomb to join the dreamer in the dungeon. That they are both below the earth accentuates the unusual depth of the unconscious that opened to the dreamer that day. Certainly, it is more than impressive—a message from von Franz, herself, not only meeting the dreamer in the underworld, but also coming out of her tomb to see him. That's quite a statement regarding its import.

The dungeon suggests a sealed place in which only the dreamer and von Franz were present, a kind of container, protected and safe from the upper outer world, held sacred in this event, and a place that seems otherwise empty. In fact, that emptiness is a clear sign of the Wise Old Woman's presence.

Von Franz begins immediately, wasting no time, her first and continuing focus on their relationship. Looking directly at the dreamer, she states she knows his purpose and presses him to speak. Her attention to their connection expresses the Wise Old Woman's presence, confirming their *eros* and implying a mutual understanding between them.

Their partnership is seen when the dreamer first responds, *eros* emphasized again when he turns his chair toward hers. She signals him to sit at her left, which means that she is then on the dreamer's right—a strong, loving, holding right arm. Von Franz looks directly at the dreamer over the top of her glasses, as if she wants no barrier between them, even if transparent.

The dreamer seems to know that he is the vessel where the transformation is to take place and points to his heart. In fact, the number 12, referring to the "twelve precious stones and twelve gates," although carrying specific meaning for the dreamer, can be understood archetypally "as a *need or a possibility to activate the inner center by all the aspects or qualities of time*" (Abt, 2005, p. 158).

The number 12 highlights time—12 months, 12 hours, 12 signs of the zodiac, for example, and refers to the cyclic nature of human development. Moreover, the number 12 conveys the archetypal meanings of receptiveness, belonging, beauty, unity, and wholeness. For example, 12, the result of 3×4, is described as the union of the soul with God (Faron, 2012).

Seen archetypally, the redundancy of the number 12 may alert us to our currently troubled times worldwide and the great need for unity. The transformation mentioned, however, focuses on the need for an *internal* change: "I point to my heart." Even a cursory review of the New Jerusalem revealed that von Franz's very direct message to the dreamer, and the reader, indeed concerns a symbolic renewal.

The symbol of transformation, the New Jerusalem, points to a re-emergence of feminine consciousness, which presents new material for attention, reflection, and experiencing. Thus, follows greater understanding and integration.

In the dream there are twelve precious stones, or "truths from good" ("Spiritual Meaning of Precious Stones," 2002), and twelve foundational gates, each made of a single pearl and guarding access to the New Jerusalem ("Gates of New Jerusalem," 2011). Von Franz states that they are to be joined to the lapis, the philosopher's stone, and goal of human development and individuation. The Wise Old Woman spirit's unique qualities—*eros* and *emptiness*—are experienced and integrated as a part of the process. They are also mysteriously connected with immortality.

Eros and *emptiness* appeared when I researched the New Jerusalem and read that in Revelation, the New Jerusalem is described in distinctly feminine ways: "the bride" or the "wife of the Lamb," for example, in

John Patmos' vision ("New Jerusalem," 2022). Of course, the city is itself a feminine symbol.

Interestingly, the New Jerusalem literature reveals words like "reunification," "gigantic" (meaning beyond human limits), "renewal," "reconstruction," "the third," suggesting the transcendent function, and "wisdom." Moreover, descriptions such as "reconciliation," "meeting place," "heavenly sanctuary," "bread of life," "restoration," "God's throne," and "peaceful," are also listed ("Spiritual Meaning of Precious Stones," 2002). Thus, the temple itself not only has a feminine motif, but these words also describe her structure.

Even at the end of the meeting, their eye contact and handshake once more reveal the Wise Old Woman's sustaining *eros*. The dream's message about the New Jerusalem can be understood as an expression of the Wise Old Woman's reemergence in our times. The von Franz dream conveys the WOW spirit's assertion of the need for heartfelt change.

Canada, Woman, 64

A Canadian woman sent me a 1995 dream.

Re my dream and request for guidance—
I began asking for dream guidance in January 1995 ... [and] the white-haired woman dream occurred in early September 1995. As I recall, my Wise Old Woman dream went something like this:

I was visiting KH in M and decided to stop at the hospital in M before heading home. I was sitting on a cement bench in front of the hospital when three nurses came out to take a break. They sat down on the bench as if I was not there and kept sliding down the bench as each nurse came out to join the others. I thought they might actually push me off the bench—so I introduced myself to the one next to me. She was an older white-haired woman, wearing an old-fashioned nursing outfit and thin grey cardigan sweater, buttoned at the top button (Same generation as Mrs. B, a nurse I used to work with when I worked at [a hospital] in 1978). My white-haired nurse from

*my dream had a similar hairstyle, chin or collar length with
waves brushed back off the face—something from the '60s I
would say).*

*After I introduced myself the white-haired woman
acknowledged me by turning to face me and looking me straight
in the eye. I felt as though she were looking right through me.
Then she said, "I see your Mother in your eyes."*

*"'My mother?" I repeated, trying to make sense out of
what she was saying. "Have you been to [a state]?" I asked (I
was born in [a city]).*

*With a knowing smile she said, "Oh no, Dear ... But she
is showing through more than you know." I was just beginning
to think she wasn't talking about my birthmother, T, when the
white-haired woman suddenly said, "Yes—you're certainly a
[Canada] girl."*

*"[Canada]!" I exclaimed and paused; then I said,
"Strange you should say that—I am thinking of moving there."*

*She responded enthusiastically, saying, "Oh, yes, Dear,
that would be wonderful!" As soon as she said that I got goose
bumps (I think of this as a "truth chill"). I pointed to my forearm
to show her how the hair on my arms was standing on end, and
I said, "Look! I have goose bumps."*

*She pushed up the sleeve of her cardigan to show me her
forearm and said, "So do I"—followed again by that knowing
smile, this time accompanied by a nod of her head.*

*As for background prior to the dream, I had been in a
long-distance relationship and was asking for next steps. H
had asked me to come live with him in [Canada] early in our
relationship in Dec 1993.*

The dreamer describes a successful practice and work life, especially
beginning the year before. Opportunities for travel appeared. She and H
had begun dating. By 1993, the dreamer was offered an unusually good
opportunity to buy the home in which she had been living. The question
addressed whether he should move to California and join her, or "if I
should uproot as my career began to swing into high gear ... ."

I am a psychic dreamer. I have been receiving information and guidance in dreams since childhood ... and I have been practicing dream incubation for over forty years. I ask the question at bedtime and wait. If no relevant dream arises, I interpret that it is not the "right time" for direction.

When I do dream incubation—my dreams are often quite direct responses to requests for guidance (like the one you identify as the WOW). Patience is key to dream incubation—though often responses are immediate (three dreams within a week or two). ... for big life-changing decisions, I rely on my dreams. So here I am, living in [Canada], residing by [a beautiful river].

Psychological Commentary

This woman has had a working relationship with the unconscious for many years now. She has come to recognize the value of guidance from the unconscious and has approached it with a specific request. Certainly, this dream offers inspiration to all who wish to develop a working relationship with the unconscious, especially with the Wise Old Woman spirit, so critically needed today.

Sometimes an individual is trying to make "a life-changing decision." In this dream, the Canadian woman received specific guidance from the Wise Old Woman spirit herself!

Not only did the WOW clearly visit the dreamer, but the context reveals a place of healing, a hospital on a mountain. Could this represent a nearness to the spiritual realm or the sacredness of the moment? Doesn't the "mountain of healing" sound like a place of being completely yourself, reflecting the wisdom of the Old Woman and her values?

Here, again, at the beginning of the dream is the Wise Old Woman's *emptiness*. The dream opens as the dreamer sits alone on a cement bench in front of a hospital. Cement benches were used by Asclepius, the Greek god of healing, who had initiates lie on a cement bench to ask for and incubate a healing dream. Three nurses arrive, one at a time, to sit on the bench. As each nurse joins the others, the first one slides over, creating an *emptiness* to make room for the next nurse.

174

Certainly, the Wise Old Woman spirit knows how to get the dreamer's attention, pushing her nearly off the bench before she speaks up. By pressing the dreamer to engage, she essentially builds a bridge, or way of *eros*, between the dreamer and herself. The dreamer had felt invisible, perhaps another state of emptiness, that is filled by her own initiative when she introduces herself.

The appearance of multiple nurses emphasizes a health-giving presence, another expression of the Wise Old Woman's *eros*. The Old Woman in the dream is white-haired and looks rather old-fashioned, reminding the dreamer fondly of a professional colleague from prior work years. Surely, *eros* is there, the Wise Old Woman spirit smiles. Importantly she appears as a nurse, which points to her capacity for healing and care.

The Wise Old Woman spirit immediately responds to the dreamer, turning to her and looking her straight in the eyes. It has often been said that the eyes are the windows to the soul. In these moments, the WOW seems to take in every bit of the dreamer who now feels totally seen, known, and understood throughout her being—"as if she were looking right through me."

The WOW spirit refers to the dreamer's mother and seems to address the dreamer's maternal energy. She sees in the dreamer the place of her beginnings. "I see a lot of your mother in your eyes." In other words, she sees the woman, deeply and beyond the present time, seeing her personal mother come through her. She sees her inner mother as well as her ancestral motherhood, which symbolizes unity. Remember, *eros* is the basic principle of the mother, the connecting principle, and welcome as a deeply felt support when giving birth to new adventures in life.

The Wise Old Woman knows the dreamer in ways that are mysterious. But she *knows*, that is for sure. "Yes—you're certainly a [Canada] girl," she says assertively. The WOW suggests that she is well-suited to Canadian life and will be a good fit for this particular community. The WOW spirit tells the dreamer it will be "wonderful" for her to move there. And it has! The Wise Old Woman spirit helped lead the dreamer, quite specifically, not only to life's joys, but also to her unique Tao.

Finally, the most intimate moment is shared (as it is in true partnerships) as the dreamer and the Wise Old Woman each disclose their own goose bumps and numinous experience. The dreamer sums up the personal significance of the dream: "My move to [Canada] was more than simply an invitation to live with H—the invitation was a point of destiny calling me, which I was being guided to accept."

India, Man, 40

This man's dream occurred around the time of a sacred journey. Traveling to a holy mountain, he had sojourned in thankfulness for an experience that was "incredibly transforming," releasing him from severe pain and immobilization.

Significantly, he had experienced a synchronicity with a woman friend, also in the outer world, with whom he had not spoken for years. She called to inquire about his welfare and upon hearing his plight, offered help and guidance. Moreover, not only was his application to travel to the holy mountain selected when three-quarters of the applications are not, he also received a month's special leave from work. Multiple synchronicities were in play.

He had the dream in 2010, a short time before the journey. He felt that the pilgrimage to the holy mountain exuded the WOW spirit's energy and healing. In fact, the dreamer felt that the synchronicity of his friend's calling, together with the trip to the holy mountain, were in and of themselves embodiments of the Wise Old Woman spirit.

Here is his dream and his own thoughts about it:

I am lying down in an open field and an older woman is behind me (towards my head). She is ruffling my hair with concern and caressing me saying, "Don't worry, it will be ok; just go ahead ... I will be there."

I feel it was a numinous encounter. ... I never thought of it in this light up until now because I was primarily seeking a Wise Old Man. This Wise Old Woman gave me the sense of protection and care, which only a mother can give. She knew it would be a journey I have to undertake, but she gave me an inner sense of security to withstand the outer chaos. As I recount this dream, I feel moved again and deeply energized ... [and] vivified.... it was in that moment I felt that there is someone wise, like a divine mother, assuring me to go ahead.

[Life] has been very tough, as much as it has been deeply enriching in the inner world and experiencing grace. The recounting of this dream gives me hope and solace—she is there, and she will take care. In India, we do not take the negative attitude to Kāli that normally Westerners do. She is the terrible one and slays but she is also the divine mother who protects. Of course, the woman in my dreams was far from Kāli, but a benign benevolent mother reassuring and comforting. I feel somewhere that the testing by Kāli and the reassurance of the nourishing mother come from the same wisdom of that Wise Old Woman. Indeed, the WOW spirit has her ways in arriving and guiding. The Cosmos was playing out to me and forcing me to look at sides other than what I was focusing on.

Psychological Commentary

The man's dream is poignant and simple. The Wise Old Woman spirit ruffles his hair and reassures him that she will always be there. She says that it will be okay and to "just go ahead."

This dream reminds me of Brad Pitt in the film *Seven Years in Tibet* (1997) when the Dali Lama ruffles his blond hair as he first bows down before him. (The Dali Lama had never seen blond hair.) Remember, from a Jungian perspective, hair, emanating from the head, is often symbolic of thoughts, ideas, and fantasies.

In contrast to the act of curiosity shown by the Dali Lama, the Wise Old Woman spirit expresses playful concern, *eros,* lovingly tossing his hair. Perhaps she is shaking up his worries and anxieties or maybe interrupting a self-critique? Taking the initiative herself, the WOW responds kindly to the dreamer's receptive pose and strokes him tenderly. Her endearing ways encourage him to trust her and his way ahead.

Lying there on the earth, outside by himself in the openness of nature (I imagine a sunny day in a golden field), the dreamer receives the WOW spirit's love and hears her urge him toward his destiny—both coming at a time of great uncertainty and risk. This openness in nature reflects the same *emptiness* from which the Wise Old Woman spirit appears—and of which she actually is. She lets him know that she is behind him, literally so in the dream. Her reassurance and caring come from a deeply maternal place of safety. Moving and numinous, her *eros* is deeply felt within the *emptiness*.

The WOW spirit shows warmth, confidence, and great personal regard for the dreamer, offering protection and revitalization. Perhaps this enabled the dreamer to see the opposites in the Wise Old Woman spirit, both testing and nourishing, with the gift of renewed strength.

Although the emptiness in his outside life was hard to bear, the feminine wisdom spirit seemed to offer the same emptiness needed to contain his inner riches at that time. It was as if he was becoming conscious then of his whole body as the symbolic vessel. This bearing of the tension of the opposites, within and without his experience as the vessel, worked to keep the dreamer in balance with himself. As he indicates, the Cosmos seemed to force him to focus on other perspectives needed at that time.

The dreamer also recognized the hearkening synchronicity of the friend's call. Perhaps she was sent by the Wise Old Woman spirit as a precursor, representing an initial and concrete outer way of receiving help and wisdom.

Perhaps the Wise Old Woman first arrives in a familiar way to prepare us for the more unfamiliar to come. Again, the role she plays helps us identify her, appearing here with a special sensitivity or intuitive gentleness guided by the quality of her *eros*.

Great Britain, Woman, 46

In 2019, the dreamer wrote about a first dream:

When I changed analysts from female to male, I remember having a dream with my Nan. She died when I was sixteen, and this was too early for me as she was a very loving grandparent with total confidence in herself. She was the only positive, loving female around me, so without realizing it at the time, an enormous blow.

The dream with the analyst was in 2013 (I was forty) and I must have been a bit rocky with things as a single parent and lots of stressful stuff going on too.

Dream #1, 2013

*She [the Wise Old Woman spirit as Nan] was giving me the
gold pound coins and I was sitting next to the analyst, and I
think that he was reading* The Red Book. *So that was the first
encounter with a wise woman figure in my Nan.*

*There wasn't really anything spoken in the Nan/analyst
dream. It was more of a one shot. I guess* The Red Book *focuses
on Jung's other inner figure that he sees as his guru. Maybe my
Nan/old woman is something similar.*

*It feels good in the dream with my Nan ... but she is running
in and out of the room with the coins—as though she is excited.
There is a real energy about her as there was in reality. Also,
when she was alive, she always used to give me a pound coin
before I left—just as pocket money. Her purse was always really
bulging with the gold coins.*

*The feelings in the dream were mixed—a calm aspect with
the book, and a vibrant, helpful figure in my Nan. I would say
that she did feel numinous—like she's got something to share
with me that is important.*

Psychological Commentary

This first dream begins as a love story about one of the dreamer's
greatest losses, Nan, her beloved grandmother. The dream is all about
relationship and *eros*. In this way, it highlights the Wise Old Woman
spirit's timely and compassionate appearance, even years later, when the
emptiness and sorrow of *eros* replace the physicality and outer reality of
a loved one.

The spirit enriched the dreamer's life by giving her a new experience
of the particular feminine qualities of *eros* and *emptiness*. Moreover,
the dreamer was not conscious in the dream that her grandmother had
died, and Nan's visit was lively and energizing. She gives gold coins,
nuggets along the way, made of an incorruptible and everlasting material,
a frequent symbol of the goal of individuation—indeed for *eros* itself,
emerging throughout the journey.

This dream is also a glimpse of how the Wise Old Woman spirit came to the dreamer's aide and encouraged the conscious development of a relationship with her, which here begins with memories of Nan's loss. Thus, the first time the dream ego met the Wise Old Woman spirit was in a dream of her loving grandmother, who had died in 1988. Twenty-five years later, the WOW spirit was apparently evoked by an outer-world event—the dreamer's changing analysts from a woman to a man. Changing therapists, especially changing the gender of the therapist, is often a significant emotional and psychological transition. Moreover, this change occurred during the dreamer's midlife crisis. It seems the WOW clearly knew that such a move in intimate work would be deeply felt at this time.

In this way, the Wise Old Woman's presence provides another experience of relationship with her while encouraging the dreamer's positive connection with the animus. This change shows a maturing of relationship between the dreamer and the WOW, presenting a brief image of one of the multiple changes that occur.

In the dreamer's case, the loss not only involved an alchemical *separatio* from her long-term analyst, but also brought back her loss of the only positive feminine energy she was close to in her first sixteen years of life. The loss is echoed by what has not been for the dreamer; save for Nan, she is absent the experience of being cherished throughout her childhood. That is, apart from her grandmother, no positive maternal energy from female or male in the outer world had been present.

However, the dreamer has held the image and feel of Nan close to her, remembering the *eros* between them. The woman especially noted her grandmother's confidence, a confidence that remained with the dreamer. Also, the memory of the WOW spirit in the form of her Nan continued to help the dreamer, giving her courage to face the difficulties of single motherhood. With the renewed energy, the dreamer found work, developed greater self-reliance, and experienced the joy of rearing her daughter.

Here in the dream, the WOW spirit is providing mandalas of gold, gifting the dreamer with new energy of highest value. This positive increase occurs at the time the dreamer is changing analysts, separating from the woman analyst to whom she is deeply bonded, as she now sits beside the new male analyst. The dreamer is physically aligned with her new mentor and animus. Clearly, the WOW reinforces the dreamer's decision to begin with a different analyst in the outer world.

The male analyst can also be considered the dreamer's analyst within as well as another manifestation of the Wise Old Man spirit. That he reads from *The Red Book* suggests that Jung's works and the unconscious are in focus, both the emotional experience and the thoughts Jung engaged, his inner work and the beginning of his many developing ideas. Thus, the woman's animus is in a guiding and collaborative role. In this way, her animus serves as a valuable conduit to the unconscious.

The Wise Old Woman and the Wise Old Man point to a possible *coniunctio*, with the dreamer serving as the transcendent function, an increasingly conscious container. The dreamer is at last experiencing the loving attention and noble parenting she deserves, moving her through the pair to renewed life.

Dream #2, 2016

The day before the dream I went into a cafe to write in my diary and had a feeling when walking in that I would be given some kind of message ... .

I'm outside and it's dark. McDonald's is in the background. Feeling and thought came as I was walking towards the cafe [McDonald's]—just before entering. There's an old woman who comes up to me, offering to give me some money to buy "food and drink." The old woman wants to help me just before I go and make an order.

But the old woman has no nose and when she talks the sound is inside the face. She is mediumistic and wants to give me pound coins (which are gold in the UK). She is cute but terrifying at the same time. I'm so terrified of her and feel the need to protect myself from her.

I'm scared of her and think that I will have to create a boundary to keep her out. She says that it's hard for her to get a sense of me because of it. She has lots of gold pound coins and gives me a few to take to McDonalds. I don't want her charity and give them back to her.

Really, she was a helpful figure, but I didn't really know this. This is a part of me that I'm not quite aware of, and in reality, when something is important that I am thinking about, I get a sensation in my nose. I try to catch the thought that I have to take notice of what it is trying to tell me. It's like the sixth sense that helps me with things.

I've been talking to an aunty and uncle (L and M). It's near to the graveyard where my mum is buried. Then I bump into another aunty and uncle (C and H). I tell her that I've already spoken to the others and that I want to go. She says "buzz off" to me as I'm walking away. I go up to her and confront her about it. Then I walk away.

I did have a dream a while back, and this figure has appeared a couple of times. With regards to my mum, I've realized through analysis that she loved [the] other siblings that I have—but not me. And she wouldn't have wanted me to have anything which was "gift" like. This has been repeated in another dream, so maybe in the nose dream, it is also difficult for me to accept the gift. [My] mother's death in 2000 [was] sudden and premature ... a six-month cancer.

Psychological Commentary

The dream begins in the unconscious, as do all dreams, but this dream seems to present particularly strange, remote, and foreign images to the dreamer's consciousness. "It's dark outside." Could this darkness be the *emptiness* of the Wise Old Woman spirit?

Emerging from the dark night are the nearby "Golden Arches" of McDonalds, a source of both concrete and symbolic nourishment, embraced by the double-arch symbol of *M. M*, or *Mu*, is an Egyptian hieroglyph similar to the ancient Greek letter *M* or *Mu*. These are ancient feminine symbols of water from the great goddess culture of 7,000 BCE mentioned earlier in the book (Gimbutas, 1989, p. 19). The double-arch

M might also be understood as the number 2, accentuating the possibility for greater consciousness by its brightness against the dark.

According to the dreamer, she had walked to McDonald's, having earlier parked a short distance away to shop. In other words, the dreamer walks on her own two feet, even though she has a car, which suggests a strength of ego functioning and sense of direction. Once inside, standing in line, the dreamer invisibly connects again with the spirit of the Wise Old Woman—the feminine who *is* the *emptiness* or non-doing in that waiting. The dreamer may be a bit shaken having just encountered the Wise Old Woman approaching her with gold coins. However, the Wise Old Woman reaches out and perseveres with support for the woman, offering gold once again.

Although the dreamer rejects the gold coins out of understandable fright and uncertainty, she is nevertheless gifted with several forms of gold symbolized by the coins. For example, the WOW spirit appears in a restaurant with the dreamer, suggesting nourishment, both a literal and symbolic type of gold. Another kind of gold is found in her feeling the day before that she'd be receiving some kind of message, a valuable gift, indeed.

Importantly, the dreamer begins to develop a conscious relationship with the Wise Old Woman spirit. Over time, the dreamer comes to realize that the old woman is trying to help and offer her protection, but the dreamer doesn't yet realize who she is. We are privileged to get a glimpse of a particular part of her development, namely, the dreamer's need to deny the gift of coins when she did. Doubt quite naturally enters as she becomes more conscious, and here, it shows.

It is to the dreamer's merit that she can live her doubts. When she returns the coins, she is in control, volunteering her entry to another kind of *emptiness*, this time a sort of protection with her refusal of the coins. Doubt can be a pause or different type of emptiness, which creates space for the creative act of expressing that doubt. By doing so, the dreamer reveals her courage and independence.

The dreamer faces the paradox of the opposites and makes a decision. Perhaps it is the emptiness of the Wise Old Woman spirit that can receive the psyche's complexity and depth, including the human process of the dreamer's doubt.

Her doubts might have been the very thing needed for her development to happen. Jung would likely tell us that the dreamer's doubt is exactly what was needed. He discusses this in his essay on "The Stages of Life."

> Our psychic processes are made up to a large extent of reflections, doubts, experiments, all of which are almost completely foreign to the unconscious, instinctive mind of primitive man. It is the growth of consciousness which we must thank for the existence of problems; they are the Danaän gift of civilization. It is just man's turning away from his instincts—his opposing himself to instinct—that creates consciousness … . Everything in us that still belongs to nature shrinks away from a problem, for its name is doubt, and wherever doubt holds sway there is uncertainty and the possibility of divergent ways … we want to have certainty and no doubts … certainties can arise only through doubt and results only through experiment. (Jung, 1981b, CW 8, paras. 750–51)

Simultaneously, the auxiliary functions appear to be growing. The dreamer describes how "feeling and thought came" as she approached the cafe.

> *"But it's been years later that I started to get the [in-the-nose] sensation sometimes. And it took me a while to put two and two together with the old lady (she looks about eighty). I think ultimately that the intuition has been blocked and when it is, it comes through the nose as a* helper with things."

In fact, one of the first things that stands out in this dream about the Wise Old Woman spirit is that, paradoxically, her nose does not stand out, or at least not visibly. Its absence is notable. How perfect, though, because the nose is associated with the *intuitive* function and that's how we begin to understand the relationship between the WOW and the dreamer. Jung describes *intuition* as an "immediate awareness of relationships," which, of course, is all about the WOW spirit (Jung, 1981a, CW 8, para. 257).

Intuition is an irrational function gifted with grasping the total situation. It is the perception of the possibilities inherent in a situation (para. 292).

The nose—that typical projectile—that goes beyond the face's surface is missing, and without it, breathing in the human world would be hampered, if not impossible. But the area for the nose in the dreamer's drawing does reveal, faintly, two tiny openings, suggesting that the WOW spirit does not require the human filtering system of the projected olfactory part.

Original drawing of the Wise Old Women spirit sent from the Great Britain dreamer. "Here's my little picture of the Wise Old Woman." This rendition of the WOW spirit with no nose suggests her nonverbal savvy and unique way of functioning through the dreamer.

After all, she is a shape-shifter! Without a nose, the intuitive function is unrestricted and direct in its knowing. Moreover, when the Wise Old Woman spirit speaks, it is her nose that seems to emit the sounds, creating further emphasis on the olfactory or intuitive function.

Intuition deals with space-time relationships, in particular, including the possibility of those in the past and future and includes subliminal factors. When first orienting, intuition approximates that which is not otherwise determinable by the remaining three functions (Jung, 1981a, CW 8, para. 257), perhaps because it mediates perception in an unconscious way (Jung, 1971, CW 6, para. 770).

The dreamer's descriptions seem to indicate that a developmental process of the intuitive function occurs for her in getting to know the WOW spirit. The effect of the Wise Old Woman's great power, an unknown one at that, truly frightens the dreamer. However, the drawing that the dreamer did looks quite innocuous, very sweet actually. Although her instincts seem to pick up the Wise Old Woman's numinosity, terrifying as it is to the dream ego, the unconscious nevertheless seems to compensate her fear in the dream and the WOW spirit appears quite friendly.

Lastly, the dreamer is near the cemetery where her mum was buried. She sees and talks with a maternal auntie and uncle and shortly after with the other auntie and uncle. Although the dreamer tried to explain that she had already talked with the first couple, apparently about a specific subject, the second auntie took offense and told the dreamer to "buzz off." The dreamer explains: "The auntie that said, 'buzz off' is a lot like my mum (domineering husband, passive, and their mother led them to believe that men are superior etc.)."

However, the dream ego returned and confronted the auntie. The bravery that appeared when the dreamer earlier expressed a doubt is the same valor she shows in response to her auntie's rejection and lack of kindness.

Ultimately, the *lysis*[16] is that the dreamer walks away, which feels like the right thing to do. She walks away from the place of her dead mum and goes out into life. It is altogether possible that the rough-edged auntie in this case is another form of the Wise Old Woman, herself.

Here we see what appears to be a darker side of the Wise Old Woman spirit. The Wise Old Woman spirit as rejecter is really a mystery; she does not always function with human customs of appropriate behavior. Remember, she is a shape-shifter. One example is found in an interpretation

---

[16] The lysis of the dream is frequently its resolution or catastrophe.

of a Grimms' fairytale "Old Woman in the Wood," where a similarly rough old woman tests the determination, endurance, and courage of the girl protagonist by entering into a struggle with her (Faron, 2017).

Could it be that this was what the Wise Old Woman spirit had in mind? The Wise Old Woman as a tough-talking auntie, seems to use such a disguise to accentuate the command "buzz off." This means "go away," or movement in the other direction. The disliked auntie may be the very best image for initiating another necessary *separatio*, a going-away that leaves the place where the dead are buried and faces the *emptiness* of the unknown, with its potential for adventure toward the fullness of life.

This harsh and rejecting sendoff might be likened to the feminine struggle throughout the ages, but both dreams show the WOW spirit giving the dreamer gold (or trying to). She's ready to offer help and support whenever it may be needed, even when it's not yet recognized.

Switzerland, Woman, 69

A woman from Switzerland also sent me two dreams. In December 2013, she first told me her dream of Emma Jung.

Dream #1, 2013

I dreamed that I was having a discussion with my husband, and at the end, he just left. It was a difficult discussion. I was alone—and it was quite a big room—it was like where you have a lecture or a meeting room or something like this.

And then, Emma Jung came in and she came straight towards me and she hugged me and she said, "Oh, you know ... I understand you. Everybody always has the feeling or is meant to know that C.G. was only a good man ..."

"That was not the thing ..." — said the dreamer, quoting Emma's words and laughing—

"He was not always a good man ... so take it easy," [counseled Emma]—and then she hugged me."

I asked the dreamer a question to clarify: "So take it easy ... it will be all right—something like that?"

"Yes. She was for me like the Great Woman."
"Yes, she was."
"Yaa!"
"The Wise Old Woman?" I confirmed.
"Yaa, yaa ... yes; she was!"

Psychological Commentary

This short but powerful dream begins when the woman is left alone in a large empty room at the end of a misunderstanding with her husband. Note that the large empty room prefaces a visit from Emma Jung. It is also significant that the *emptiness* unique to the WOW spirit is at the *beginning* of this dream, highlighting the possibilities that arise out of such a void.

The dream depicts difficulties in relationship, one of the Wise Old Woman spirit's specialties. So here is Emma Jung again, appearing in a woman's dream as the "Great Woman" or Wise Old Woman spirit. Arriving in today's dream world, the WOW spirit as Emma begins her greeting by showing a loving *eros* toward the dreamer, hugging her affectionately. Emma, as the Wise Old Woman, immediately shows compassion for the dreamer, saying that she understands and giving her reassurance things will be all right.

It's as though the WOW spirit has come to comfort and advise the dreamer, appearing in the person of Emma Jung because the dreamer knew about Emma's personal experiences with marital difficulties.

The Wise Old Woman as *eros* carries the archetype of relationship. It seems that she knows how to help in this particular situation and has decided to come forth. Once again this is one of those times when she initiates the encounter. The WOW's specific instructions recognize what she intimately knows about the hearts of this particular woman and her husband.

"That was not the thing" is Emma's way of telling the dreamer to expect somewhat less of her husband and that even the best man is still a very human fellow. A good man doesn't mean good all the time, she explains.

While the WOW spirit affirms for the dreamer the harsh realities of human relationship, she encourages a positive relating toward the Self. Indeed, when the dreamer welcomes and receives the *eros* extended by Emma, it is her own *emptiness* that makes room for a right relationship with the Self.

As she gives her another hug, Emma seems to say, "Take it easy, stay with yourself, relax and tune into yourself, and remember who you are." Maybe this is another time of *emptiness* from which something new can spring, even if a painful labor accompanies it.

The Wise Old Woman spirit can say these things because she realizes that *eros*-love exists between them, when you care about the other person as you care about yourself. She sees they are committed to meeting one another in the middle way and open to accept the opposites in each other.

Dream #2, 2014

In 2014 I had again a dream ...
... of Emma in which she just stood at my side giving me protection and filling my heart with her loving feminine spirit!

Psychological Commentary

This second dream came a year later during a period of great emotional and physical suffering for the dreamer. It describes the ongoingness of their relationship—the WOW spirit and the dreamer—a partnership of familiarity, comfort, and awareness of feeling.

When the Wise Old Woman spirit appears and stands by the dreamer's side, the dreamer realizes a kind of safety filled with loving feminine energy. The dreamer's own *emptiness* seems to come from the intimate relationship with one who symbolizes *emptiness*. The dreamer is ready to receive and welcome the Spirit's presence again. The WOW contains her weary psyche and affirms the *eros* between them, the faithful and eternal bond.

Arkansas, Man, 70

Here is a powerful dream I had many years ago. I was feeling a great deal of emotional pain and grief over a relationship that was not working out and likely ending.

That night I dreamed that I was walking in an enormous field of grain, during which I felt great peace come over me and an abundance of love all around and in me. Then the scene shifted and I was viewing the field from a distance. Now, however, I could see that it was not a field of grain in which I was walking, but an enormous flower, which felt feminine and oh so loving.

The experience was so numinous, the feeling that I was loved stayed with me even after I awoke from the dream.

Psychological Commentary

In a huge field growing with grain, the dreamer walks close to Mother Earth. Here, the dreamer, so overcome with sadness and grief, nevertheless takes the first step, and walks with the Wise Old Woman spirit. He doesn't really know it is her at first; he just breathes in the utter peacefulness and soaks in the love that surrounds him both outside and inside. Surely, this experience is blissful and numinous.

Then, the dreamer suddenly sees the scene from a distance and realizes the field was actually the center of a giant flower, a loving and feminine flower, there for him to bask in and be upheld in unspeakable tenderness. He was literally "centered" or, perhaps, centered in the Self.

When, at a distance, the dreamer could see where he'd been walking, he became conscious of his path through the center of a living feminine energy. It was a flower of love. "The primary feeling was love," the dreamer remembered. "I also felt peace, amazement and awe … [when] … the field turned out to be the center of a flower."

This dream underscores again the WOW spirit's loving *eros* extended to the dreamer during a time of great loss and sorrow. As the unconscious responds to the dreamer's pain, it gifts him with a most beautiful dream. This is a dream remembered, its cherished thoughts and feelings remain and can be replayed whenever they are needed.

The huge flower is a wonderful image, a "yantra," as James Hollis would say,[17] coupled with an amazing feeling of contentment and support. The dreamer experienced an abundance of peace and love. The Wise Old Woman's emptiness is surely present; the dreamer is alone, just walking along, being carried by the field's healing energy.

It also calls to mind the dream given to me by the man from India. It came during a profound experience of emptiness, with misery and loss in the outer world for both men. Yet something inside this man from Arkansas is born of heartache and beauty, somewhat different from the Indian's need for shaking up his worries.

This dream is surely compensation for the loss of outer love—lovely and loving *eros*, appearing as a beautiful flower. In both dreams the men are alone in a field. Each experience of the Wise Old Woman spirit yields energized and numinous feelings, including a loving attitude, peace, assurance, and abundance.

The Arkansan's dream is complex; indeed, two different angles or dimensions are depicted, one in each part of his dream—the immediate emotions and the distant view. It seems that a *separatio* has occurred— from where he was at the beginning of the dream to where he is at the end of the dream. The dreamer now stands independently.

The second part of the dream offers a new perspective. Perhaps it is meant to help him fix his gaze on the eternity of love. The flower he sees is the flower of divine love. Maybe it's a reminder, too, that separating isn't the end. That is, all the experiences, especially the positive ones that he knew in the relationship, remain in felt memory, remain in all sensate memory—a part of him now, forevermore.

A picture he created is shown here. Notice how the colored corollas of the flower turn up around the center, creating a cup-like receptacle or vessel; how the flower's orange color suggests warmth and vitality, a color that's been described as "the wisdom of a spiritualized passion" (Abt, 2005, p. 98).

---

[17] Hollis differentiates between a "yantra" and a mantra; he writes that the yantra is a "centering image," and not a "meditating image." The "mantra" is typically considered a sound or group of sounds that are repeated (See Hollis, 1997, p. 7).

The painful breakup has most likely left the dreamer exhausted and drained. Nevertheless, it created the dreamer's emptiness and openness, allowing for his experience of the mystery, of the magic, and of the WOW's healing. The emptiness of the Wise Old Woman spirit provided a place, most of all, for an unlimited and unconditional love.

The notion of grain, moreover, calls up Demeter, the goddess of the harvest. She symbolizes the spiritual bread or the bread of life,

Original collage from Arkansan dreamer: Flower of *eros*-love and wisdom.

the bread of the earth, fertility, and the cycles of life and death. In fact, the dreamer himself recalled the Egyptian myth in which "wheat is also associated with Osiris, and thereby death and rebirth." In both senses, renewal for the dreamer is promised and revealed.

Northern California, Woman, 76

In 2019 a woman from California described her "Wise Woman Dream":

In the dream I am on some kind of a trip in the outdoors with a small group of people (outdoor trips are something I had done many times, and was a pretty familiar and comfortable setting). What I remember about the dream, sometime in the mid-80s:

There is an older woman, kind of roundish and a little dowdy but very active and helpful and having a good time also. At first I don't notice her very much, and when I do, I am not too interested; she doesn't capture my attention or my imagination.

But she persists in a cheerful way with interacting with me in helpful but not subservient ways. Slowly I begin to actually notice her as a person who is unique and worth knowing, but still not very attractive to my imagination. The image that really changes it all and that I remember clearly is when we are on a raft trip with the group, and she is in the raft with me (I had done a number of rafting trips before this dream over the years on both fairly quiet water and also in some pretty tough rapids). It may be just the two of us. The water becomes very turbulent, a 4–5 rapids, and I am scared; it is moving very, very fast and it is dangerous now, I need to really hang on and am not sure we will get through this; this is when I see she is both really enjoying it, very alive and vibrant, and also very skilled and helpful in getting the raft around the boulders and pointed in the right direction, "setting" it up correctly so we don't overturn. I notice how surprised I am that she has so much life and so much knowledge when she has been so low key throughout the journey together. At one point she is lying on my body and laughing uproariously, thoroughly enjoying herself and the life energy of what we are doing. I feel an intense connection between us and an incredible feeling of safety in being with her, something completely unexpected.

Waking and thinking about the dream over days, I realized she is a new feminine image from my psyche, where before the images had been more easily recognizable as numinous, divine figures. She is of nature, but comfortable, belonging to a life in nature, still human, and so much wiser than I had imagined doing the ordinary tasks with her in the periphery of my awareness.

I then realized and felt her "wise-ness," her depth and solidity and named her my Wise Woman figure. She reminds me of some images of older Indian women I had seen and heard stories about.

The dreamer's primary outer-world experience with a helpful older woman was her grandmother. She remembers close times between them.

Her grandmother was a healer. The grandmother and child were together during the dreamer's infancy through toddlerhood, but when the dreamer moved away, she never saw her grandmother again. She continues:

She was in some sense ageless but definitely weathered. I couldn't guess her age really, except older than I was. She had the aspect of an old peasant woman perhaps and that is why I also mention the Native American connection, but no, she was not in fact Native American ... she was "generic" in some sense while also very specific. I think especially she was not "special" or "divine" or set apart from the real human lived experience, so it was a gradual understanding of her innate power and wisdom gained through the lived experience the dream described (of course the river journey is a familiar archetypical motif for me re life's spiritual journey).

But this woman was much more independent and alive and vibrant than any actual woman I had known. As I am writing this, I realize that it was after this dream, a year or two later, that I felt a strong need to go on a "walkabout" solo, in my pickup truck camping, so for about twelve to fourteen years after that I went every summer for three to four weeks on such a solo adventure, many times in the American Southwest areas, especially the high desert, but also up the Pacific coast and into Canada. I would pick a general direction each year, but not have specific plans and would make up the itinerary as I went. I always knew there would be some kind of great test that would happen during the journey, something dangerous from which I could not be sure I would survive, something totally unexpected, and that was a very important reason why I had to do this. The excitement and danger of the truly unexpected. These are wonderful memories; it was an important part of bringing balance to my life in those years when I was working many hours a week ... I learned so much.

Psychological Commentary

This dream is like an action film, revealing again how unlimited the manifestations of the Wise Old Woman spirit are. How boundless her energy and ability appear in what it is she does. Here we can literally see what we've already discovered: that she is a spirit "of nature," being spirit and nature, and showing gradations in the particular experience the dreamer has of her.

The dreamer is surrounded by nature, camping with a few friends, when the dream begins. Right away the Wise Old Woman spirit brings *eros* between the dreamer and nature, coinciding with the *eros* of companionship with the others. That is, the dreamer loves being outdoors and lovingly relates to her friends and natural surroundings.

This is familiar territory to the dreamer who had many years of such outdoor adventures, each time bringing her close to the earth and close to the spirit of the Wise Old Woman. In fact, the dream depicts how the relationship did, indeed, bloom over time. The dreamer's story about gradually getting to know the Wise Old Woman spirit is lovely. It resonates with the idea of the human psyche's developmental process that evolves over time.

In the dream, the WOW spirit is "older, kind of roundish, and a little dowdy ... ageless but definitely weathered." Moreover, this "active" spirit is persistently helpful, but "not in a subservient way." She is "cheerful" and "having a good time," but otherwise unnoticeable, according to the dreamer, sort of nondescript.

The dreamer wrote that she felt her initial experiences of the WOW were uninteresting and unattractive to her imagination ... perhaps, unimaginable or "nothing going on," as von Franz would say. This represents a kind of *emptiness*, which may provide an inner readiness for the emergence of the Self.

Invisibly, the Wise Old Woman spirit *is* the *emptiness*, present *as* the *emptiness*, and holds the dreamer's great potentials. It's no surprise that the woman remembers this dream because of its immediacy, vividness, and life or death imagery. Such an experience can be life changing.

Not that the WOW spirit can't appear in majestic form, but this dream depicts a different kind of experience. The dreamer literally feels the Wise

Old Woman spirit as physically close, near to humanness, and not at all a goddess to be worshipped. The dreamer slowly and increasingly sees the WOW as "unique and worth knowing." Eventually, the dreamer realizes that the WOW is "so much wiser than I had imagined."

That discovery occurs when the dreamer is paired with the WOW on a rafting trip. She and the WOW are almost immediately caught in dangerous, turbulent waters that understandably scare the dream ego. She hangs on, fearing for her life, and then looks over at the Wise Old Woman.

Before her is a lively, fun-loving, vibrant, and skillful partner, negotiating the rapids with deference (maybe with grace) and glee. The dreamer watches in surprise as the WOW makes sure to miss boulders and stay on course to not overturn. She shows she is someone who has "been around ... and knows the ropes" ... or oars, in this case.

The dreamer sees the Wise Old Woman spirit truly enjoying herself, laughing throughout the quest. In fact, the water is so rough that at one point the WOW lands on top of the dreamer:

> ... at the time I didn't understand why she was being so physically close; there was nothing that made her intent clear, and also there was some sense that it was just due to the turbulence we were enduring on the journey in the raft. Later in thinking about it, I realized it was to emphasize the fact of our "embodiment," both hers and mine, and that was the form of our intimate knowledge and connection to each other, i.e., this is not an abstract relationship, it is actual and embodied.

The dreamer wrote how she felt in the dream at various stages, particularly when the WOW made physical contact. She described an "intense connection ... and an incredible feeling of safety." Here again is the felt vision that Jeff Raff has described, noting that sometimes people may have a profound experience, but not actually see the figure (like when the Wise Old Woman is on top of the dreamer). Visions are not just about sight. Remember that, at times, the dreamer feels (or senses) a physical effect in her body.

The dreamer's word *embodiment* describes a vital quality in connection with the WOW, making visible, or literally felt, the loving container that *emptiness* and *eros* both provide. Recall how safe the dreamer felt. The WOW is not, as the woman suggests, set apart from "real human lived experience"; that is, indeed, just the point. She is *in* but not *of* the reality of today's world.

Thus, this dreamer begins a *conscious* thirty-year relationship with the WOW spirit. Over the years, the woman has continued to relate to the Wise Old Woman archetype through dream work and exploring the outdoors. Many dreams of a helping old woman have come her way since this first one, forerunner to the remarkable unfolding of her life with the Wise Old Woman spirit.

Her dream presence is felt as numinous but, in this case, "still human, yet beyond humanness or beyond human limits." The Wise Old Woman spirit certainly navigates the dreamer through troubled waters. She has stayed with the dreamer through thick and thin and laughed through it all. The dreamer later realizes the great value of this wisdom figure and spontaneously calls her the "Wise Woman," confirming her identity.

The dream shows how the Wise Old Woman spirit can help in any context, applying skill, know-how, good humor, and courage as she guides the dreamer down the river of life. Here, the WOW reveals an unexpected confidence and great love for life itself, indeed, an *eros* for life.

This Wise Old Woman raft-trip dream is a life-changing event, not only for the dream ego and the outer ego, but also for the beginning of a great rebalancing in the dreamer's life. Not only did the WOW spirit dream offer compensation for her immediate circumstances—"many hours of work"—but she also guided her journeys for a decade and a half into the future.

That is, the prospective role, so well-known in wisdom figures, means that the WOW likely anticipated her walkabout journeys. The Wise Old Woman spirit came and guided her with "strong feelings" toward a yet unknown and unrealized future. Assuredly, the Wise Old Woman spirit does know our destiny and probably does as much for our future as she does in the now. It appears that the raft adventure functioned as a prototype for the rebalancing required for a full participation in life. Essentially, the dreamer continued to live out a similar experience to the one in her extraordinary dream—over and over again. How wondrous!

Switzerland, Woman, 67

I would like to share some experience with the Wise Old Woman I made in the last few weeks.

I had a dream in which she asked me to comp her on the piano whilst she would give a concert. She was a singer. She gave me a sheet of music with notes for the concert. We stood before a large wooden door. Behind that door there was the concert and we listened both to the vocalist (a woman) who was singing in a very beautiful way, and we also heard the piano that comped her. We had to wait, and we knew that we were next to enter the hall and give our concert. While we were waiting, I nod my head to say I would be ready to comp her; this was difficult for me, because I was afraid to play to such a large audience. Then she embraced me in a very cordial way. I felt it physically during the dream and always feel it when I am pondering about this dream.

After this dream I feel a connection to her, and I made different active imaginations. She is my guide and helps me in different situations, especially in handling of my mother complex ... (I take care of my mother who is ninety-eight years now and am often confronted with that complex ... as my relation to my mother was not the best in the past [childhood included].)

To describe her: She is an older, beautiful Lady. When I met her in the dream she wore a very light veil, in the colour bright blue/grey (pastel). I remember her tall eyes, brown coloured, and her long cloth in the colour of her veil.

Maybe it has to do with the feeling function (music) to learn to express her love and give her a voice, maybe it has to do with the ability to trust in the feeling, in the love she gave me with her embracement?

Psychological Commentary

This dream reveals a beautiful partnership between the Swiss woman and the Wise Old Woman spirit—they make music together!

198

Here the WOW spirit is an older beauty, wearing a colorful veil of feminine pastels, blue and gray—colors of the ocean, the sky, the mood, or emotion. Different from a wedding veil, funeral veil, or veil of political repression, the Wise Old Woman's veil maintains her regality, privacy, and mystery. The dreamer's descriptions of her "cloth" of the same colors suggest a softness and flow, and her brown eyes are remarkably disconcerting. As the dreamer writes, they look "tall."

The Wise Old Woman's veil seems to separate her from the collective world, a *separatio* alchemically speaking, a veil between the divine and human realms. Although not fully seen, the Wise Old Woman spirit is present, embodied, confident, and loving. The veil doesn't seem to get in the way of true intimacy. "Half-concealing, it invites fuller knowledge" (Chevalier and Gheerbrant, 1994, p. 1063).

J. E. Cirlot cites M. Schneider (1946, p. 50) in his book, asserting that "all symbolic meanings are at root musical ..." and we remember that "singing, as the harmonization of successive, melodic elements, is an image of the natural connexion between all things, and, at the same time, the communication, the spreading and the exaltation of the inner relationship linking all things together" (Cirlot, 1962, p. 215).

How could there be a deeper connection? The Wise Old Woman spirit's *eros* pervades the encounter. The WOW's singing and the dreamer's playing of the piano calls up Emma Jung's love of music and her understanding that it resides in the depths where spirit meets nature, offering potential for a religious experience (Jung, 1968j, CW 10, para. 8)."

For example, as mentioned briefly in Chapter 3, a man once told of being alone in the woods one day and being suddenly confronted by a huge moose (personal communication). The largest of all deer species, the moose is an enormous creature that can charge if it feels provoked or startled. A powerful musical connection occurred when the man, in an effort to protect himself, began humming to the moose. When that happened, the moose began to wiggle its ears and listen. After a short time, the moose slowly ambled away. The man felt relieved and moved by the power of the *eros* that connected them. Might this not be such a "religious experience"? Perhaps this life-saving crooning was sent by the Wise Old Woman spirit!

Singing as a way to lull and calm also occurs in an episode of *MASH* (1974–1982), in which an enemy patient lies flailing on the operating table when an intense struggle ensues. Worst of all, the patient is still holding the hand grenade from which he has pulled the pin, then thrown it. A frantic search is made for the pin. "Put him under, quickly," but the first breathing tube they find is broken. The surrounding doctors and nurses continue to think out loud on how to contain the patient.

In the meantime, the surgeon, having only his own strength to hold onto the man and the grenade the patient is clasping, strains with great effort and fear. In quiet desperation he begins to sing: "Hush, little baby, don't you cry," and the rest of the staff joins in slowly and softly together. This lullaby calms him enough so that he can finally be put to sleep.

This scene is reminiscent of Jung's description of an early memory of being carried in his father's arms as he paced back and forth while singing to the restive baby Jung. One song in particular was soothing. "To this day I can remember my father's voice, singing over me in the stillness of the night" (Jung, 1965, p. 8).

Thus, singing is an ancient and eternal form of human and animal expression, vocalizing emotion, feeling-toned thought and image. Jung observed that sometimes a tune could be hummed while the words are still repressed, this often being when a complex has been unconsciously activated. In other words, singing has to do with naturalness, harmony, and relating with feeling. It also has to do with ordering, connection, and, sometimes, celebration. Moreover, song is often offered up during spiritual prayer and rituals. Emma Jung has written that a wonderful melody radiates from the Grail (E. Jung & von Franz, 1970, p. 297).

Returning to the dream, note how the Wise Old Woman might be on either side of a petition. The WOW begins this time by making a specific request of the dreamer. Will the dreamer accompany her on the piano while she sings? The Wise Old Woman spirit seems to know that performing in front of a big audience will be especially difficult for the dreamer.

In support of the dreamer, the Old Woman provides sheet music showing the exact notes to play on the piano. Like all sheet music, symbols noting rests are an integral part of the temporal relationships among the sounds. Here is her *emptiness* again, coming intermittently as it helps shape the melody. How can the presence of the Wise Old Woman's *emptiness* provide for our need for rest? Or even just to help us pause?

The dreamer will be singing with the keys, in harmony with the Wise Old Woman's song. This is *eros*. When might you or I be the one who provides both the steady background and invisible support for another's time in the spotlight? This might be *eros*! How would it look in our lives to be psychologically in tune with each other? Could this be *eros*?

When a person has it all together, aren't we really describing her or his inner unity? Don't others feel it whether it's spoken or not? Whether it's conscious or not? What is right relating to each other and ourselves? Could it reduce the dissonance that we currently bear?

The Wise Old Woman spirit and the Swiss woman engage in making beautiful music that moves out from their relationship and serves as a model for the witnessing collective. Their performance, an inspiration for the unity it represents, underscores the world's great need for *eros*.

Another external and literal application of the magical powers of music is a community sing along. Such events happened in Italy in the 1990s when people gathered outside the Assisi town church, for example, in late afternoon, spontaneously breaking out in song for about fifteen minutes. And during the COVID-19 pandemic, as Italy was swept by the virus and the country locked down, its citizens sang to each other from their balconies. Whether the 1990s or 2020, the singing offered more than just a sense of the picturesque; it offered a sense of belonging and unity and was felt regardless of the language or the words.

Returning to the dream, as the Wise Old Woman spirit and the dreamer wait, they hear the voice of the singer on stage and the pianist accompanying her, a divine echo of their relationship projected and creating wholeness with the number 4. The dreamer and the WOW spirit stand at the door, the threshold to their concert together.

Waiting suggests the quality of *emptiness* particular to the Wise Old Woman spirit, and a prelude, in this case, to an extraordinary depth of experience with each other. The space between the stage performers and the waiting WOW spirit and dreamer is a deliberate, conscious boundary; the big wooden door is humanmade and both a physical and psychological entry. This forethought provides the *emptiness* required for creative relationship.

Just before the performance, when the dreamer nods her agreement to play, the Wise Old Woman spirit reveals her understanding and compassion. She embraces the dreamer who then enters a beautiful and numinous depth of feeling. Upon reflection, the dreamer wonders if the music in her dream refers to her feeling function and ponders how to express the Wise Old Woman spirit's love ... to be her voice. The dreamer seems encouraged to trust in this feeling—that is, to trust in the love that the WOW gives when she embraces her.

Importantly, the Wise Old Woman spirit helps the dreamer with her inner and outer mother (and complex). The sacred WOW, like Isis, is the source of light to be found in the darkness. The Swiss woman lives daily with this darkness, but through her dreams and active imaginations with the feminine wisdom spirit, the dreamer has become more aware and protective of her vulnerabilities. In this way, the Wise Old Woman spirit has given the dreamer more freedom from possession by the negative mother complex. Her ongoing relationship with the Wise Old Woman spirit is as powerful and moving as it is as simple, and as natural, as singing a song.

Spain, Man, 59

The next dream was contributed by a therapist born and living in Spain. Unless otherwise shown, quotation marks signify descriptions by the analyst. This is a lovely story about the Wise Old Woman spirit as seen in the dream of a Spanish woman. She is forty-five years old and presented the dream in her therapy. It is a short, sweet dream that, nevertheless, shows so much ... and does so much.

"One of my patients, of middle age, in a moment of stagnation in her therapeutic process, had the following dream:"

I was in the chapel of my village, in front of the image of the Virgin Mary (although it was a statue it seemed very lifelike) and with a well-known male singer in my country. In the dream I remembered that in my youth I sang in a choir. I contemplate the image of the Virgin and I feel a very strong feeling, I wake up wanting to cry.

"Note: … the statue seemed to her to be full of life and gave off a certain brightness."

The woman's therapist wrote his interpretation as follows:

"In her youth, the woman had participated in a choir that sang at mass in church, a fact that she remembers as something gratifying and that made her feel good. This woman, who in her real life does not have any particular religious beliefs and who could even be said to be an atheist, in the dream finds herself before a goddess, although in the form of a statue (the same thing happened to many dream incubators in late antiquity with the presence of the god Asclepius). It is not strange that the presence of the goddess impregnated the dreamer with the function of feeling: in many Valencian towns in Spain, the cult of the Virgin is expressed through a devotional feeling of great intensity, as was evident in the associations of the patient. On the other hand, the presence of the singer, the creative animus, is a fundamental aspect with which the patient must relate in order to develop her creativity in harmony with her feeling. The goddess who appears in the dream guides the dreamer towards feelings that can stimulate her creativity."

Psychological Commentary

The several ways in which the Wise Old Woman spirit appears to this woman reveal the main theme of the dream—the relationship or *eros* she experienced with the WOW spirit. In the moments she gazes upon the feminine deity, the woman is brought to the edge of tears. The image, this *yantra*, this lively vision, "impregnates" her with the feeling function. The woman's numinous connection with the Virgin brings her to her soul life. What a wonderful *lysis*, the feelings of great intensity, of which she was so needful, came forth.

Madonnas and other statues of the feminine have been seen shedding tears on numerous occasions ("Weeping Statue," 2022). Remember how a psychological understanding values tears—they are like precious jewels or golden rays of the sun—and they have a healing effect on the woman.

In this case, tears offer a watershed inspired by her connection with the Wise Old Woman spirit, as seen and felt through the Virgin Mary.

In this dream, the analysand's deep emotional experiences also underscore the nonverbal nature of her relationship with the WOW spirit. This may have to do with WOW's loving powerfulness, which requires no words to be felt—maybe, as seen before, she can only be felt in the woman's silence.

This dream is a good example of how the Wise Old Woman spirit may appear in the form of a traditional deity so that she may be recognized by this individual. Her appearance and behavior are tailored and interwoven with the dreamer's needs and experiences. The WOW spirit is related to all the goddesses throughout time who serve to amplify the WOW spirit today.

The analyst indicated the dreamer had been stuck—perhaps in a depression; that *negredo* stage seemed to hold her feelings until she was ready for the WOW's appearance. The Wise Old Woman spirit contains the intensity of her feelings within her *emptiness* until the woman is able to cry. In fact, the woman's depressive symptoms, according to her analyst, were "related to a certain sense of emptiness and lack of direction in her life."

The great need the woman had for accepting her own experience of *emptiness*, so misunderstood and disparaged across the world, was finally felt for the dark beginning it was. In other words, the *emptiness* she felt could be understood as her experience of the Wise Old Woman spirit, here as an alchemical container. The woman's sense of *emptiness* offered the very place needed for a constellation of the Self and a subsequent transformation.

The analyst had also been holding the woman's painful stillness. When the dream came, the analyst's interpretation conveyed his own *eros*-love, offering a compassionate comprehension of the woman's struggle and need for a talented (creative) animus. The presence of the male singer adds nicely to the dreamer's emotional *solutio* and potential for the further development of her masculine side, "creativity in harmony with her feeling."

It's interesting that the Wise Old Woman spirit, who appears in the form of the Sacred Virgin, the Mother of God, did, indeed, "give birth

to a creative project," according to the analyst. That is, the WOW spirit
seemed to help the woman give birth to herself!

Brazil, Man, 58

Here is a dream I had back on January 12, 1999:

*I started thinking about the Mother of Jesus, Mary. She took me
and went with me in the middle of that place where that entity,
Jesus-Evil, had thrown the coffin. Mary was not really walking;
she rather slides besides me.*

*When we crossed that reddish light, I could see a very
ugly place. There were packs of people, kind [of] alive but
also in decomposition. There was a lot of suffering and I was
very fearful and tried to avoid looking. I wanted to get out of
that place, but Mary said I should be there. And I asked what I
should do and she told me to pray. But pray to whom? I asked—
"for her, for Christ?" And she said to pray to God the way she
was (she is making clear that she, herself, is as Divine as any
God). So, while we were praying, some of those "souls" would
leak out of that place, while others would still stay there.*

*Mary insisted that I should penetrate deeper in that place
for she would be with me. I was still horrified! I saw myself
being caught by an evil-like entity. It tied my hands in a cellar
compartment and started whipping me. I couldn't feel pain, but
just anguish. So, I decided to "confront" it, such as "Hey, let's
see what is going on here!" And immediately this evil-like entity
melted away and disappeared.*

*Mary continued to walk with me and took me to a very
huge fireplace. It was awfully hot and frightening. I felt myself
completely dried and became very thirsty. We continued to walk
and I saw a very beautiful stream and I want to jump in it to
drink some fresh water. But Mary said no. I had the sensation
that she wanted to show me 5 more things, but all of the sudden,
I could see flashes of a nice garden with white flowers and*

*green grass. We walked a little more and Mary decided that it
was enough.*

When I wrote the dreamer, I asked him two questions:
1) "What does 'thrown the coffin' mean?" He answered, "It means
that that entity had disposed the urn where a dead body was kept."
2) "What does 'reddish light' indicate? e.g., crossing into hell's
territory?" He said, "It was a place illuminated by a red light ... I
cannot say that it was hell ... maybe it was ... I don't know."

Psychological Commentary

I humbly acknowledge that much more could be said about this
dream than I can say here; indeed, an entire book could easily be written
about this one dream. The scope of this chapter limits, however, the
infinite ways in which the dream can be understood. Nevertheless, I will
highlight the unique qualities of the Wise Old Woman spirit and how and
when they appear, especially as the dreamer and the WOW relate to and
walk with each other.

This powerful dream is filled with the *eros* and *emptiness* symbolized
by the Wise Old Woman spirit. These qualities seem to alternate with
each other throughout the dream and sometimes appear at the same time.

Among its many complexities and images of antiquity, however,
is the undeniable masculine patriarchal emphasis at its beginning, and
an undeniable ending amid flashes of the feminine beauty of nature—
white flowers as mandalas and the green growth of grassy earth. Surely,
this is a dream in which the Wise Old Woman spirit wisely, firmly, and
very gently, guides the dreamer. That she glides suggests her absence of
connection to the material earth. She is above the ground, detached from
matter. She is not altogether of this world.

Note that the dream begins with the dreamer's reflection and thinking
about the Mother Mary or Wise Old Woman spirit. It is as though he
has known the WOW in the past, and they are already familiar with one
another, perhaps in prior developmental passages.

The dreamer's thoughts are like a bridge of *eros* that connects him to
the WOW who responds immediately with her presence. In fact, we will
see that the WOW's presence is critical to the dreamer's entire process

of transformation. She accompanies the dreamer throughout an intensely felt and fierce rite of passage.

The dream begins at the "middle" of a great *emptiness*, like the loss of the urn where a body is kept or perhaps, as in the Christian myth, the empty tomb where the stone was rolled away. The dream begins with relationship and emptiness, both qualities unique to the Wise Old Woman spirit and both providing the loving container needed for change.

My best understanding is that the dream continues by depicting a part of the alchemical process, which begins in the *rubedo*, a stage usually depicted as an end goal in the process of individuation. Moreover, the emphasis is on a painful spiritual shadow process that the dreamer is suffering. It is as if the dreamer had moved through the alchemical process before and had paused or not proceeded for some reason and has to now return to this *rubedo* stage.

The crucial question is why did the Wise Old Woman spirit as the Mother Mary appear in this dream to guide, teach, and serve as companion? Why was it important for her to be in the lead? Certainly, it is apparent that this journey is a necessary one—Mary's insistence—and its course suggests a number of stages or places, the first being when Jesus-Evil has "thrown the coffin," with only *emptiness* remaining.

This particular *emptiness* in the dream, with Mary by his side, allows for a direct crossing of the "reddish light." Is this illuminated scarlet light a consciousness of passion? Or is its message meant to bring a greater awareness of rage, heat, or blood? Is the dreamer's experience a kind of tinted seeing and, if so, in what way is his vision tinted or tainted, and by what? Is crossing that light like a borderline between consciousness and the unconscious? Or does its crossing have to do with overcoming an obstacle? (Jung, 1967, CW 5, para. 327).

Surely, the dreamer confronts in anguish the alchemical stage of *putrefactio* ... "a very ugly place," where "there were packs of people, kind [of] alive but also in decomposition." The dreamer sees the suffering masses and the dream ego is very fearful and tries to not look. Are these many parts ones that have been discarded or are they decomposing due to neglect?

Nevertheless, Jung reminds us that the goal of the opus cannot be reached without "the putrefactio, the corruption of one is the generation of the other, an indication that this death is an interim stage to be followed by a new life" (Jung, 1968b, CW 12, p. 105, fig. 48; 1966, CW 16, para. 467).

Cirlot says it another way, "From a psychological point of view, putrefaction is the destruction of the intellectual [or other] impediments in the way of the evolution of the spirit" (Cirlot, 1962, p. 255).

Of course, the dreamer wants to get out of that place, but the Wise Old Woman spirit denies his request and says he must stay. More than likely, she has another vision and understanding beyond the present torture.

Keep in mind that the WOW spirit surrounds the situation in *eros*. She is always there. Her presence in consciousness is paramount. The dreamer needs to be present himself, staying conscious throughout the process. That is, the dream ego consciously witnesses and participates in this way, which could be understood as his role in their partnership (perhaps, now partially conscious).

A tender example of the significance of presence is shown in the film in which Jane Fonda and Robert Redford star as Addie and Louis, in *Our Souls at Night* (2017). Presence essentially makes up their non-erotic relationship when this widow and widower begin sharing a bed together to heal their mutual loneliness. Their presence with each other in the *emptiness* of their silence becomes a presence without words or touch. Their relationship evolves and eventuates in their telling each other their stories of life lost and suffered. A *coniunctio* occurs through *emptiness*, presence, and the developing *eros* arising between them.

Returning to the dream, the man asks the WOW, "What should I do?" and the Spirit instructs him to pray. He asks for further direction, "Pray to whom or for whom?" he implores. Mary says to pray to God the way she is: "She is making clear that she, herself, is as Divine as any God."

This is the Wise Old Woman spirit, as revealed in the Mother Mary's Declaration of Divinity. She leaves it to no interpretation. The Mother Mary just says it matter-of-factly, "as Divine as any God," affirming her equality to the higher powers. Needless to say, the influences of this realization are infinite and await further exploration and articulation; this direct communication is a powerful gift from the WOW spirit, especially at this time.

From a Christian perspective, the Mother Mary, Jesus, and the Father-God themselves make up a new divine trinity—Mary or the Wise Old Woman being the figure that was previously missing! If you want to add the Christian religion's Holy Ghost, that makes the Father, the Mother, the Son, and the Holy Ghost, the quaternity Jung describes as the needed step toward wholeness—the quaternity that includes the feminine divine.

However, with Mary praying too, it is apparent that she and the dreamer are praying to God the Father of the Catholic tradition. This can be understood, archetypally, as the Great Father or the Wise Old Man spirit, psychologically speaking. Like most of the other great religions, it is based on the masculine principle. As I discussed at length earlier, the patriarchal God has been incomplete; his help by itself isn't working. Sadly, women as well as men are steeped in the patriarchal masculine, and both continue to need to integrate the feminine more fully.

While Mary and the dreamer are praying, some of the souls for which they are praying, "leak out," suggesting liquidity is involved in their soul saving. Perhaps this shows how the patriarchal God is barely squeezing it out, or maybe he is just worn out from being so lopsidedly burdened. Also, liquid, like water for instance, is associated with the feminine, which may offer a clue to the *lysis* of this dream.

Some process of differentiation seems to be occurring while the dreamer and the Wise Old Woman pray. Some souls are set free, and some will have to stay in that place. The dream shows that praying to the father-god leaves some who do not escape the suffering where the reddish light occurs.

However, the reddish light illuminates the area. Could that mean the reddish light works like the light that enables one to see in the dark? Sometimes referred to as *infrared*, this equipment can be used to allow night vision (Psychics Central, 2020). Psychologically speaking, does the reddish light make the unseeable seeable? Is consciousness enhanced by the reddish illumination? What is the dreamer's experience? Does he see what he hasn't seen before? Does he realize that something is terribly missing?

Horrified, the dreamer is pressed by the Wise Old Woman to "penetrate deeper," beyond the stage of putrefaction. She assures the

209

dreamer that she will be with him, *eros* holding. Still terrified, he suddenly "saw himself" being "caught by an evil-like entity." This suggests that he has some emotional distance, this *seeing* a sign that he is indeed staying conscious throughout the ordeal.

The entity ties his hands behind his back in a cellar, a frequent symbol of a shadow area. This shadow, this unknown part, often approaches from behind, where it can't be detected. Could this be an archetype that is constellated and then activated as a complex in the dreamer?

Certainly, the dreamer is *disarmed*. This evil-like archetype takes over and begins whipping him, the dreamer feeling anguish but not pain. Note that the whip is a symbol of the Terrible Mother and the entity's negative *eros* connection: the whip induces deeply felt emotions in the dreamer.

Might the dreamer's helplessness be likened to another experience of *emptiness*, in which he has to *be* or witness and not *do*? Could the Wise Old Woman spirit be in collaboration with the Terrible Mother? Is the Terrible Mother animus possessed? What is the lesson to be learned from this agonizing experience of thrashing?

Von Franz quotes Jung: "Demonic powers are archetypes in an initial stage of moving toward consciousness" (1995, p. 151). It's like the archetype is changing along with humans, this man, in the process of initiation. The dreamer's creative energy born out of this emptiness reaches the dreamer's consciousness, which then "decided to confront it." Thus, the dreamer asserts himself: "Hey, let's see what's going on here?"

The evil-like entity immediately "melted away and disappeared." The dreamer's facing the archetype has the effect of melting it. Has liquid been introduced again? *Solutio*? If so, the softening and breaking up of the material is instantaneous, really magical in this case. Moreover, the confrontation is respectful and courteous.

That's all it took. A simple request to see, and low and behold, he does! That is, he learns through the experience itself, that facing into the wind without anything but yourself—just *eros* and *emptiness*—can be the saving grace.

This is reminiscent of the children's story *Dizzy and the Dreams,* which is really a book for all ages (Newton, 2019). In her dream, Dizzy has been threatened by a giant bull when another dream figure suggests finding out what he may want. So, when the bull comes at Dizzy again, nearly reaching the place where she's standing, she feels a surge of power and strength. At first ready to run, she suddenly pivots and faces the bull, asking that very thing, "What do you want?" Instantaneously, the bull hands her a paintbrush! In analytical terms, these facing-the-wind acts might be understood as the beginnings of active imaginations, the powerful method described by Jung for connecting with an inner figure.

Returning to the dream, Mary or the Wise Old Woman takes the dreamer to a huge fireplace that is tremendously hot and frightens him. Psychologically speaking, fire is the great judge and reduces all to its bare essentials. Although contained, the fire is enormous and still very threatening. The dreamer becomes very hot and dry and longs for drink. He feels the need for water. The masculine energy, the spirit, the dryness, the heat, the power, the immortality of spirit, is not enough. It does not quench his thirst.

In fact, when an image of that very quenching appears—a beautiful stream—and the dreamer wants to plunge into it and drink its fresh water, the Wise Old Woman says, "No" and declines his urges. It's as though she wants him to hold a greater perspective. It's as if she wants him to fully see this enticing vision. Perhaps it beckons. Perhaps, the dreamer needs to see the life that only the addition of the feminine could make whole—a life including *eros* and *emptiness*, a place from which the Self could emerge.

The dreamer senses that the number 5 is involved, the number of the quintessential, a human number for fingers and toes, a number that goes beyond the four elements, and a number for life itself.

Three plus two is about the union of the masculine directional dynamic and the "steady oscillating rhythm" of the feminine, the opposites of feminine and masculine, equivalents in the number 5. In fact, the number 5 has been described as an "awakening and regeneration" and oversees the *hieros gamos*. In this way, the number 5 can be described as a motif that signals a "possibility or necessity of relationship and its realization in life" (Abt, 2005, p. 135).

Moreover, the number 5 is the "most spiritual and refined unity imaginable among the four elements, not as the fifth element nor added to the four, but symbolic of its presence and refinement from them" (Abt,

2005, pp. 132–35). Importantly, 5 is also 4 plus 1, the wholeness of the four, with the fifth at its quintessential center. The middle of the number 5 can be seen as a cross in the center of a diagram of the 4, and "uniquely integrates both the experiences of suffering and the achievement of eternal life and wholeness" (Eastwood, 2002, pp. 100–5). Eastwood continues: "Five ... is seen psychologically as the fresh insight and higher consciousness necessary for new life and transformation" (p. 105).

This is the *lysis* of the dream: the dreamer and the Wise Old Woman together approach a place of growth in nature and divine feminine beauty, a place that Mary says, "Is enough."

At the end, the Wise Old Woman spirit and the dreamer suddenly see flashes of a garden of white flowers and green grass. They arrive to glimpse a place of the beauty and growth of Mother Earth. Are these flashes the scintilla of increasing consciousness? Are they glimpses of a place where the feminine can be accessed, a feminine divine that can heal with balance and beauty?

Australia, Man, 49

Dream #1—May 30, 2013

> *I am at a race or a ceremony it appears, with crowds lining both sides of a street which is on a bend. A car comes around the corner and it appears so strange as it is only the top one-half to two-thirds of the car. It is an old Citroen. There are four guys in the car, and I cheer as I can't believe what I am seeing. I look at the edges and the image of the car almost lost like it's CGI [computer-generated image]. The whole crowd cheers. They turn around and go back the other way. I hear someone in the car say something about not having enough fuel, power, or momentum to keep going.*
>
> *I have cheered but now I am finding it hard to breathe; my lungs are filled with crap. I try to cough it up but can't seem to get anything up. Nearby over the road I hear and see Sacred Heart boarders cheering too. I am leaving, perhaps with my family, and am trying to find a Ventolin [salbutamol] inhaler.*

I am in a church. Here again I am struggling for breath, with my lungs filled with gunk. I ask everyone if there is a doctor in the church as I need Ventolin. An older woman (who is a doctor) steps forward to help me.

The dreamer wrote this about the first dream:

A few ideas in unpacking the dream: This dream was at an interesting time. I'd been working across a number of GP surgeries for approximately three years. ... two doctors in one surgery [was particularly difficult] ... and at the time seemed to be an issue. I was also about to get sick with a flu ... and you can see here that I am running myself into the ground.

The Citroen, Citroen DS in particular, is a car that I always wanted, still do ... those ugly ones ... I wanted the ugliest car on the road ... I actually wrote a song about the Citroen when I was about twenty-six. ... It's a pretty crap song, but it was fun at the time.

I went to boarding school from 1987–1989. I failed the first year as I spent a lot of time skipping school, drinking, partying. There's a book called "the making of them" where the author nails the situation for boarders ... The first thing you learn to do as a boarder is lie. If you don't learn to lie, then you won't survive. ... Those years are not fond years in my memory.

That church reminded me of the church/chapel from the movie version of Les Miserable, but in my dream, it is more decrepit and in disrepair. But instead of a priest there is a doctor ... Also the lungs have to do with breathing which is to do with air and air is pneuma. ...

Psychological Commentary

The dream begins "at a race *or* a ceremony," which immediately raises the question, "Which one?" Together they suggest the tension of the opposites.

On one level, the "race" has to do with time and energy, and in this story, the draining thereof, and also with competition. A race car is often seen as positive masculine energy, and auto racing is a popular sport worldwide.

Psychologically speaking, a car could be considered the way one gets from one place to another, but the energy here is running out and the dreamer is depleted. Is the car sputtering like what can't be coughed up? Does he feel like he's trapped in a rat race? Alas, we see the dreamer's words, "I am running myself into the ground."

Note that both Jung and von Franz have written that all haste is of the devil (Jung, 1965, p. 296), or haste comes from the devil (von Franz, 1997a, p. 103), but the crowds are cheering with excitement. In fact, the dream depicts the collective all around, unknown others on both sides of the street, which is perhaps another reference to division in the dreamer's psyche.

In *The Red Book*, Jung also states, "Through haste and increased willing and action we want to escape from emptiness and also from evil. … But the right way is that we accept emptiness" (Jung, 2009, p. 288).

So, the dreamer is running on empty, as if the Wise Old Woman showed up just in time.

Is this the kind of *emptiness* that comes from racing around without enough rest? A common way of getting out of balance is when we take on too much, thinking we can do more than we can, feeling like there is really little choice. Or could it be a dark sacred *emptiness*, a holding place from which the creative may appear? Does either kind of *emptiness* likely constellate the Wise Old Woman spirit?

The featured car that's running out of fuel, an old but beloved Citroen, is "the ugliest car on the road." It's a car the dreamer always wished he'd had and still does. Perhaps this is a counterculture effort to be oneself, whether conforming to the average or not. It might also be understood as symbolizing an integration of his shadow.

The car the dreamer loves best appears from around the corner of the unconscious—in a curve on the left, received by a cheering collective. The left is typically associated with the unconscious side of things, which is conveyed by its magical and strange appearance.

The image of the Citroen, revealing only the top one-half to two-thirds of the car, appears as if it has been computer generated. The dreamer can't believe what he is seeing—no wheels are visible—and now there are cheers from the whole crowd. Is the dreamer feeling "edgy" or perhaps a bit "on edge"? Thus, the Citroen races without wheels—the four missing mandalas only suggested by memory. Moreover, the Citroen might also point to a process, which is as yet incomplete or unconscious.

However, the racing car turns around, going back in the direction from whence it came. The dreamer hears one of the four men in the Citroen saying something about being out of gas or lacking momentum.

Could this be a turning point in the dreamer's conflict? Here, the four men in the car is a kind of masculine wholeness, but it's missing the feminine principle completely. Perhaps it is more like 2×2, than the wholeness that 4 typically represents. As 2×2, the emphasis potentiates the 2 as a coming to greater consciousness. Perhaps that greater awareness recognizes something is missing; something needs to be retrieved in order to go forward and complete the mandala around the track.

Note that the dreamer has difficulty breathing just at the moment the fuel is running out in the car. "My lungs are filled with crap," he writes, just after the dreamer has cheered. It sounds like the last hurrah. The dreamer's struggle means trouble with pneuma, as he correctly observes, and highlights a need for spirit or spiritual nourishment. That is, blockage has occurred in the spiritual realm.

So "coughing it up" does not work in this case. Apparently, it's not going to be a straight-up affair. Might he not need to learn through experience? Cheers from the Sacred Heart (SH) boarders are heard. What might that evoke in the dreamer? Were the sounds from the Sacred Heart boarders a reminder of a difficult time from his adolescent past?

Next, the dreamer leaves, probably with family, and looks for an inhaler, looking for help to breathe. In the outer world, he was familiar with a bronchodilator called Ventolin that relaxes muscles in the airways and increases airflow to the lungs.

Referring to the beginning of the dream, there is the possibility of the dreamer's being at a ceremony, which is anything but a race, and traditionally held in somber and deliberate slowness. A ceremony is often intended to be thoughtful, reflective, and quiet—a ritual, so to speak. A ceremony is a ritual of *eros*, of relationship and devotion, and the dreamer feels drawn to the spirit of the WOW.

At the end of his first dream, the dreamer finds himself in a chapel reminiscent of the one in the movie *Les Miserable,* which took place in the 1780s in France, with its cold, dark, large and ornate arches of stone. Note that the chapel in the Australian's dream is "decrepit" and in "disrepair." The film takes place in this dreary setting, akin to the dark and drastic poverty of the dreamer's spiritual condition and his psychic and emotional depletion.

However, a place of worship such as a chapel is a feminine symbol and, from a Jungian perspective, a container, which might be understood as a *temenos* or sacred circle. The chapel *holds* and provides a safe place of stillness, of non-doing and calm. The chapel is, of course, a vessel or a container of *emptiness* as well as a container for *eros* and positive relating to the Godhead, both inner and outer in nature.

Surely, the dreamer feels the need for *emptiness,* and it is this *emptiness* that is the Wise Old Woman. The dreamer searches in earnest, not yet conscious that she is there, not yet seeing her. However, he continues to reach out, asking everyone if there is a doctor in the church, unceasing in his search for an inhaler. In the *lysis* of the dream, it is not the usual priest, but a physician who responds—an older woman coming to heal and help. The Wise Old Woman spirit steps forward.

Dreamer's Active Imagination

> *And through an active imagination she tells me her name is ... Dr. Grace and that doctors weren't always the way they are now. ... They were shamans, doctors, healers. ... And that is what she is ... she is someone I should again start to revisit.*

Psychological Commentary

So out of nowhere, out of the *emptiness* the Wise Old Woman not only steps forward, showing responsiveness to the dreamer's plea, but also extends the *eros* between them by telling the dreamer her name, "Dr. Grace."

216

The moment the dreamer sees the Wise Old Woman come forward, he feels "a sense that healing was coming." He knew that he had done all he could in searching for help. According to Jung, a person cannot make grace happen, but through his or her presence, the individual can participate in divine grace (Jung, 1968c, CW 9i, para. 205).

The dreamer appears, not just at any chapel, but at the chapel associated with deep misery and neglect. He sees it for himself … dilapidated. That is ego's part—out of desperation, he makes himself present and reaches out for help.

Returning to the meaning of grace, Jung writes that grace is felt when an individual glimpses her or his own wholeness (Jung, 1968e, CW 12, para. 7). Maybe the dreamer's own experience of not being able to breathe awakened him to the feminine divine, the vital and missing spiritual fourth? Or maybe the cultural dissonance of a woman doctor also filled this silent quarter?

Did the Australian feel a sense of numinosity? Was his experience of grace like a religious experience or the irrational phenomenon of which Jung writes? He states that grace "cannot be discussed any more than can the 'beautiful' or the 'good.' Since that is so, no serious quest is without hope" (Jung, 1968l, CW 13, para. 143).

Thus, acts of grace are beyond human control and come from the outside, not from the individual (Jung, 1968d, p. 13, n. 8). And, indeed, the Wise Old Woman spirit appears, bringing hope and understanding, love and faith—all gifts of grace according to Jung. He affirms, and we observe, that grace happens through experience and cannot be produced (Jung, 1969c, CW 11, paras. 500–1).

As seen, the dreamer sees who the Wise Old Woman spirit is and confirms that a return to her is needed. In this way, he acknowledges he has known her before. He writes, "She is someone I should again start to revisit." A renewal of his relationship with the Wise Old Woman spirit beckons.

In the dreamer's active imagination, Dr. Grace, as the Wise Old Woman spirit, introduces herself. *Eros* surrounds the two of them forthwith. She describes shamans and doctors as healers, not the same as doctors today. Perhaps she speaks of healers of the soul. It seems as though she knows a sacred kind of healing and may consider the technology of today more about diagnosis, at the expense and neglect of the psyche and soul. It seems the dreamer knowingly translates the medical equipment to a soulful healing.

The following is a painting that emerged as the dreamer sought to express the Wise Old Woman spirit. He wrote about staying with the process, working as he trusted his hands to reflect what he was feeling and experiencing, smearing, and blurring the canvas with paint until a vision appeared.

Original oil painting from Australian man—"Dr. Grace" steps forth and emerges. The dreamer follows the paintbrush in his hands to reveal the form and color of the Wise Old Woman spirit, shown here with a sacred heart.

I've done a painting. ... it's the first painting I've done in a long time ... it's not pretty ... but I kept going over it and smudging things out till something emerged ... as I painted a figure started to emerge. Her dress is a dirty brown on the lower and blue on the upper ... it occurred to me to add some red, which ended up being something of the sacred heart.

Yes, Sacred Heart (SH) is a school for teens. It was purely a masculine environment. The monk I liked the best showed no emotion ... the reason I liked him is I knew where I stood with him. If I'd been caught doing something wrong, I would be punished. Because SH was a football school, the footy players were the gods of the school. I didn't play footy but as a rock musician could safely fly under the radar.

Re Sacred heart ... I don't think of the place much these days, but this has brought it up. From what I understand people started having visions of the sacred heart when da Vinci was dissecting people to find that a heart was nothing but a pump ... and so there was a compensation needed.

Funny enough, medicine has discovered that people can die from a broken heart, one such pathology is "Takotsubo cardiomyopathy" (TC), which was discovered in Japan in older couples where one would pass away and the other would pass away from Takotsubo cardiomyopathy shortly afterwards ... the heart changes its shape to resemble a Takotsubo [Japanese octopus pot/trap] and this causes a heart attack.

Psychological Commentary

In the last two stories, the heart prevails. The Wise Old Woman spirit, a shapeshifter as we know her, appears not only as herself but also as the heart—each a symbol of *eros*.

In his first account, the dreamer is drawn to wholeness; he cites the opposites. Da Vinci's dissection showed the heart as "nothing but" a pump, but the people continued to need *eros*, or heart, as their emotional foundation, its ethics and values. Had the visions been spawned by the felt *emptiness* of a medical discovery?

According to the dreamer, heart visions were first reported in the eleventh and twelfth centuries and continued at the time of da Vinci as compensation. At that time, visual images of the heart were embraced by the Catholic devotions; the heart was a symbol of unlimited and unconditional love. In other words, the heart stands for divine love and mystical unity ("Sacred Heart," 2022).

Moreover, the heart alone was left in the body in the mummification process in Egypt. The heart was considered "indispensable to the body into eternity" (Cirlot, 1962, p. 134). Traditionally, the heart was understood as "the true seat of intelligence" (p. 135). This is reminiscent of Jung's experience with Chief Mountain Lake, a Native American who observed that the Natives thought with their heart, not with their head.

The heart is a good example of our concrete and psychic experiences of *eros*. *Heart*, in a psychological sense, is like the word *grace* and cannot be comprehended. However, one could say that the heart circulates the body's lifeblood as well as the continual nourishment of psyche and soul. The dreamer describes a balancing of the two sides through compensation and that balance fosters hope. Heart may be considered the psychological loving of our life.

In Japan, Takotsubo cardiomyopathy (TC) can reveal the strength and endurance of *eros* between two people, often an older couple married for a long time. Positive *eros* can be imagined as the Wise Old Woman spirit in the center of a loving couple. In this example, the actual changing of the heart's shape, a broken heart, if you will, evidences the irrational power of *eros* and love. The dreamer told of TC cases that resulted in a heart attack, which in turn led to reunification with the dead partner. Symbolically, this might be seen as an alchemical *coniunctio*. Note that in Greek, the heart is the emblem of *eros*.

As the heart changes shape, it resembles a Japanese octopus pot or trap. The octopus, in turn, is associated with the number 8 or 2×4. The four, a symbol of wholeness, is more differentiated and potentiated by its doubling. The many meanings of the number 8 include "wise" (Eastwood, 2002, p. 156), "regeneration," "endlessness," "splendor," "perfection," "death," "grief," "symbol of the Great Goddess of life and immortality," "divine love," "fertility," "earth," "health," "understanding," "a sense of rightness," "conscience," "courage," "the soul," and more (de Vries, 1984, pp. 159–60, 243–44). Also, because the dreamer is a pianist and lover of music, it should be noted (perhaps synchronistically) that the number 8 is also an octave on the piano.

Psychologically speaking, the appearance of the number 8 in dreams like this one symbolizes a need or possibility for consciousness based on inner developmental gains by the dreamer (Abt, 2005, p. 148). This next

220

dream could be said to reveal those gains, especially in relationship to the
Wise Old Woman spirit.

Dream #2—May 9, 2016

*I am in a classroom; it seems to be not at class time though. It
has the feel of SH in Mr. G's classroom. There are 4 students
here to my left practicing singing together. There are 2 boys
and 2 girls. ... Or men and women. I don't know how they feel
about me being in there. I might be doing some work, but I am
seated at the piano.*

*When they finish I get ready to play the piano. An older
woman, who reminds me of Susan Faron, comes into the room on
my right, walking past a drum kit saying "oh no." I can see that
she wanted to use the piano. I start to play anyway. I am joined
on both sides, a woman to my left who was in the singing group I
think, and the Susan woman to my right. There is complex music
in front of me, but I start to play quite automatically. Music just
pours from my fingers on the keyboard. I am improvising and it
sounds amazing. It's far more complex than anything I've done
before. It might look like I am reading whatever it is in front of
me, but I am not.*

*In looking at this dream from 2016 ... Mr. G is the music
teacher from SH. He was a nice enough bloke. Music was my
saviour and escape at SH. It was a source of fantasy, and it was
something I was good at ... and something other people had
fantasies for me it turned out. As I was leaving school many
people imagined that I'd go on to be some sort of "rock star."*

*If you asked me what you would have represented to me
back in 2016, I would have said someone I seemed to gel with
someone with whom I could lock in with when I played piano
and you percussion. I also saw you as well ahead of me in life,
almost finished the course. ... And perhaps more true to yourself
than me.*

Psychological Commentary

This second dream of the Wise Old Woman spirit occurs one month shy of three years later. It is spring again and set in a place of learning, yet no formal class is in session. It's also the time of year of the dreamer's birthday, so renewal is in the air.

The dreamer is in his Alma Mater, Sacred Heart boarding school, and feels the familiarity of his music teacher's classroom. He sits at the piano, unsure of his purpose, unsure of his welcome. The dreamer describes "2 boys and 2 girls … Or men and women," as a group of singers on his left. Is he relating to the youth of his adolescence or being politely proper for the time?

He waits for the four singers on his left to complete their practice. Are these moments of *emptiness* for the dreamer? Is the masculine-feminine *coniunctio* of "fourness" a presage of what is to come?

As the students finish, the dreamer prepares to play. An older woman reminiscent of Dr. Faron comes over from his right. Thinking of this woman as a percussionist, he nevertheless hears her decline the drums as she joins him at the piano.

The dreamer begins to play. At the same time, one woman from the four singers comes over to the dreamer's left and she sits at the piano on his other side. The sounds of music, both melody and keys, convey the emotional energy surrounding the dreamer inside and out.

Moving to the dream's ending, it is within this euphonic context that the *lysis* of the dream occurs. The dreamer begins to play quite automatically, his hands oblivious to the complexity of the music in front of him. "Music just pours from my fingers on the keyboard," he writes. "I am improvising and it sounds amazing."

The feminine on either side of the dreamer mysteriously enables his very best play; indeed, he plays beyond his best play ever—which undeniably arises from the unconscious. Thus, the dreamer's animas, two of them—one an analyst crone and one a singer—serve to connect him with the Self. The older woman like myself is clearly symbolic of the dreamer's inner analyst, this one associated with the image of the Wise Old Woman spirit.

Declaring the soul-nourishment of music "my saviour," the dreamer followed this gift until he left a music career for a different kind of art, to train as a Jungian analyst. This dream and the Wise Old Woman spirit clearly guided him toward an analytic life that is unique to his music-making self and not necessarily the kind that's entertaining.

The three years between the first and last dreams, including an active imagination in between when "Dr. Grace" first steps forward, show a remarkable shift from the sputtering-car race to the side-by-side trio of wisdom, dreamer, and song. Sitting together, creative sounds come forth; surrounded by the feminine, the dreamer plays like he's never played before.

Not only does the dreamer call for, and later receive, the spirit of the Wise Old Woman, but his dream life reveals how the power of relationship with her may deepen and develop. The first dream depicts a lopsided masculine accompanied by illness and exhaustion. In this last dream, the feminine doubles up, compensating the four racing men and bringing balance. It is clear that the WOW spirit's presence can be profound and even joyful. We can see, hear, and feel the promise of what can be when connected with the Wise Old Woman spirit by just listening to the music within.

CHAPTER 7
Epilogue

Nature Mandala (Photo: Susan Faron)

Yes, indeed, the Wise Old Woman spirit is upon us! Uppermost, the Wise Old Woman spirit's remarkable qualities of *eros* and *emptiness* are just what we need and just when we need it most. The point is for you, the reader, to see for yourself how each account may help you launch or relate to your own connection with the Wise Old Woman spirit.

She can shape-shift, like the Mother Mary from Spain or von Franz in the tomb, or even be the center of a most vibrant and beautiful flower. She can be powerfully present and silently observing the creative works of a Norwegian, or active and skilled as on the California raft journey. She sings to a Swiss woman's accompaniment on the piano and ruffles an Indian's hair to cheer him up. She literally pushes gold upon one in need, and encourages another to suffer the fiery depths. For another, she guides without hesitancy toward a huge move and positive future. In still another, the Wise Old Woman appears as Emma Jung herself ready to share her own disappointments, providing understanding, affection and grounding with gentleness in realistic expectations. Wherever she's needed, the Wise Old Woman spirit comes forward and companions us as we live the analytic life, our way of individuation.

These glimpses of the unfolding ways she is manifest bring us the overarching message of her infinite variety of helping ways that can guide us to find balance. She can be a stranger or a more familiar deity from the past, depending on the individual's life experience and how their relationship to the Wise Old Woman bears upon it.

As I have thought and written about her, studied and learned more of her ways, I have realized her unpredictability, liveliness, immediacy and real presence. I have known and seen her *eros* and *emptiness* and help. I have felt her love.

Remember, she is a part of us. From the beginning, with the growing wisdom of self-knowledge, she has become humanized in us over time. That's the potential—the partnership of which I've spoken. Critically, it's the Wise Old Woman who is most missing and needed in today's world. This part of us is vitally needed.

These images of experience with her, so beautifully portrayed, reveal how she's been shaped by our outer lives, as well as inner dreams, active imaginations and other unconscious material. All those things help make up our alliance with Wise Old Woman spirit. The dreams and active imaginations depicted here are filled with a depth of riches and much for us to reflect upon. May they tempt us to follow our curiosity and discover for ourselves what a relationship with the Wise Old Woman spirit can be—what true *eros* and *emptiness* can provide.

References

"Active Imagination. (2002, February 9). In *Wikipedia*. https://en.wikipedia.org/wiki/Active_imagination

Abt, T. (2005). *Introduction to picture interpretation according to C.G. Jung*. Daimon Verlag.

Adler, G. (Ed.). (1973). *C.G. Jung letters: Vol. 2, 1951–1961*. Princeton University Press.

Ann, M. & Imel, D. (1993). *Goddesses in world mythology: A biographical dictionary*. Oxford University Press. (Originally published in 1993 by ABC-CLIO)

Anthony, M. (1990). *Jung's circle of women: The Valkyries*. Nicholas-Hays.

Archive for Research in Archetypal Symbolism (ARAS). (2010). *Book of symbols*. Taschen.

Avila-White, D., Schneider, A., & Domhoff, G.W. (1999). The most recent dreams of 12–13-year-old boys and girls: A methodological contribution to the study of dream content in teenagers. *Dreaming, 9*, 163–171. https://dreams.ucsc.edu/Findings/12-13.html

Axiom of Maria. (2022, January 21). In *Wikipedia*, https://en.wikipedia.org/wiki/Axiom_of_Maria

Bair, D. (2003). *Jung: A biography*. Little, Brown and Company.

Bar H. (2021). COVID-19 lockdown: animal life, ecosystem and atmospheric environment. *Environment, Development, and Sustainability, 23*(6), 8161–78. doi: 10.1007/s10668-020-01002-7

Baring, A., & Cashford, J. (1991). *The myth of the goddess: Evolution of an image*. Viking by the Penguin Group.

Bem Sex Role Inventory. (2021, October 7). In *Wikipedia*. https://en.wikipedia.org/wiki/Bem_Sex-Role_Inventory

Birkhäuser-Oeri, S. (1988). *The mother: Archetypal image in fairy tales.* Inner City Books.

Brome, V. (2001). *Jung: Man and myth.* House of Stratus.

Chevalier, J., & Gheerbrant A. (1994). *Penguin dictionary of symbols.* Penguin.

Chinaroad Löwchen. (2000–2008) *Names of gods and goddesses.* http://www.lowchensaustralia.com/names/gods.htm

Circle of Mithras. (n.d). *Zoromitharism.* https://circleofmithras.wordpress.com/zoromithraism/

Cirlot, J.E. (1962). *A dictionary of symbols.* Routledge and Kegan Paul.

Cowan, L. (2003, November 22). *Dismantling the animus.* Shambhala.

Crisp, T. (1999–2010). Archetype of the wise old woman – wise old man. [Blog post]. *Dreams, Health, Yoga, Body Mind & Spirit.* Retrieved from https://dreamhawk.com/dream-encyclopedia/archetype-of-wise-old-woman-wise-old-man/

de Vries, A. (1984). *Dictionary of symbols and imagery.* North Holland Publishing Co.

Douglas, C. (2000). *The woman in the mirror: Analytical psychology and the feminine.* An Author's Guild Backinprint.com. (Original work published 1990)

Eastwood, P. (2002). *Nine Windows to Wholeness: Exploring Numbers in Sandplay Therapy.* Sanity Press.

Egyptian Gods: Isis. (n.d.) In *Egyptian gods and goddesses.* http://egyptian-gods.org/egyptian-gods-isis/

Ellenberger, H.F. (1970). *The discovery of the unconscious: The history and evolution of dynamic psychiatry.* Basic Books.

Esoteric Theological Seminary. (n.d.) *The Christian Goddess.* http://www.northernway.org/goddess.html

Faron, S. (2012). *The seven-pointed star and the two houses around the corner: Interpretation of a dream.* [Unpublished manuscript]. Research and Training Centre for Depth Psychology according to C.G. Jung and Marie-Louise von Franz, Zurich.

Faron, S. (2017). *Interpretation of Grimms' "Old Woman in the Wood"* [Unpublished manuscript].

Faron, S. (2019, March and April). *The Wise Old Woman spirit: Help as a partnership* [Paper presentation]. San Francisco Analytical Psychology Club, San Francisco, California.

Ganz, D., Jung, A., Michel, R., Rohrer, J., & Ruegg, A. (Ed.). (2009). Stiftung C.G. Jung Küsnacht. In *The house of C.G. Jung: The history and restoration of the residence of Emma and Carl Gustav Jung-Rauschenbach* (pp. 18–19, 119). Stiftung C.G. Jung Küsnacht (C.G. Jung Foundation Küsnacht).

Gates of New Jerusalem. (2011). Tour of heaven. http://www.tourofheaven. com/eternal/new-jerusalem/gates.aspx

Gimbutas, M. (1982). *The goddesses and gods of Old Europe, 6500 to 3500 BC: Myths and cult images.* University of California Press.

Gimbutas, M. (1989). *Language of the goddess.* HarperSanFrancisco.

Global Peace Index. (2021, October 10). *Vision of humanity.* https://www. visionofhumanity.org/maps/#/

Goddess Gift. (n.d.) *Isis: Egyptian goddess of magic and giver of life.* http://www.goddessgift.com/goddess-myths/egyptian_goddess_isis. htm

Goddess-guide.com. (2007–2022) *Goddess names.* http://www.goddess-guide.com/goddess-names.html

GreekBoston.com. (n.d.). *Birth of Eros – God of Love.* https://www. greekboston.com/culture/mythology/birth-eros/

Grimms. (1972). *The Complete Grimm's Fairy.* Random House.

Hall, Manly. (1928). *The secret teaching of all ages.* H.S. Crocker Company. In *Sacred-texts.* http://www.sacred-texts.com/eso/sta/ sta10.htm

Hannah, B. (1976). *Jung, his life and his work.* Putnam.

Hauck, D.W. (n.d.). The AZoth ritual. http://www.azothalchemy.org/ azoth_ritual.htm.

Henderson, J.L. (1982). C.G Jung, Emma Jung, and Toni Wolff. In F. Jensen & S. Mullen (Eds.), *C.G. Jung, Emma Jung, and Toni Wolff: A collection of remembrances.* The Analytical Psychology Club of San Francisco.

Hollis, J. (1997). The image behind the emotion: Practicing active imagination. *Review of Contemporary Contributions to Jungian Psychology* (January–February).

Howes, E.B. (1982). Memory of Emma Jung. In F. Jensen & S. Mullen (Eds.), *C.G. Jung, Emma Jung, and Toni Wolff: A collection of remembrances*. The Analytical Psychology Club of San Francisco.

Isis. (2016, January 1). In *Wikipedia*. https://en.wikipedia.org/wiki/Isis

Jacobi, J. (1964). Symbols in an individual analysis. In *Man and his symbols*. Princeton University Press.

Jacobs, B. (2015, March 31). *Feminine in religion* [Blockcourse 41]. Research and Training Center in Depth Psychology according to C.G. Jung and M.L. von Franz. Bethanien, Switzerland.

Jaffe, A. (Ed.). (1979). *C.G. Jung: Word and image*. (K. Winston, Trans.). Princeton University Press.

Jung, C.G. (1959). *Mandala symbolism*. Princeton University Press.

Jung, C.G. (1960). On the nature of the psyche. In W. McGuire (Ed.), *The structure and dynamics of the psyche: Vol. 8. The collected works of C.G. Jung*. Princeton University Press. (Original work published 1947/1954)

Jung, C.G. (1965). *Memories, dreams and reflections*. Vintage Books.

Jung, C.G. (1966). Psychology of the transference. In W. McGuire (Ed.), *The Practice of Psychotherapy: Vol. 16. The collected works of C.G. Jung*. Princeton University Press. (Original work published 1946)

Jung, C.G. (1967). *Symbols of transformation: Vol. 5. The collected works of C.G. Jung*. (W. McGuire, Ed.). Princeton University Press. (Original work published 1911–1912, rev. ed. 1952)

Jung, C.G. (1968). *Aion: Vol. 9ii. The collected works of C.G. Jung*. (W. McGuire, Ed.). Princeton University Press.

Jung, C.G. (1968a). Commentary on "The secret of the golden flower." In W. McGuire (Ed.), *Alchemical studies: Vol. 13. The collected works of C.G. Jung*. Princeton University Press. (Original work published 1929)

Jung, C.G. (1968b). Concerning mandala symbolism. In W. McGuire (Ed.), *Archetypes and the collective unconscious: Vol. 9i. The collected works of C.G. Jung*. Princeton University Press. (Original work published 1950)

Jung, C.G. (1968c). Concerning rebirth. In W. McGuire (Ed.), *Archetypes and the collective unconscious: Vol. 9i. The collected works of*

C.G. Jung. Princeton University Press. (Original work published 1940/1950)

Jung, C.G. (1968d). Individual dream symbolism in relation to alchemy. In W. McGuire (Ed.), *Psychology and alchemy: Vol. 12. The collected works of C.G. Jung*. Princeton University Press. (Original work published 1936)

Jung, C.G. (1968e). Introduction to the religious and psychological problems of alchemy. In W. McGuire (Ed.), *Psychology and alchemy: Vol. 12. The collected works of C.G. Jung*. Princeton University Press.

Jung, C.G. (1968f). The phenomenology of the spirit in fairy tales. In W. McGuire (Ed.), *The archetypes and the collective unconscious: CW 9i. The collected works of C.G. Jung*. Princeton University Press. (Original work published 1945/1948)

Jung, C.G. (1968g). The philosophical tree. In W. McGuire (Ed.), *Alchemical studies: Vol. 13. The collected works of C.G. Jung*. Princeton University Press. (Original work published 1945/1954)

Jung, C.G. (1968h). Psychological aspects of the mother archetype. In W. McGuire (Ed.), *Archetypes and the collective unconscious: Vol. 9i. The collected works of C.G. Jung*. (Original work published 1938/1954)

Jung, C.G. (1968i). Religious ideas in alchemy. In W. McGuire (Ed.), *Psychology and alchemy: Vol. 12. The collected works of C.G. Jung*. Princeton University Press. (Original work published 1937)

Jung, C.G. (1968j). The role of the unconscious. In W. McGuire (Ed.), *Civilization in transition: Vol. 10. The collected works of C.G. Jung*. Princeton University Press. (Original work published 1918)

Jung, C.G. (1968k). The spirit Mercurius. In W. McGuire (Ed.), *Alchemical studies: Vol. 13. The collected works of C.G. Jung*. Princeton University Press. (Original work published 1943/1948)

Jung, C.G. (1968l). The visions of Zosimos. In W. McGuire (Ed.), *Alchemical studies: Vol. 13. The collected works of C.G. Jung*. Princeton University Press. (Original work published 1938/1954)

Jung, C.G. (1968m). Women in Europe. In W. McGuire (Ed.), *Civilization in transition: Vol. 10. The collected works of C.G. Jung*. Princeton University Press. (Original work published 1927)

Jung, C.G. (1969a). Answer to Job. In W. McGuire (Ed.), *Civilization in transition, Vol. 11: The collected works of C.G. Jung*. Princeton University Press. (Original work published 1952)

Jung, C.G. (1969b). New paths in psychology. In In W. McGuire (Ed.), *Two essays on analytical psychology: Vol. 7. The collected works of C.G. Jung*. Princeton University Press. (Original work published 1912)

Jung, C.G. (1969c). Psychoanalysis and the cure of souls. In W. McGuire (Ed.), *Psychology and religion: Vol. 11. The collected works of C.G. Jung*. Princeton University Press. (Original work published 1928)

Jung, C.G. (1969d). *Two essays on analytical psychology: Vol. 7. The collected works of C.G. Jung*. Princeton University Press. (Original work published 1928)

Jung, C.G. (1969e). The role of the unconscious. In W. McGuire (Ed.), *Civilization in transition: Vol. 10. The collected works of C.G. Jung*. Princeton University Press. (Original work published 1918)

Jung, C.G. (1969f). Transformation symbolism in the mass. In W. McGuire (Ed.), *Psychology and religion: Vol. 11. The collected works of C.G. Jung*. Princeton University Press. Princeton University Press.

Jung, C.G. (1970). *Mysterium coniunctionis: Vol. 14. The collected works of C.G. Jung*. (W. McGuire, Ed.). Princeton University Press. (Original work published 1955–56)

Jung, C.G. (1971). *Psychological types: Vol. 6. The collected works of C.G. Jung*. (W. McGuire, Ed.). Princeton University Press. (Original work published 1921)

Jung, C.G. (1977). *C.G. Jung speaking: Interviews and encounters*. W. McGuire & R.F.C. Hull (Eds.) Princeton University Press.

Jung, C.G. (1980a). Depth psychology. In W. McGuire (Ed.), *The symbolic life: Vol. 18, The collected works of C.G. Jung*. Princeton University Press. (Original work published 1948)

Jung, C.G. (1980b). Jung and religious belief. In W. McGuire (Ed.), *The symbolic life: Vol. 18. The Collected Works of C.G. Jung*. Princeton University Press. (Extracts from H.L. Philip, Jung and the problem of evil, 1956/1958/1959)

Jung, C.G. (1981a). The stages of life. In W. McGuire (Ed.), *The structure and dynamics of the psyche: Vol. 8. The collected works of C.G. Jung.* Princeton University Press. (Original work published 1930–31)

Jung, C.G. (1981b). Psychological factors determining human behavior. In W. McGuire (Ed.), *The structure and dynamics of the psyche: Vol. 8. The collected works of C.G. Jung.* Princeton University Press. (Original work published 1937)

Jung, C.G. (1984). *Dream analysis: Notes of the seminar given in 1928–1930.* (W. McGuire, Ed.). Princeton University Press.

Jung, C.G. (1989). *Memories, dreams, reflections.* Vintage Books.

Jung, C.G. (2009). *The red book: Liber novus.* (Sonu Shamdasani, ed.). W.W. Norton & Co.

Jung, E. (1985). *Animus and anima.* Spring Publications. (Original work published 1957)

Jung, E., & von Franz, M-L. (1970). *The grail legend.* Princeton University Press. (Original work published 1958)

Kotschnig, E.P. (1982). Memory of Emma Jung. In F. Jensen & S. Mullen (Eds.), *C.G. Jung, Emma Jung, and Toni Wolff: A collection of remembrances.* The Analytical Psychology Club of San Francisco.

Lockhart, R.A. (1983). *Words as eggs: Psyche in language and clinic.* Spring Publications.

Lynn, P.C. (1982). C.G. Jung, Emma Jung and Toni Wolff. In F. Jensen & S. Mullen (Eds.), *C.G. Jung, Emma Jung, and Toni Wolff: A collection of remembrances.* The Analytical Psychology Club of San Francisco.

MANANcigogne (2011, September 23). Granny Evergreen. *Binding Birches blog.* http://bendingbirches2010.blogspot.com/2011/09/granny-evergreen.html

McGuire, W. (Ed.). (1974). *The Freud/Jung letters.* (R Manheim & R.F.C. Hull, trans.). Princeton University Press.

McLynn, F. (1997). *Carl Gustav Jung.* St. Martin's Press.

McVane, B. (2012, April 17). *McCarthy and the Bible* [Online forum post]. CormacMcCarthy.com. https://www.cormacmccarthy.com/topic/mccarthy-and-the-bible/page/5/

Moon, S. (1982). Memory of Emma Jung. In F. Jensen & S. Mullen, (Eds.), *C.G. Jung, Emma Jung, and Toni Wolff: A collection of remembrances*. The Analytical Psychology Club of San Francisco.

Moore, Faith. (2018, August 18). Why can't the princess be ugly? Fairy tale symbolism and why it matters. *Faith Moore blog*. https://faithkmoore.com/2018/08/17/why-cant-the-princess-be-ugly-fairy-tale-symbolism-and-why-it-matters/#:~:text=A%20fairy%20tale%20princess'%20outer,in%20order%20to%20be%20good

New Jerusalem (2022, February 22). In *Wikipedia*, https://en.wikipedia.org/wiki/New_Jerusalem

Newton, M. (2019). *Dizzy and the dreams*. Chiron Publications.

Nichols, S. (1982). Memory of Emma Jung and Toni Wolff. In F. Jensen & S. Mullen (Eds.), *C.G. Jung, Emma Jung, and Toni Wolff: A collection of remembrances*. The Analytical Psychology Club of San Francisco.

Pinch, G. (2006). *Magic in Ancient Egypt,* University of Texas Press/ British Museum Press.

Psychics Central (2022, September 30). https://www.physicscentral.com/explore/action/infraredlight.cfm

Purrington, Mr. (2020, March 7). Carl Jung on the "Hieros Gamos" and "Eros." *Carl Jung Depth Psychology Blog*. https://carljungdepthpsychologysite.blog/2020/03/07/carl-jung-on-the-hieros-gamos-and-eros/#.Y0b7JC-B3rA

Raff, J. (1997). The felt vision. In D.F. Sandner & S. Wong (Eds.), *The sacred heritage*. Routledge.

Raff, J. (2006). *The practice of ally work*. Nicolas-Hays, Inc. (Original work published 1997)

Rasmussen, K. 1988. Von einer Frau die sur Spinnne wurde (Eskimo Tale of the Moon Spirit). In *Die Gabe des Adlers*. (K. Rasmussen, Trans.). Zerling Clemmens.

Robb, C. (1992, January 26). Top archaeologist suggests women ruled ancient world. *The Contra Costa Times,* p. 6.

Sacred Heart. (2022, April 19). In *Wikipedia*. https://en.wikipedia.org/wiki/Sacred_Heart

Schneider, M. (1946). *El Origen musical de los animales-símbolos en la mitología y la escultura antiguas* (*The Musical Origin of Animal-Symbols*). Barcelona.

Segaller, S. (Director). (1990). *Jung on Film* [Film]. Stephen Segaller Films. (Originally released in 1957)

Smith, B.M. (2010). *The Greek dialogues*: *Explorations in myth*. Xlibris.

Solutio. (2020, December 9). In *ARAS*. https://aras.org/concordance/content/solutio

Spiritual Meaning of Precious Stones. (2002). Bible Meanings. http://www.biblemeanings.info/Words/Natural/Preciousstones.htm

Toub, G. (2021, February 22). Re: Arni Mindell's presentation, Camarillo State Hospital, intern seminar, 1975.

von Franz, M-L. (1964). The process of individuation. In *Man and his symbols*. Princeton.

Von Franz, M-L. (1974). *Shadow and evil in fairytales*. Spring Publications.

Von Franz, M-L. (1980). *Alchemy: An introduction to the symbolism and the psychology*. Inner City Books.

Von Franz, M-L. (1982). *Individuation in fairy tales*. Spring Publications.

Von Franz, M-L. (1983). *Shadow and evil in fairytales*. Spring Publications.

Von Franz, M-L. (1987.) *On dreams and death*. Shambhala.

von Franz, M-L. (1993). *The feminine in fairytales*. Spring Publications. (Original copyright 1972)

Von Franz, M-L. (1995). *Creation myths*. Shambhala.

Von Franz, M-L. (1996). *The interpretation of fairy tales*. Shambhala.

Von Franz, M-L. (1997a). *Archetypal dimensions of the psyche*. Shambhala.

Von Franz, M-L. (1997b). *Archetypal patterns in fairy tales*. Inner City Books.

Von Franz, M-L. (1999). *The cat: A tale of feminine redemption*. Inner City Books.

von Graevenitz, J. (1982). Memory of C.G. Jung. In F. Jensen & S. Mullen (Eds.), *C.G. Jung, Emma Jung, and Toni Wolff: A collection of remembrances*. The Analytical Psychology Club of San Francisco.

Wagner, S. (1999). A conversation with Marie-Louise von Franz. *Psychological Perspectives, 38*(1), 12–39.

Walker, B. (1983). *Women's Encyclopedia of Myths and Secrets.* HarperSanFrancisco.

Weeping Statue. (2022, March 15). In *Wikipedia.* https://en.wikipedia.org/wiki/Weeping_statue

Wehr, G. (1989). *An illustrated biography of C.G. Jung.* Shambhala.

Zeta, A. (2007). *Encountering the shadows: Embraced by the dark goddess.* Isisbooks online, https://www.isisbooks.com/Encountering-the-Shadows-s/372.htm

Susan in front of stone at Bollingen

Susan K Faron, PhD, is a psychologist and Jungian analyst and graduate of the Jung and von Franz Centre, Switzerland. She received her undergraduate degree from UC Berkeley, Magna Cum Laude, with high honors in psychology, Phi Beta Kappa. She completed her PhD at the California School of Professional Psychology. Dr. Faron has numerous academic honors and is a member of the California Psychological Association. Currently focused on the feminine wisdom archetype, she began her research in 1983 exploring adult development. She has lectured at the San Francisco Analytical Psychology Club and presented internationally in other forums.

The heart of Dr. Faron's work is through private practice, in which she specializes in dreams and their spiritual direction. Susan, mother of six, grandmother to nine, is convinced the real-life experience of the Wise Old Woman spirit serves as foundation for the loving *eros* and vital *emptiness* needed in the world today.

Printed in the USA
CPSIA information can be obtained
at www.ICGtesting.com
LVHW040100071123
763116LV00003B/241